Tom Taylor's Civil War

Albert Castel

Tom Taylor's Civil War

University Press of Kansas

Published by the University Press of Kansas (Lawrence, Kansas 66049), which
was organized by the Kansas Board of Regents and is operated and funded by
Emporia State University, Fort Hays State University, Kansas State University,
Pittsburg State University, the University of Kansas, and Wichita State
University

Library of Congress Cataloging-in-Publication Data

Taylor, Thomas Thomson, 1836–1908.
    Tom Taylor's Civil War / [compiled by] Albert Castel.
      p. cm. — (Modern war studies)
    Comprises Taylor's diaries and letters to and from his wife, Margaret
Taylor.
    Includes bibliographical references and index.
    ISBN 0-7006-1049-9 (alk. paper)
    1. Taylor, Thomas Thomson, 1836–1908—Diaries. 2. Taylor, Thomas
Thomson, 1836–1908—Correspondence. 3. United States—History—
Civil War, 1861–1865—Personal narratives. 4. Ohio—History—Civil
War, 1861–1865—Personal narratives. 5. a United States—History—Civil
War, 1861–1865—Campaigns. 6. Taylor, Margaret Antoinette White,
d. 1913—Correspondence. 7. Soldiers—Ohio—Diaries. 8. Soldiers—
Ohio—Correspondence. 9. Married people—Ohio—Correspondence.
I. Castel, Albert E. II. Taylor, Margaret Antoinette White, d. 1913.
III. Title. IV. Series.
E601 .T295 2000
973.7'82—dc21   00-041162

British Library Cataloguing in Publication Data is available.

Printed in the United States of America

10 9 8 7 6 5 4 3 2 1

To ALAN BROWN—

true gentleman and scholar, whose friendship
it has been my good fortune to enjoy for twoscore years:
it always has been and always will be cherished.

Contents

Preface

I MET TOM TAYLOR in October 1976—not in person, for he died in 1908, but in the form of his letters and diaries at the Ohio Historical Society in Columbus where I was doing research for a history of the Atlanta Campaign. Instantly I realized he was well worth knowing. His accounts of what he saw and did while serving with Gen. William Tecumseh Sherman's army in Georgia in 1864 contained valuable, sometimes vital, information to be found nowhere else. Furthermore, they possessed a high literary quality: Taylor, a lawyer by vocation and a sometime newspaper editor by avocation, could write as well as fight, and he did a great deal of each, both with a flair. Then and there I vowed that someday I would endeavor to make it possible for others to become acquainted with Taylor and his Civil War. This book fulfills that vow.

The person who enabled me to meet Taylor was Helen Taylor Steinbarger, the daughter of his oldest son. In 1962, when almost seventy-five, she donated his Civil War letters and surviving diaries to the Ohio Historical Society along with a file of letters written to him between 1861 and 1865 by his wife, Margaret Antoinette White Taylor. These letters total 272, and they average six pages in length and cover a time span beginning in April 1861 and ending in August 1865 with the termination of his military career, which saw him rise from lieutenant to brevet brigadier general. The only long breaks in this correspondence occurred while he was at home on leave, engaged in recruiting duty in Ohio, or participating in military operations that precluded access to the mails, as, for example, during the march to the sea from Atlanta to Savannah in autumn 1864.

Although it is evident from his letters that Taylor kept a diary while campaigning in West Virginia during 1861 and 1862, the only diaries that remain are those for the latter part of 1863 and most of 1864—which is fortunate, as it was then that he took part in those events possessing the greatest historical interest (Battle of Chattanooga, Atlanta Campaign, march to the sea). The vast majority of the entries in these diaries, which consist of small, black-leather-bound volumes of a type widely used by Northern soldiers, are brief, but some that describe battles in which Taylor played an active role cover numerous pages and subsequently became the basis for letters and official military reports. Because the letters are more detailed and better written than the diary versions, most of the quotations in this book derive from them. Only when the diaries contain significant or interesting information not present in the letters, or provide a convenient narrative bridge, do I (as a rule) quote lengthy passages from them.

Netta Taylor's letters number 150 and are written in a small, neat script on light-blue stationery. They are quite literate: before her marriage, she taught school, presumably the same one presided over by her father, one of whose students was a boy who as a man became a general and then president of the United States (his last name was Grant). They are not as long and eloquent as her husband's, deal in large part with family affairs and other domestic matters, and all too often are so faded with age that they are difficult if not impossible to read, either in whole or part, with the result that sometimes it was necessary to deduce the essence of their contents from Taylor's replies to them. Nevertheless, they contain much of interest and offer something that is rare among Civil War primary sources; a detailed conversation by mail between a soldier on the battlefront and his wife on the home front. Thanks to them, I have been able to present not only a firsthand narrative of Taylor's military activities but also an intimate view of the relationship between him and his wife—a relationship that at all times was passionate and sometimes turbulent. When I started writing this book, I did not expect, much less intend, to tell a love story, yet to some degree I have done so and in the process revealed aspects of married life in mid-nineteenth-century America that readers perhaps will find intriguing, even surprising.

Neither, when I began work on this book, did I foresee that I would end up writing what in effect is the biography of a junior Civil War officer (Taylor was a captain from August 1861 to April 1863, then a major until June 1865). To my knowledge, few, if any, such biographies exist, yet I believe it was worthwhile writing this one, both for its own sake and because of what Taylor's experiences convey about the role of low-ranking officers in their units and in combat. Taylor, to be sure, was not a typical officer—apart from being a lawyer, he was too intellectual, emotional, and fluent with his pen to be that—but on the other hand, he was not that unusual when it came to motivation, experiences, attitudes, and conduct on and off the battlefield.

Concerning battles, his descriptions of them will help explain why, at the close of the Atlanta Campaign, in which Taylor performed superbly, Sherman wrote that in his victorious army, "We have good corporals and sergeants, and some good lieutenants and captains, and these are far more important than good generals."

I assume, safely enough I am sure, that the majority of readers will be interested primarily in Taylor's accounts of the military operations in which he took part. They will not be disappointed. Despite having been written hastily and often under adverse conditions, his verbal depictions of marches, skirmishes, and battles are vivid, dramatic, detailed, generally accurate, and filled with exciting incidents and perceptive observations. To the professional historian, as I know from personal experience, they offer a golconda of highly useful information. For readers who simply wish to learn about, or increase their knowledge of, what Civil War soldiering and combat were like, Taylor's narratives will provide them with what they desire and will do so in a most revealing and stimulating fashion. In particular, they will discover that by the latter part of the war infantry tactics had become quite complex and sophisticated, with skirmishers performing a role that in importance and technique foreshadowed subsequent developments in warfare.

Unlike the usual compilation of letters or diary entries, which presents the texts of these documents in full with only brief introductions and is accompanied by notes containing identifications, explanations, and corrections, large portions of this book consist of brief quotations from Taylor's writings intermixed with my own prose. Even the long quotations do not contain all that he wrote and every so often give way to historical commentaries designed to provide readers with a better understanding of his accounts of military events. I adopted this format out of necessity. First, the sheer magnitude of Taylor's correspondence, not to mention his diaries, would have resulted in a monstrously long book had I employed conventional editorial methodology. Second, Taylor spent the first two years of the Civil War in what soon became a military backwater or else on recruiting duty in Ohio, and although he had some personal experiences well worth recording, much of what he did and saw possesses little historical import. Hence there was a need to cover this phase of his career as succinctly as was possible, consistent with gaining and retaining (it is hoped) reader interest.

Third, by taking this approach, I left ample space in which to quote lengthy passages from Taylor's letters and diaries once he became involved, as he did starting with the Siege of Vicksburg, in major military operations, and also in which to make maximum feasible use of Netta's letters, thereby further developing the relationship between her and Taylor and so turning this book into the story not only of a soldier at war but also of a man and his wife during that war. And, fourth and finally, by placing my historical commentaries within Taylor's accounts of battles and other military operations, I made it possible for readers to obtain useful, in some cases needed, information and interpretations concerning what he describes while at the same time maintaining the narrative flow of his accounts—a flow that could not be sustained if readers constantly had to refer to notes, especially if the notes followed the text, as is now so often the case. Moreover, this method had the advantage of enabling me to keep notes to a minimum, especially for the chapters pertaining to the Atlanta Campaign, Taylor's descriptions of which constitute the heart of this book.

I have made, I realize, some big claims for this little book. The only way to judge their validity is to peruse what follows. Prepared to abide by their verdict, whatever it may be, I now invite readers so to do.

Acknowledgments

THE WRITING OF HISTORY IS, by its very nature, a lonely task. Yet it cannot be done alone and so requires the assistance of others. Hence it is my duty, as well as my pleasure, to thank those who helped me to do what I have done in this book. (Needless to say none of them is in any way responsible for what I have failed to do.)

First and foremost I thank Larry and Priscilla Massie of the Allegan Forest for, when it came to securing the maps and most of the illustrations that appear in this book, yet again making possible what otherwise would have been impossible. Their awesome collection of rare books and vintage magazines is surpassed in magnitude only by their friendship, which I value as one of the great privileges I have had the good fortune to enjoy during my lifetime.

Next I take this opportunity to record my gratitude to the staff of the reading room at the Ohio Historical Society for its efficient and courteous assistance. In particular I wish to acknowledge the help of John Haas, Gary Arnold, and (alas, no longer with the OHS) Bonnie Link.

Then a very special thanks to Mrs. Pat Donaldson of Georgetown, Ohio, who on a Friday morning early in November of 1995 opened up to me, after I called her at her home by way of a sidewalk pay phone, the door and the holdings of the Brown County Historical and Genealogical Society where I was able to photocopy certain source materials that proved valuable, indeed vital, to this work. And when, long past noon, this ravenously hungry historian asked her where I could dine, she directed me to a curiously situated restaurant with the unusual name of The Golden Rule where I staved off starvation with two bowls of a delicious homemade vegetable beef soup. Tom Taylor left Georgetown with bitter memories, but I departed it, as a result of Mrs. Donaldson's hospitality, with fond ones.

As before, and as I trust will be the case again, I am indebted to Linda Moore, Judy Leising, and "Squeaky" Barnett of the Hillsdale College Library. They too rendered aid that was essential in its results and did so in a manner that was thoroughly professional, yet with a personal touch that was and is much appreciated.

My thanks, too, goes to Jemie Hannon, whose work on her computer transformed my disreputable looking, and in places barely legible, second draft into a respectable and readable final draft, and who did this, moreover, during the Christmas holidays under the pressure of a tight deadline.

As has been the case several times before, I owe much to the staff of the University Press of Kansas. To be specific, I begin with the director of that press, Fred Woodward, concerning whom I could and would like to say many things, but will limit myself to stating that although he tends to expect more of me than he should, he redeems himself by always realizing when I fail to meet those expectations and telling me so and why. I also extend my thanks to Susan Schott, assistant director of the press, who is entitled to credit for the title of this book and (I am sure) much more besides; to Melinda Wirkus, senior production editor, who oversaw the transformation of my manuscript into a book; and to Claire Sutton, whose skillful copyediting of said manuscript greatly enhanced it by correcting what I had done wrongly and by improving what I did rightly. Blessed be the competent copyeditors of the publishing world, for they enable creeping prose to walk upright and turn verbal dross into, if not gold, intelligible prose.

Unusual as it may seem, I must also express my gratitude to Arlan Gilbert and Merton Dillon, emeriti history professors of, respectively, Hillsdale College and The Ohio State University, and to Art Hammond, who does not claim to be a scholar but who does not need to claim to be what he so manifestly is—a true and fine gentleman. They are my weekday breakfast companions at a restaurant named The Finish Line and their morning camaraderie often gives a boost to my spirit that carries me to the finish line of whatever I hoped to accomplish on that day.

Finally, and as always, I offer my thanks as well as my love to my commisariat, cook, and wife. For forty-plus years she has served in these capacities and in so doing provided the foundation for my life and my life's work.

With the above I meant to close, and normally would, but at my wife's urging—I'll not say command—I add a word about Randall, our orange, energetic, rascal-cat who, as a result of a photograph showing him sitting at my writing desk and looking very studious, has been dubbed my "amanuensis"—an appropriate appellation if "amanuensis" can be defined to mean a critter that scatters the pages of a manuscript, chews on them, sometimes (in effect) hides them, and who with unerring instinct jumps onto my desk, purring to be petted, at precisely those times when I am desperately trying to untie some literary knot. But the very sight of him—and of our senior felines, Calico Kate and Clarence the Gentle Giant—fully compensates for such minor faults, and so I not only forgive him but love him all the more.

Prologue: The Heavy Tramp of Thousands
April–August 1861

A T 4:30 A.M., April 12, 1861, a shell exploded above Fort Sumter in the harbor of Charleston, South Carolina. Immediately, dozens of other Confederate cannons opened fire. A civil war had begun. On April 15, Pres. Abraham Lincoln called on all loyal states to furnish 75,000 volunteers to serve three months for the purpose of suppressing the Southern rebellion. Two days later a meeting took place at the Brown County courthouse in Georgetown, Ohio, a small town forty-five miles southeast of Cincinnati. After speakers urged the formation of a company to "leave at once for the service of their country," thirty-some men enlisted. Then, in true democratic style, they cast ballots for officers. Chosen captain was thirty-seven-year-old Dr. Carr B. White, a veteran of the Mexican War, during which he had attained the same rank. Elected second lieutenant was his brother-in-law, Thomas Thomson Taylor, age twenty-four and prosecuting attorney of Brown County.[1]

Tom Taylor was a handsome man, strikingly so, with a broad forehead, fine yet strong features, light-blue eyes, and thick blond hair so pale that it seemed almost white.[2] His face projected great force of mind and will, revealing what he was—an ambitious man, determined to rise in the world, to achieve position and prestige. By so doing, not only would he fulfill his ambition, but he also would redeem with his own success the failure of his father.

That father was Hiram Taylor, born in 1800 at Saratoga Springs, New York, a descendant of John Taylor of Haverhill, Sussex County, England, who in 1630 crossed the Atlantic with fellow Puritans to found a "city upon a hill" in Massachusetts. Ensuing generations of Taylors moved to Connecticut, then to New York, always prospering and sometimes achieving prominence in civil and military affairs.[3] Hiram, though, proved to be an exception. Little is known of his career, but a letter he wrote to his wife Mary on June 12, 1836, from Matagorda Bay, Texas, tells the essential tale.[4] In it he spoke of "the inexorable will of providence against my stopping in any place," of being driven to "the verge of poverty, ruin and contempt," and of how "the unpleasant situation of yourself and the children continually stareing [*sic*] me in the face, chafed my mind nearly to a PHRENZY," with the result that "in a

Tom Taylor the Soldier.
MOLLUS Collection, USAMHI

moment of enthusiasm I agreed to join the expedition to *Texas*," where the American settlers had revolted against Mexican rule. In brief, Hiram had deserted his wife Mary, his four-year-old daughter Sarah Jane, and his two-year-old son Ziba. Moreover, while he possibly did not realize it when he went off to fight for the independence of Texas, he left his forty-year-old wife pregnant with another son. He was born on November 27, 1836, and named Thomas Thomson.[5]

"Mary," Hiram's letter continued, "I have in . . . too many instances done wrong and acted wayward both in the sight of God and in the eyes of man." In Texas, where he had joined the staff of a general, "I have cast myself in a contentious crowd," where "I have to struggle for the palm with thousands, to obtain the wayward and far spreading renown which rends the air with the loud huzzas of praise."

Hiram never heard those huzzas. By the time he arrived there, Texas already had gained its independence at the Battle of San Jacinto, April 21, 1836, and no more fighting took place afterward. Unable to pursue a military career, and unwilling to return to his family in disgrace, Hiram remained in Texas, where, sometime in 1845, he died near Houston.[6] His sole legacy to the son he never saw, and who never saw him, was his fate, a fate that Tom Taylor resolved to avoid by winning, not losing, in the "struggle for the palm," or, as he himself sometimes would put it in his letters, the "battle with the world." Yet in waging this struggle, he would display traits that revealed him to be very much his father's son. When he died in 1908, among his possessions was the letter that Hiram wrote at Matagorda Bay in 1836.

Mary Taylor, following Hiram's departure for Texas, resided with her children and widowed mother at Stone House Farm, four miles west of Freehold, New Jersey, on land acquired by her great-great-grandfather, John Thomson, in 1664. Here Tom Taylor spent his boyhood, attended the "common schools," and read voraciously—in his letters, he frequently quotes the standard English poets, in particular Byron. In summer 1855, he went to Georgetown, Ohio, where he lived at the home of and studied law under William Wall, the husband of his mother's sister Elizabeth. On December 8, 1857, having attained the legal age required to engage in legal practice, he was admitted to the bar in Columbus, with his certificate of admission being signed by, among others, Morrison R. Waite, a future chief justice of the U.S. Supreme Court, and William Dennison, who two years later became governor of Ohio.[7]

When the cannons thundered in Charleston harbor, Taylor already had achieved a certain eminence, albeit local and modest. Besides being prosecuting attorney, a post to which he was elected by a large majority in 1860, he owned a half-interest in a drugstore and for a while had been the co-owner and editor of a Georgetown newspaper. By 1861, he also owned a small farm on the outskirts of Georgetown, where he resided in a house called Elmwood

Cottage with his wife, Margaret Antoinette, and two infant sons, Miles and Thomas Thomson Jr. "Netta," as Taylor usually addressed her, was the same age as he, short, fashionably plump, and well educated, having taught school before their marriage on January 17, 1858. She provided Taylor with intellectual companionship, emotional support and comfort, and—important to an ambitious man—influential family connections. Her father, Hugh Donaldson White, who died in 1856, had been a many-termed member of the state legislature and taught a school attended by a Georgetown boy named Hiram Ulysses Grant, who, when he went to West Point, found that the army had changed his name to Ulysses Simpson Grant. Furthermore, she had two brothers, one of whom, Carr B. White, was a physician who became captain of Georgetown's three-month volunteers. The other brother was Chilton A. White, thirty-five, a lawyer, a former state senator, and a Democratic member of the U.S. House of Representatives. Obviously, Taylor's brothers-in-law gave him models to emulate and a means to help him do so.[8]

They, however, were not his only models. Another, and one of long-standing, was his father's younger brother Miles. Like Hiram, Miles Taylor was born in Saratoga Springs, New York. Unlike him, his life had been successful. Migrating as a young man to Louisiana, he practiced law in New Orleans, married well, acquired a plantation and slaves, and served in Congress from 1855 to 1861, when he resigned after Louisiana's secession from the Union. Tom Taylor knew of his uncle's career—his older brother Ziba had gone to live with him—and it must have been a source of pride and stimulation to him, given that his oldest son bore the name Miles. Perhaps, too, he repaid a compliment by so naming his firstborn, for Uncle Miles's only son also was named Thomas. Several years younger than his Yankee cousin, this Tom Taylor, upon the outbreak of war, joined the Eighth Louisiana Infantry as a "high private," for, considering his father's status, he easily could have obtained an officer's commission. Likewise, brother Ziba supported the Confederacy, but not as a soldier. Instead, he became a blockade runner.[9] Manifestly, the men of the Taylor family were not ordinary in either their aspirations or their attainments, and Tom Taylor of Georgetown, Ohio, was no exception.

Given his Southern ties—ties that were strengthened by his marriage to Netta, whose Virginia-born parents came to Ohio from North Carolina by way of Kentucky—it might seem strange that Taylor was so quick to volun-

Carr White.
MOLLUS Collection, USAMHI

teer to fight against the South. But along with the great majority of other Northern Democrats—and he was, like his congressman brother-in-law Chilton, a staunch Democrat—he was devoted to the Union, and Taylor believed that the Southern rebellion must be suppressed. If it was not, as he soon would tell Netta in a letter justifying his decision to become a soldier, then the nation would be divided between North and South, who could "never dwell together on the same continent in unity, peace and brotherly friendship" but "would ever be involved in war and pillage." In this struggle "one or the other must conquer, one must yield—which shall it be?" Not the North: "We can never submit to the slave oligarchy" and its "overbearing" and "insolent" sway. Therefore, "men must go to the field and fight"—and he would be one of the men.[10]

Patriotism, however, was not the sole motive that impelled Taylor to go off to war. Although he no doubt knew from having read Thomas Gray's "Elegy in a Country Churchyard" that "the paths of glory lead but to the grave," he knew also that those paths could lead as well to what his father had termed "spreading renown" and with it promotion to higher rank, attributes that would give him a prestige in time of war that could be carried over into peacetime, where it would serve as a springboard to professional success, or political power, or financial affluence. Taylor, who described himself as an "orphan" and believed that he must "carve my own road through life," craved all these things and was determined to have them. "If I survive the war," he told Netta, "I hope there is a bright future for me." Clearly he expected to survive the war, and his chief concern was that it would last long enough for him to have the opportunity to prove himself on the battlefield and thereby gain the glory and the rank and all that went with them.[11] The war, of course, would last long enough—far longer than he could possibly foresee.

Tom Taylor's military career began, mundanely enough, on April 24, 1861, when he and 114 other Brown County volunteers, all of them destined for service in the Twelfth Ohio Infantry Regiment, traveled in wagons from Georgetown to Cincinnati. The next morning, after breakfast at the Broadway Hotel, they took a train to Columbus where they arrived at 4:00 P.M. and marched to Camp Jackson on the city's northern outskirts. Here they enjoyed "a very substantial supper," following which they were assigned quarters in the basement of the state capitol, where the floor was covered with straw, making it a "perfect livery stable." Taylor toured the building and found it "filled with troops from the dome to the basement, the gas burners shedding a mellow light on all." Then, sitting at a desk in the chamber of the Ohio House of Representatives, he penned Netta a letter. It was the first of nearly three hundred letters he would write her during the next four years and five months.[12]

Three days later, he addressed her again, doing so beside a campfire in Camp Jackson where the Brown County contingent occupied wood shanties in which the men slept on nine-by-seven-foot plank bunks, five men to a bunk. Although Sunday, "the day of all others we are required to keep holy," everything was "noise and bustle—now we hear the quick beat of tenor and now the deep tone of the bass, and again the chill notes of the fife and heavy tramp of thousands as they march to drill. Everyone is smiling, all appear joyous and in excellent spirits."

So far the volunteers had neither uniforms, weapons, nor any of the other accoutrements of soldiers. Worse, the lack of order in the camp was "absolutely disgusting—there is no system, no arrangement about it, all is confusion." Meals came at irregular times or not at all, the food was "of an inferior quality," and the civilian contractors who supplied it charged "an exorbitant price—twenty cents a meal for each man." And as if all this were not bad enough, it seemed that thirst would become a problem when a rumor swept the camp that Rebel spies had poisoned the wells. "Many men were almost benumbed with fright, in fact horror-stricken." Taylor "laughed at the report," and after some of the "boys," at his urging, drank from the wells without ill effect, the scare ended.

The would-be soldiers of the Twelfth did not have to worry long about fiendish Confederates poisoning them in the middle of Ohio. On May 7, they traveled by train to newly established Camp Dennison, fifteen miles northeast of Cincinnati and situated, Taylor wrote Netta the following day, in a vale "bounded by a beautiful range of hills." Better still, he proudly informed her, "I have been elected First Lieut. of our company," receiving seventy-seven votes, and had a uniform in which "I look very well." The coat and pants were of "dark blue cloth, vest of fine buff marsailles, buttons gilt," and his shoulder straps had gold leaves on them. "I would like," he added, "to come home very much but don't expect that I shall get an opportunity, [and so] you must not expect me. If I come, it will be as winds come, quietly and unexpectedly."

The Twelfth Ohio, according to Taylor, anticipated being "ordered into active service in a short time," and "our boys are all eager for the contest." Instead, it received orders to reorganize as a three-year regiment; all its men who did not wish to serve that long would be discharged at the end of their three-month enlistment. Most of them agreed, but a large number refused. Among the latter were nearly all the members of Taylor's company. Their recalcitrance stunned Taylor. He had hoped, in fact expected, to obtain a captain's commission and command the company. Now he faced the prospect of doing neither. He blamed the "green eyed monster jealousy." Certain persons in the company either wanted to be captain themselves or else resented his becoming first lieutenant. Since they could not have these positions themselves, they denied them to him by inducing the company not to extend its enlistment.

"How desolate, how lonely, I sometimes feel," he wrote Netta, informing her of the setback to his ambitions. "The inner man ill, in mourning— the outward lively, careless, indifferent. In other words, mentally sick, physically well. I must come home to you for a season, lay my head on your bosom and inhale new inspiration." He denounced the "trickery" and "conniving" so rife in the army yet admitted that "I am but mortal and claim no higher excellence for myself than I am willing to give to others," for when it came to advancing oneself, "aspiration begins and ends in vigilance." Obviously, a failure to be vigilant had cost him his company and his captaincy. "I am going," he concluded, "to come home before very long, as soon as I can get a leave of absence. I can do no good here now—nor anywhere else at present."[13]

A few days later, both Taylor's mood and plans changed. He had found that there was some "good" he could do after all by remaining with the regiment. That was to help prevent John W. Lowe, colonel-designate of the Twelfth Ohio, from being confirmed in that post by a majority vote of the officers. Lowe, Taylor believed, "triggered the whole thing" of the Twelfth's being transformed into a three-year unit. Consequently, "my principal ambition," he informed Netta on June 22, "is to defeat Lowe," and "I think . . . the prospect is very fair to do so." Along with a number of other anti-Lowe officers, he was working to secure the colonelcy for Capt. Jacob Ammen, a West Point–trained veteran of the regular army. Should "we succeed . . . I think that I will stand a good chance to be appointed regimental quartermaster," a position "involving no danger, except from sickness, and paying well."

Aware and fearful of the movement to make Ammen colonel, Lowe deftly countered by having Governor Dennison appoint that officer to the command of the Twenty-fourth Ohio. For a while, Taylor considered trying to obtain the colonelcy for Carr White but then concluded that "there wouldn't be perfect union on him" and so mounted a campaign to have his brother-in-law chosen lieutenant colonel. This succeeded. On June 28, during the mustering-in of the Twelfth as a three-year regiment, the officers elevated White to this rank, making him second-in-command to Lowe.[14]

A week later, the Twelfth set out for the battlefront in western Virginia. Left behind at Camp Dennison were the three-months men, Taylor among them. When his company refused to serve for three years, the only way he could remain with the regiment, other than to become quartermaster or to secure some other staff assignment, was to sign up as an enlisted man—a move, to put it mildly, that did not appeal to him. Moreover, since he was slated to be mustered out July 25, his military career, unless he did something about it, would soon come to an abrupt and inglorious end.

Fortunately, there was something he could do about it. A new regiment, the Forty-seventh Ohio, was being organized at Camp Clay, four miles east of Cincinnati. Its sponsor was a wealthy businessman of that city, Charles F. Wilstach, in whose honor it had been unofficially dubbed "the Wilstach Regiment."[15] Thanks to his munificence, it was well provisioned. But it needed men; the great wave of patriotic fervor that had swept over Ohio, along with the rest of the North, following Fort Sumter, had ebbed. If Taylor could raise a company for the Forty-seventh, he would become a captain after all.

Early in July, having obtained leave prior to the departure of the Twelfth for western Virginia, Taylor returned to Georgetown. There he set to work recruiting throughout Brown County. His efforts seemed to succeed; eighty-three men promised to join his company. On July 27, accompanied by Netta, he went into Georgetown, expecting to find them there, ready to travel to Camp Clay. Instead, only twenty-six of the eighty-three were present. Many of the townspeople laughed and jeered at Taylor as he set forth with his meager band of recruits.[16]

"You witnessed our departure yesterday," he wrote Netta from Camp Clay, "[and] saw how humiliating it was, how distressing to me. I endured it, passed the ordeal although it seared me to the quick and I am yet smarting under it." Not only did he feel "sold, badly sold," but he also feared that he would be unable to obtain a captain's commission, for army regulations stipulated that a company must contain a minimum of 101 soldiers before it and its officers could be mustered into service. Should he again be denied because of a lack of men to command, then "I shall shake the dust of Georgetown from my feet and go where the people are at least patriotic—or do something else."

On July 29, the Forty-seventh moved to Camp Dennison. On arriving, the men discovered that quarters, blankets, and rations could be obtained only by requisitioning them. None of the officers, including the quartermaster, knew how to prepare the necessary forms save Taylor. This he proceeded to do, laboring until midnight, with the result that the regiment was able to eat, obtain blankets, and occupy barracks where the men slept on the "soft side" of long plank bunks, twelve to a bunk.[17]

Taylor's display of military know-how—a skill obviously in short supply in the Forty-seventh—perhaps explains why his company, despite its miniscule size, was among the first three to be mustered, an event that took place August 7. Furthermore, he was designated its captain and thus could don shoulder straps with four bars on them. Even so, he remained apprehensive that "unless we raise our company full," his commission as captain, which he had yet to receive, would be withheld by the governor. Should that happen, he informed Netta in a letter written on the day of the mustering, he would "stick by the boys" he had recruited by going "into the ranks with them and trust to luck for promotion."

In the end, all turned out well. On August 21, the tenth and last company of the Forty-seventh was mustered, bringing the regiment's strength to 830. Four of its companies consisted entirely of Germans, almost all of them from Cincinnati. "Americans" composed the majority of the other six companies, one of which (Company B) was from Michigan. Taylor's Company F was by far the smallest, numbering a mere thirty, and he worried that it would be consolidated with another undersized unit, which could result in his being denied a captain's commission or being reduced in rank to lieutenant.[18] Neither he nor anyone else could foresee that the time would come when the Forty-seventh's companies would average less than a dozen men apiece.

On August 25, the regiment received uniforms and weapons. For eight of the companies, the latter took the disappointing form of smoothbore muskets. Only the flank companies—A and B—were issued rifles (i.e., muskets whose rifled or grooved bore gave them much better range and accuracy than the smoothbores). They were Enfields, imported from England, and by 1863 they became, along with the virtually identical Springfield, the standard firearm of both armies.[19] At this stage of the war, however, they were the exception rather than the rule, and the Forty-seventh actually was better armed than many other Union regiments and most Confederate ones.

The Forty-seventh's troops had little time to familiarize themselves with their firearms. On August 27, after the whole regiment had been officially mustered into service, the colonel, Frederick Poschner, a forty-five-year-old former Austrian officer, announced that it would leave the next morning for Columbus and from there for the battlefront. The men cheered long and lustily, then spent the rest of the day and most of the night getting ready to go off to war, doing so with great enthusiasm, much confusion, and not a little intoxication. In the morning, some of them looked "red about the eyes" and had "quite an unmilitary gait" as they boarded the boxcars carrying them to Columbus.[20]

Hardly had the train started moving when Taylor engaged in his first combat of the war. It was with a member of his company, Pvt. Josephus Davis, who although he wore a uniform and carried a musket, had refused to be mustered. Now he was drunk and obstreperous. Taylor ordered him to shut up and sit down. He refused, whereupon Taylor grabbed him by the collar. Davis in turn knocked off Taylor's $1.45 beplumed dress hat and kicked it out of the car. Taylor had the train stop, then consulted Lt. Col. Lyman S. Elliott. Despite not having any previous military experience, or perhaps for that very reason, Elliott, who was from Michigan, advised Taylor to bind Davis "hand and foot," and if that did not quiet him, to shoot him. Instead Taylor, probably realizing that such drastic treatment of a local boy would have an adverse effect on the people back in Georgetown, did neither but managed to keep Davis quiet, "comparatively," for the remainder of the trip.

About a mile east of New London (present-day London, Ohio), Taylor noticed a team of horses hitched to a wagon "dashing across the country at a fearful rate." On reaching the railroad tracks, the horses turned and galloped along a road paralleling them. At a crossing, the locomotive struck them and the wagon. The train stopped. From his boxcar, Taylor saw "one horse dead, the other struggling in its harness, [and] something white lying beside the track." Two children were in the wagon bed. One was dead, the other "wounded mortally." In a sense, they were casualties of the war, killed by ill chance amid the peaceful farmlands of central Ohio.

Toward sundown, the train arrived at the Columbus depot, where the Forty-seventh partook of a supper ordered for it by Governor Dennison, "bread and butter, bologna sausage, ham, cheese and hot coffee." Dennison also distributed to the officers their commissions. Taylor placed his in a trunk, at long last relieved of all uncertainty and worry about his military status. His sole immediate problem was the still recalcitrant Josephus Davis. He referred the matter to Colonel Poschner. Declaring he would "fix him," Poschner personally commanded Davis to swear the soldier's oath. Davis swore that he would not. Poschner thereupon instructed Taylor to have Davis disarmed and stripped of his uniform. Not wanting "to see him made nude in Columbus," Taylor instead deprived Davis of his musket and other equipment, then turned him "adrift" to make his way back to Brown County.[21]

That evening, the Forty-seventh boarded a train of the Central Ohio Railroad and headed—not west toward the Mississippi River and Missouri, where the officers and men expected to go—but east toward the Ohio River and Virginia. Neither the regiment nor Taylor could have realized it, but a decisive event in the careers of both thus took place, one that would largely determine what they accomplished and did not accomplish during the next year and a half.

Also on its way eastward that evening was a letter that Netta had written to Taylor the night before, unaware that he had his coveted captain's commission and was about to set off, at least figuratively speaking, for the battlefield. She wrote: "Your friends all say come home. Oh my dear let me beg and implore you to come. I will go with you any place, make any sacrifice, only *come home*. You know how happy I would be."[22]

It was not the first such plea Netta had made and it would be far from the last. She did not share Taylor's patriotic fervor, and she preferred a live husband to a dead one, regardless of how gloriously he died. With him gone from Elmwood Cottage, she had declared in a May 5 letter, Georgetown was "Fort Desolation."

The time would come when Taylor himself was more than willing to return home. That time, though, had not come yet. As the train carrying the Forty-seventh Ohio chugged through the August night, Taylor looked forward eagerly to being in Virginia. There he would do battle not only with the Rebels but also with the world itself—a battle he was resolved to win, determined not to go down in dismal defeat like his unknown, yet unforgettable, father. He asked only for a chance to fight both those battles, and in Virginia, he was confident, he would have it, and soon.

I Want to Distinguish Myself

September–December 1861

"**Y**OU DOUBTLESS WILL BE SURPRISED at the point from which this letter is written," Taylor began a letter to Netta dated Weston, Virginia, September 1, 1861. "Before I narrate my trip," he continued, "I shall state for the benefit of my particular friends that I now have my commission as Captain for three years safe in my trunk. As I have marched along the road, I have frequently wondered what master hand guides my course."

Most of the remainder of the letter described the Forty-seventh Ohio's journey to Weston, in what became in 1863 the state of West Virginia but which then was part of Virginia, albeit separated geographically from the eastern portion by the Allegheny mountain range. On August 29, the regiment crossed the Ohio River to Benwood and boarded another train that took it by way of Fairmont to Grafton, where it transferred to a train that carried it to Clarksburg, which it reached the next morning. From Clarksburg, the men marched to Weston, arriving there at noon on September 1 after an overnight encampment. During the first day's march, which covered sixteen miles, "Will Kirpatrick came near giving out," whereupon Taylor "took his knapsack and carried it six miles" before putting it in a wagon, then "took Pugh Haggerty's gear and carried it the balance of the way," an act he repeated the second day. The march left him with "only one foot slightly blistered" and enhanced his reputation in the regiment, where "I am known as 'the white haired Captain who is as mean and tough as hell.'"

The Forty-seventh had been rushed to the front, Taylor explained, because "Gen. Lee is pressing Rosecrans and the general report is that a battle will occur in a short time." By "Gen. Lee" he meant none other than Robert E. Lee, and Rosecrans of course was William S. Rosecrans, at this time a brigadier general but destined to be one of the top Union commanders until fate turned against him at Chickamauga Creek in Georgia two years later. Earlier

The Forty-seventh Ohio Crossing a River in West Virginia.
  J. Nep Roesler, Portfolio of Lithographs of the War in Virginia and West Virginia
  (*Cincinnati: Ehrgott, Forbriger, and Company, 1862*).

in July, executing a daring plan that he himself had conceived, Rosecrans had driven the Confederates from a supposedly impregnable position atop Rich Mountain near Beverly, Virginia, thereby giving the Federals control of the northwestern corner of the state.[1] Now Lee had come from Richmond, in his first campaign of the war, to redeem the lost territory. Half of his small army he personally led, its objective Cheat Mountain Pass; taking it would open the way for a Confederate sweep northward through the Tygart Valley to Beverly. The other half, two brigades headed by Brigadier Generals John B. Floyd and Henry A. Wise, sought to defeat a Yankee column that had advanced to the Gauley River near where it and the New River join to form the Kanawha River, about seventy miles to the southeast of Cheat Mountain. To this end, on August 22, Floyd had crossed the Gauley at Carnifex Ferry and routed a Union detachment at Cross Lanes. Since this victory put Floyd and Wise in position to cut off a Federal force under Brig. Gen. Jacob D. Cox at Gauley Bridge, twenty-some miles downstream from Carnifex Ferry, Rosecrans intended to move against them as quickly as possible and with all available troops—among them, those of the Forty-seventh Ohio.[2]

On September 3, Rosecrans set out from Weston with 8,000 men. Taylor, however, was not among them. "Yesterday," he wrote Netta the next day, "six companies were taken from our regiment, and the remaining four left as a garrison." While others marched off to battle, he had to stay behind guarding supplies, the consequence of commanding so small a company.

In a long September 9 letter, he complained to Netta:

> We are still in garrison at this place, and Lord only knows how long we shall remain here. If I had a conception of the duration of the time I would send for you and the children to stay with me. This is a long and tedious track to tread. We come on duty every four days, remain all day and night, but it is a glorious cause and that gives us the requisite endurance. We are aroused in the night by false alarms and all are compelled to turn out. . . . Everything is strict, very strict—the boys grumble at discipline and I have to almost goad them into obeying. I have no orderly, no one with me who understands the drill, and I have to take it [the drilling] six and one `half hours per day and then make out the morning report, the detail for guards, for fatigue and do all the other duties which an orderly has to perform, then I have to sit on court martial and make out reports and everything related to it. It appears that the Col. [Lieutenant Colonel Elliott, who was left in charge of the Weston garrison] thinks I am able to do all these things. I am the senior captain in our camp, therefore in the absence of the Col. I had to officiate at dress parade, &c., &c.[3]

On the evening of September 10, Taylor, whose tent was pitched atop a hill overlooking Weston, heard the rumble of cannon fire coming from the south. It was Rosecrans attacking Floyd, who had retreated to the north bank of the Gauley River at Carnifex Ferry. Here his 2,000 troops, fighting behind log barricades, held the Federals at bay until dark, whereupon Rosecrans, who had been able to employ only a portion of his army owing to the rough terrain and dense woods, fell back with the intention of resuming the battle in

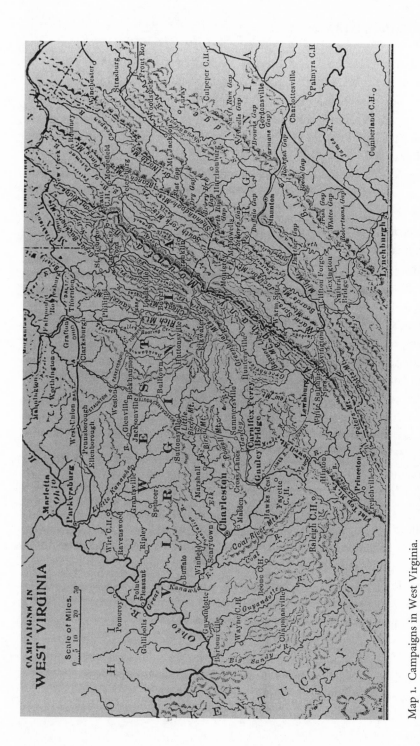

Map 1. Campaigns in West Virginia.
Jacob D. Cox, Military Reminiscences of the Civil War. 2 vols. New York: Charles E. Scribner, 1900.

the morning. He did not get the chance. Floyd, who had compelling personal reasons to avoid capture, used the cover of the night to cross his forces to the other side of the Gauley by way of a footbridge and flatboats, which he then destroyed. Without pontoons or any other means of bridging the river, Rosecrans could not pursue. Even so, his counterthrust not only caused the withdrawal of Floyd but also that of Wise's Confederates from the Gauley River. More important still, on September 12, an attempt by Lee to penetrate Cheat Mountain Pass failed when the commander of the brigade who had been sent to outflank its defenders lost his nerve and turned back. Had he succeeded, Lee would have been in position to occupy most of northwest Virginia. Instead, Union control of the region was assured, never again to be seriously challenged.[4]

In the Carnifex Ferry fight, the six companies of the Forty-seventh neither lost men nor gained glory, for although deployed, they did not engage. Taylor's old regiment, however, the Twelfth Ohio, did advance against the enemy and suffered three casualties, one of whom was Col. John Lowe, shot dead. As a consequence, Taylor's brother-in-law Carr White assumed command of the regiment, and his rank was soon elevated to full colonel.[5] Manifestly, combat offered opportunity as well as peril—to those who survived it.

Denied, for the time being, that opportunity, Taylor endeavored to make the best of Weston, as these passages from a September 15 letter to Netta indicate: "The Colonel [Frederick Poschner] has given me permission to recruit here and I have secured three recruits; somehow as I get settled my spirits revive, my courage strengthens and I start off on the future like a locomotive." "I have" he added, "been out several nights,—there is a secret band of traitors which meets in town nightly and I was detailed to smell them out. I think I have succeeded but am not certain." Meanwhile, "Last week I took possession of a secession printing office and was engaged for three or four days doing job work for the regiment." And "Today I took dinner over in town. Last week Lieut. Col. Elliott invited me out and we had a royal time. I got acquainted with the *bon ton* of this place."[6]

Taylor never identified the secessionist conspirators in Weston; neither did he again hobnob with that village's "*bon ton*." On September 18, orders arrived for the four companies to join the rest of the regiment at Cross Lanes. "I regret leaving," Taylor notified Netta that evening, adding that "although I feel glad to move and am rejoiced at the prospect of getting into active service, I hate to go to service with only 39 men and that is the number I have with me now. However nothing ventured nothing gained, and [as] it is with honor, so [it is] with success—the path is never strewn with roses, nor passed with perfect ease."

At 10:00 A.M., September 19, the four companies set out from Weston. Their march to Cross Lanes lasted a week and traversed close to one hundred miles of some of the most spectacular but also rugged mountain terrain in western Virginia. The road, which was little more than a trail hacked through the wilderness, twisted "around and over a succession of steep hills" and was turned by incessant rains into "one continuous struggle." Taylor had his men toss their knapsacks into a wagon, an example followed by the other companies. Even so, at the end of the first day, a soldier in Company G fatally shot himself after declaring "if he was going to be killed by marches, he might as well die first as last." Sometimes the wagons fell so far behind that the troops were left without rations when they bivouacked for the night. After several such occurrences, Taylor's "boys" came to him and asked, "What about getting a pig?" He replied, "It is not necessary for a Captain to see or know everything." The next day, while on the march, he received "a piece of fresh pork finely roasted." Henceforth, everyone ate well, even though the "houses along the road are deserted and everything is barren, barren, barren!" Foragers, though, needed to exercise caution, for the "country is full of secesh," and on the night of September 21, three soldiers were killed by bushwhackers.[7]

On September 26, the little column reached Cross Lanes, "a crossroads formed by the intersection of the Gauley and Clarksburg Pike and some neighborhood road which intersects the Summerville and Lewisburg Road." By then Taylor, who a month ago had left Camp Dennison attired in a dress uniform and his soon-to-be-lost plumed hat, wore "a blue blouse, two grey flannel shirts, coarse heavy blue pants, [and] no shoes or socks"; because of the rain and mud he had decided to "let my feet take it" for the nonce. "Soldiering in Western Virginia," he wrote Netta on September 27, "is jolly! Though rough work, hard on a weak frame, a feeble constitution." At first, he had feared he would "yield to it," but so far he had "stood it first rate— not a cold, no stiffness, no soreness, nor anything calculated to injure my health; indeed, my dear, I now weigh 161, when I left home I weighed only 149½." Moreover, life henceforth would be easier, for he had been joined by

George Herrick, a black barber whom he hired in Ohio in August to serve as body servant. Herrick was "as good a Negro as ever lived, polite, kind, with eyes everywhere,—needs no telling and can keep secrets, at least he never told anyone when he got a large *louse* out of my hair while cutting." He also kept Taylor well supplied with fresh "grunter" and made "soft bread and pie and cake" and "the best soup you ever tasted," using an oven that Lieutenant Colonel Elliott "found disconnected from a building the other day."[8]

By September 27, Rosecrans's army, including the main body of the Forty-seventh Ohio, had advanced southeastward to Big Sewell Mountain on the road to Lewisburg. Here it faced a large and growing Confederate force commanded by Lee in person. Taylor believed that soon a "battle will come off" that "will decide the fate of Western Va.," one that "I hope I shall be permitted to participate in," for "I want to distinguish myself." Instead, his company remained at Cross Lanes with the rest of Elliott's detachment, once more guarding supplies. Taylor experienced renewed frustration. "I am sorely puzzled," he told Netta on September 30, "at the prospects of my ultimate success."

But if denied the opportunity to distinguish himself on the battlefield, he would, he resolved, strive to do it where he was. South beyond the Gauley River, bushwhackers infested the country, terrorizing local Unionists and sniping at Federal troops.[9] On orders from Elliott, Taylor conducted a series of "nocturnal scouts" during which his men "impressed" horses and livestock belonging to suspected guerrillas and took prisoners. These expeditions were hazardous—a lieutenant drowned while attempting to cross the Gauley—and also arduous. During one foray, Taylor's patrol traveled thirty miles, much of the way "down ravines, through laurel brakes, [and] in a thunder shower," with the "night as dark as could be." His enterprise and energy gave him a measure of what he craved. "I am quite famous on the scout with this portion of the regiment," he bragged to Netta on October 9.

In the same letter, Taylor also reported that Rosecrans was retreating. With his army reduced by sickness and detachments to 5,200 effectives, without adequate supplies owing to roads that were "endless quagmires," and opposed by a much larger Confederate force holding a virtually impregnable position, Rosecrans's sole hope for victory was to have Lee attack him—a choice that Lee declined, with his poorly equipped and ill-trained troops, many of them militia. Finally, on the night of October 5, Rosecrans stealthily evacuated his works and withdrew to Gauley Mountain near the confluence

The Gauley Mountain Camp.
Roesler, War in Virginia and West Virginia.

of the New and Gauley Rivers. Here he passed the rest of the month and all of November awaiting a Confederate counteroffensive, but apart from some probes by Floyd none occurred. For any strategic purpose, the 1861 campaign in western Virginia, actually decided at Rich and Cheat Mountains, came to a soggy, anticlimactic end.[10]

The bushwhackers, however, remained active, and Taylor continued to hunt them. On the morning of October 13, armed with an Enfield rifle, a revolver, and a bowie knife, he set forth with Lt. Henry King of his company, fifteen soldiers, and two civilian guides, both Unionists from the Gauley River region. One of them had had a son, the other a brother-in-law, murdered by secessionists. They were "burning for vengeance."

At midnight, Taylor's party approached the house of "a notorious scout by name of Nutter." After having his men surround the place, Taylor knocked on the door, and Nutter's wife opened it. He told her that he had orders from General Floyd to obtain her husband's services as a guide. She answered that he was at his brother's house beyond the Meadow River. Taylor thereupon dropped the pretense of being a Confederate officer and, using a torch made from a piece of board, peered beneath a bed where Lieutenant King, who also had entered the house, reported that someone was hiding. He saw a man "standing on all fours, his back close up to the tick" of the mattress. Cocking his Enfield, he ordered him to come out. He did so, "the wildest looking man I ever saw and all from fright."

"Your name, sir!" Taylor demanded. "Nutter." "David?" "Yes." "Put on your britches." Nutter put them on, along with his shoes and coat. While he dressed, Taylor took a rifle that was standing by the bed, then escorted Nutter outside where the soldiers tied his hands and led him away. Before leaving, Taylor warned Mrs. Nutter that if she told "any one about our visit the consequences should be visited on her husband's head."

Taylor next searched the house of a bushwhacker named Odell, but he was not there. Then a local Unionist informed him that Capt. John T. Amick, "chief of the rebel scouts," was at his home and planning to leave it that day. Accompanied by King, a guide, and six volunteers, Taylor proceeded to Amick's residence, arriving at daylight. A dog "having let loose its gab," Taylor ordered his men to rush the place. He reached it first, cocked his Enfield, and entered by a side door, "smiling as you please." He beheld a man sitting at a table eating breakfast with his wife and children. "Are you Captain Amick?" he asked the man, who replied "No." "John T. Amick?" persisted Taylor. This time the answer was "yes." "You are the man I want, get your coat." Amick stood, then suddenly dashed from the room, through the parlor, and to the front door, only to meet Lieutenant King brandishing a revolver. Turning around, Amick said to Taylor, "I will get my coat now, if you will let me," then sprang past Taylor and ran out the side door. Taylor pushed aside Mrs. Amick, who tried to stand in his way, and followed him. As Taylor emerged from the side door, a bullet fired by one of his own men whizzed "within an inch of my head." He in turn fired at the fleeing Amick and saw "blood start in two places apparently on his back." Even so, Amick kept running until another bullet struck him, whereupon he cried "Oh! Oh! Oh!!!" and fell to the ground. Taylor went to him—"I wanted," he subsequently informed Netta, "to kill him" but "couldn't do it while he was helpless"— and found that a bullet, presumably the one he had fired, "had passed entirely through his body and come out near the right arm."

Taylor had Amick carried into the house where, after his wounds had been bandaged, he left him, for obviously he was in no condition to be moved. Describing the affair two days later to Netta, he expressed the opinion that Amick "is dead by this time as he appeared to bleed inwardly." So it was that Tom Taylor got his first taste of actual war, in the sense that he had (probably) killed a man and come close to being killed himself, albeit by what a later generation would call "friendly fire." To be sure, it was not war as he had envisioned it—a battlefield where massed armies clashed amid drumbeats and bugle peals. Instead, the scene had been an obscure mountain "holler," the action had consisted of shooting a fleeing unarmed man in the back, and the accompaniment was the wailing of Amick's wife as she stood by his bed, two small children by her side, a baby in her arms. "I felt deeply for her," Taylor told Netta, "but made her be quiet."

Taylor and his men made a "lively trip" from Amick's house—they were behind enemy lines—until they reached a secure place in the forest where they rested for a couple of hours. They then resumed their scout, searched "many houses," and captured another "secesh" before halting again to sleep until it became dark. On awakening, Taylor found that he had been joined by Capt. Hananiah D. Pugh of the Forty-seventh, who informed him that his expedition had been reported to be surrounded by Confederates and that seventy men had been sent out to rescue it. Taylor enjoyed "a good hearty laugh," then returned to camp where Elliott and the other officers congratulated him on putting out of action Amick, who "had taken more prisoners, shot more men and run off more cattle" than any bushwhacker in the region.

The next day (October 16), Taylor penned a long, at times somewhat incoherent narrative of the expedition to Netta, concluding it with these words: "The business [of tracking down bushwhackers] suits me. I like it, stand it well. . . . I am not trammeled by orders and directions but all is left to me and I go when and where I please. . . . I came out here to make a reputation some way and I am going to try for it."

Soon after (supposedly) killing Amick, Taylor further enhanced "my reputation as a scouting chief" by leading another successful foray across the Gauley. During it, he rounded up five prisoners, seized their horses, and acquired for himself sundry plunder that included a saddle, "a splendid bolster and one comfort," a glass goblet, a copy of Charlotte Brontë's novel *The Professor,* and "some religious books." Describing this raid to Netta, he boasted,

"Now my position is almost impregnable" with Poschner and Elliott. "Captain Taylor," he added, "stands very high—I have been favorably mentioned in reports and have had many reports go directly to Gen. Rosecranz [*sic*]. 'Oh vanity of vanities, & c.,' as the preacher says—but still it is natural for one to be ambitious and to be glad when he knows he stands well with his superior officers."[11]

Presumably because he stood well with his superior officers Taylor was able to obtain a leave of absence for the entire month of November. Certain passages in his October letters indicate that the official purpose of the leave was to recruit more men for his company, which remained the smallest in the regiment. But he also had another and personal motive for returning to Georgetown, one revealed in an October 9 letter to Netta:

> This is night, a quiet, calm and lovely night, speaking to us but too distinctly of the hoar frosts which e'en now are brewing and making ready to pay us defenders of liberty and the Constitution a glorious visit, robing us in white, clear and sparkling vesture, as the breath of heaven which falls on higher and holier things, but too forcibly, [with the result] that man, poor weak, wayfaring man . . . will need more covers and a lump of flesh about five feet in height and weighing between one hundred & fourteen & one hundred & twenty, called woman, to look after creature comforts and darn stockings.

Although Taylor spent most of his leave in Georgetown, he did devote considerable time—more than Netta liked—to recruiting and succeeded in signing up thirty-plus men before bidding his wife and children good-bye on November 29 and going to Cincinnati to take an Ohio River steamboat back to western Virginia.[12] While waiting to embark, he sauntered about the city and came upon a used bookstore where he purchased for twenty-five cents a copy of Edward Bulwer-Lytton's 1834 novel, *The Last Days of Pompeii*. This, he wrote Netta the following day from Gallipolis, Ohio, "is the best thing of the kind I ever read. I would not take five times what I paid for it."

Two days later, Taylor traveled by steamer up the Kanawha to Charleston and from there by wagon to Carrolton, where Carr White's Twelfth Ohio was stationed. Throughout September and October, Taylor had made repeated efforts to visit White but always in vain, and this time proved no exception. As he informed Netta on December 4, "to my astonishment" White had gone home to Georgetown. Had he been present, Taylor "intended to make some arrangement with Carr by which I could get in his regiment in some capacity." Nice though it was to be in an "almost impregnable position" with Poschner and Elliott, evidently he thought that it would be nicer still to be in a regiment commanded by his wife's brother.

Quite possibly another reason Taylor hoped to rejoin the Twelfth Ohio was that it had been ordered to Charleston for the winter, whereas the Forty-seventh was to remain at Cross Lanes and Gauley Bridge. He disliked the prospect of spending the winter there and hoped that a rumor that Brig. Gen. Robert L. McCook, commander of the brigade to which the Forty-seventh had been assigned, "has promised to get us out of this infernal region" proved true. Yet orders were orders, and on December 5 he set out for Cross Lanes, only to discover that he could not get there because the "road is almost impassable for foot travellers being eighteen inches to one foot in depth in mud."

Hawks Nest, Gauley Mountain.
Roesler, War in Virginia and West Virginia.

Perforce he stayed at a farm being used as headquarters by the sutler of the Forty-seventh (and a scoundrel, according to the regimental history).[13] From there he sent Netta a letter the next day in which he described the country-side—"great destruction and loss is apparent on every side"—and informed her that "I just got a [Colt] navy revolver that will carry about four hundred feet for twenty-five dollars" because "I did not feel like tramping through the country without the proper safety guard." His old revolver he had left at home where, he declared, "I would like to be but I cannot, therefore I am compelled to like to be with the 47th Reg."

By December 10, when he next wrote Netta, he was back with the regiment in a camp located two-and-one-half miles from Gauley Bridge. "We are again an outpost but are well provided with defenses. . . . All the commanding eminences are occupied by our posts," which mounted "ten field pieces, three of them Parrott guns rifled, one a twenty pounder, two ten pounders and the rest smooth bores. We have Sibley tents and good stoves."

While at Charleston, Taylor had become acquainted with Maj. S. A. Stafford, paymaster for the Department of West Virginia, "a fine-looking gentleman, six feet two inches in height" and "always ready for a joke, a laugh or a funny expedition." Therefore, when Stafford visited the Forty-seventh to perform his duties, he employed Taylor as an assistant, then asked him to accompany him on a trip to pay several other regiments. Delighted—"it is much better to be lucky than rich"—Taylor agreed, subject to the approval of Colonel Poschner, who granted it, remarking that he "must have one in his regiment who understands making up pay rolls." During the latter half of December, Taylor traveled with Stafford and three other officers to Charleston, Barboursville, Guyandotte, and Winfield, "improving my geographical knowledge very much" and generally having a "most pleasant trip," even though the "main portion of the inhabitants have the same sullen, downcast expression of countenance for which all Western Virginians are noted." Moreover, he was "making many acquaintances among officers and men," he expected to have ninety men in his company when "the balance of my recruits arrive" from Ohio, and he now was "fourth in point of seniority" among the officers of the regiment, where "I am a favorite" and "can carry it almost solid for anything." If only Netta and the children could come to stay with him at the Forty-seventh's camp, he would be completely content; but since "we live in tents" this "would be too severe" for them, given the winter weather.[14]

On December 26, he wrote Netta from Gallipolis, where Stafford's group had stopped for several days before going on to Wheeling. After describing some of the places he had visited, a false alarm of a Confederate attack at Guyandotte, and the murder of two Union couriers by bushwhackers who had been urged on by a woman who wished to "dance in their blood," he continued:

> Christmas I spent in this place, had roast possum and turkey for supper. The day was very tame, no amusements, no entertainment of any character. In the evening I received an invitation to attend a "Hasty Hop" and would have gone had we not been compelled to start for Winfield and spend all night on the boat sleeping.
>
> After my trip to Wheeling I shall rejoin my company. . . . I cannot tell how long before I will be able to revisit you. Oh, how it would delight me to be at *home* again, my dear home, the feeling, the desire become so strong that I am actually childish—but never mind, the war will be over before many more years and then I can enjoy it all the more.

This was Taylor's last letter to Netta in 1861. He had been in the army for eight months, three of them on active campaign. He had his much-desired and treasured captain's commission, he hoped for—indeed expected—promotion to major before long, and he possessed (according to his account) great prestige and popularity in the regiment. Yet the closest he had come to combat had been his antibushwhacker expeditions, about which nobody back home knew anything except Netta, members of the family, and a few close friends. And because the Forty-seventh had not participated in any major engagements, little had appeared in the newspapers about it, not even the Cincinnati ones. To former newspaper editor Taylor, such a lack of press coverage was galling and perhaps explains his sarcastic tone in a December 12 letter to Netta:

> We have an accomplished German artist in our Regiment whom we have excused from all duty in order to embalm our advent to and march through this State in picture. Other Regiments are extolled by Reporters. Our artist and his true pictures will extol us in future and when the poor newspaper is passed away, and the memory of what they [*sic*] contained gone, then our pictures will present us viv-

idly before the eyes of the world and as long as there are lovers of the grand, beautiful and sublime, the 47th Reg. will be known and cherished. Who says that the 47th is not ahead. Hurrah for the gallant, the sturdy 47th. I will have a full set. Our camps, our marches, our crossing at Carnifax [*sic*] by torchlight, our bivouac and everything of interest, then all that is grand in nature . . . will be associated with us and heighten the effect. Won't it be glorious?[15]

As 1861 ended and 1862 began, Tom Taylor clearly was a frustrated young man. Would the new year give him what he craved—glory, promotion, some spectacular successes in his battle with the world? It is a question he surely asked himself. If he could have foreseen the answer, just as surely he would not have liked it.

2

What Have I Accomplished?
January–December 1862

"**A** S A NEW YEARS GIFT," wrote Taylor from Wheeling on January 1, 1862, "please accept a photograph of myself." The photograph showed him in "my dress suit but not full uniform"—no sash, sword, or belt. Accompanying it was a second photograph, this one of Taylor with Maj. S. A. Stafford and three army surgeons. After identifying them, Taylor commented: "We have had a most excellent time together. They are witty, humorous and generous to a fault. Preserve the picture for my sake. I want to enjoy it in after life." Meanwhile, he concluded, since Stafford had completed his paymaster tour, the next day he would "start on my return to camp. Then hurra [*sic*] for business and work and by close application I trust that I shall merit one months leave in March."

By January 8, Taylor was back at Camp Gauley Mountain, his "abode" a Sibley tent perched on the side of the mountain. Here he and the rest of the Forty-seventh Ohio spent the winter, with only an occasional reconnaissance or antibushwhacker scout to relieve the monotony of drilling and camp routine. During this period, Col. Frederick Poschner was in Cincinnati on sick leave, which left Lyman Elliott in command of the regiment. Hitherto Taylor had enjoyed a friendly relationship with the lieutenant colonel. This quickly changed. Elliott refused to withdraw charges against several members of Taylor's company who had been involved in a "row" even though Taylor, while in Wheeling, had arranged with the departmental judge advocate to have them released from arrest if this were done. Angered, Taylor denounced Elliott to Netta as "the most vindictive man I ever saw" and told her that if his "boys" were shot he would resign. They were not shot and he did not resign, but he resolved to "settle" Elliott and hoped that Poschner, "a warm friend of mine," soon would resume command.[1]

Also drawing Taylor's ire was Netta herself. Twenty days passed in January without his receiving a single letter from her. Writing on January 28, he accused her of neglecting her wifely duty as a correspondent and, in effect, threatened her with infidelity if she did not perform it in proper fashion:

> In a few days we may be ordered to Lewisburg . . . and then you will not hear from me so frequently and perchance I may be able to serve my country by shedding my blood for liberty, won't that be glorious? At Lewisburg, if I should have the good fortune to be ordered there, I shall find nice rebel lasses and there perhaps I will need all your matronly care to keep me from temptation. Who knows—arching eyebrows, raven hair, dimpled cheeks and pouting lips, all rosy with life and radiant with beauty are great seducers & then a scarlet sash and brass buttons carry love wherever they go—

On reading these words, an indignant Netta picked up her pen on February 10 and wrote to "My Dear Husband":

> You cannot imagine what my feelings were when I read your letter of the 28th in which you have accused me of neglect and indifferences . . . [and] throw it up to me that there are other "bright eyes, dimpled cheeks, and pouting lips." What does all of this mean . . . ? I have written twice a week since the first of January, and if you have not received the letters, then God in Heaven only knows where they have gone. I often think of the way you are situated in camp and of the temptations strewn around you, and for that reason I have . . . wrote [sic] long letters and endeavored to make them interesting to you, and every night ere I close my eyes in sleep . . . I pray for you that God may watch over and protect and shield you from every temptation. Oh my dear, put a guard over yourself, do not sink into dissipation of any kind.

Following this exhortation, and after once more imploring Taylor to leave the army and return home, Netta concluded somewhat sarcastically: "Well my dear I shall close in the hope that after you read this, you will think better of your little wife, who has always endeavored to do her duty in every respect. And hereafter my dear, if you do not get my letters, it will be the fault of the mails and not mine, for I shall be very particular."

Taylor read Netta's rejoinder on February 14—Valentine's Day. By then, a number of her letters, all posted in January, had reached him, providing proof that she had not been remiss in writing. Furthermore, in one of them, that of January 24, she had noted that his January 1 letter, containing the photographs, had not arrived until January 22; and therefore, he realized that he was not the only one to have waited a long time without receiving mail.

Taylor could only try to put the best face possible on his letter about finding "nice rebel lasses" in Lewisburg. It was not a very good face: "You misread my letter. . . . The expressions 'pouting lips,' etc. do not apply to you but to myself. I say and meant that possibly such graces, etc. might provoke me to a break of vows and entice me temporarily [*sic*] from fidelity to you if you did not stretch forth a hand to save."[2]

Even as this bit of arrant nonsense traveled to Georgetown, Netta "stretched for a hand to save" her husband from "infidelity" in a most effective manner: "I shall," she wrote Taylor on February 16, "expect you [to come home] on leave next month and will be very much disappointed if you do not come. I wish to—

'Feel the soft clasp of your hands
And your breath warm on my cheek
And hear you breathe those passions
I so often have heard you speak.'"

Understandably, these lines intensified Taylor's desire to obtain leave in March. But orders from army headquarters made this impossible, and it was neither practicable nor safe for Netta to visit him at Gauley Mountain, where the only habitations were tents and the soldiers assumed that any young woman entering the camp was a prostitute and acted accordingly. The best Taylor could do was to arrange to meet Netta in Charleston on Sunday, April 6—the same day, incidentally, that the biggest and bloodiest battle of the war thus far began on the banks of the Tennessee River at a place called Pittsburg Landing, near a log church named Shiloh. In West Virginia, it was a "bright, beautiful day" and presumably Netta experienced the "soft clasp" of her husband's hands—and all the rest.[3]

Hardly had Taylor restored peace with Netta when he became embroiled in another quarrel with Elliott. On April 14, the lieutenant colonel "interfered" in his "domestic affairs" by expelling his body servant, George Herrick, from the camp for having struck a soldier, who had called him a "damn black son of a bitch," in the arm with a hatchet. Taylor went to Elliott and told him that he had "no power to do so under the regulations," to which Elliott answered that "power or no power, he would take the responsibility." For a while Taylor "had a good mind to send in my resignation," then thought better of it and instead drew up charges against Elliott for exceeding his authority. "We will," he informed Netta on April 15, "have him up."

The new tiff with Elliott deepened Taylor's dissatisfaction with being stuck in the wilds of West Virginia with the Forty-seventh. Everywhere else, he declared in the same letter, Union armies "are advancing, glorious battles are being fought and triumphant victories are being won." In contrast, the Forty-seventh could not even move, much less fight, because in West Virginia "it rains on an average two days a week," turning the roads into quagmires. To be sure, the regiment had seen action at Carnifex Ferry and Big Sewell, but "all of these were as skirmishes compared with Bull Run, Donelson & Pittsburg [Landing]." Even worse:

> All the fellows who have gone from Georgetown, except myself, have been in a good fight. I have been in more dangerous service and had to "kill my man" in order to save myself, yet people don't look on it with the same respect, regard, and honor as the other description of fighting. I think I am just drifting, a waif upon the vast ocean of life, and whether for weal or woe I cannot tell.

By spring 1862, West Virginia formed part of what had been designated the Mountain Department under the command of Maj. Gen. John C. Frémont, who had replaced William Rosecrans at the end of March. At President Lincoln's behest, Frémont initially proposed marching with an army of 10,000 men due south to Knoxville for the purpose of liberating East Tennessee, where the majority of the inhabitants, as in western Virginia, remained loyal to the Union. When this proved to be a logistical impossibility—at least 1,000 wagons and their teams would be needed to supply such a force for such a distance in such terrain—Frémont prepared a plan whereby two Union columns would advance into southwestern Virginia, unite, and then swing into East Tennessee by way of the Holston River Valley toward Knoxville.

Frémont himself took charge of the largest column, which would move south by way of Cheat Mountain Pass and Staunton. The other and smaller column consisted of Brig. Gen. Jacob D. Cox's Kanawha Division, stationed at Gauley Bridge. It was to advance in two sections, with the main one, headed by Cox, passing over Flat Mountain to the Narrows of the New River. The other section, Col. George Crook's brigade, of which the Forty-seventh formed a part, would seize Lewisburg so as to safeguard Cox's left flank and rear.[4]

Word of the impending offensive revived Taylor's drooping spirits. He anticipated a battle "which will rival Pittsburg Landing" and was confident that, unlike two other officers from Georgetown, "I shall *not* run six miles from [my] company" or "from a dozen *Federal Cavalry* scouts." As for his company, it now numbered eighty-three men, "all big, hale, hearty fellows," the shortest of whom was five feet, six inches and the tallest six feet, one inch. They would, he assured Netta, "follow me to the cannon's mouth" and "shoot the man who runs."[5]

On May 1, having received orders from Elliott to reinforce a scouting party that had been sent to Big Sewell Mountain, Taylor set forth with his company, filled with high hopes of participating in a full-scale battle and gaining the "honor" he so strongly craved. But again, he was doomed to disappointment. The only Confederates he encountered were local bushwhackers and some roving cavalry; his sole exploit was to lead a small party into enemy-held territory where it rescued some Unionist families from secessionist persecution; and the closest he came to a battle was an encounter at Lewisburg on May 12 with some local militia, which, as he wrote Netta immediately afterward, "was not an extensive fight" but more like a "race." Furthermore, although the Federals occupied the town, every night they withdrew to a ridge west of it from fear of being attacked by a superior enemy force. Not until the rest of Crook's brigade arrived on May 15 did they abandon this prudent practice.[6]

That same day, Taylor again reported to Netta:

We are now beginning to learn what soldiering is, and to have no tents. . . . I have not had a clean shirt for two weeks. The officers' baggage is all stored at Camp Gauley Mt. And I do not know what I shall do. I have nothing but a rubber blanket, a blouse & pair of common pants—none but a captured sword. I am ashamed of my appearance. My outfit was quite expensive and it may be a total loss—

General Jacob D. Cox.

Jacob D. Cox, Military Reminiscences of the Civil War, *2 vols.* (*New York: Charles E. Scribner, 1900*), *1: 118.*

Nevertheless, he continued, "I like the service and the excitement attendant upon it." What he did not like were the people of Lewisburg:

This is the bitterest place I ever saw—people are all secesh except one and that one keeps his mouth shut. The women say they would like to cut our throats & [one of them] even said so in the presence of one of our officers. . . . I told a man today that . . . our men were rapidly coming to the same conclusion in regard to the Secesh, that hereafter we might adopt the same doctrine—that is to cut their throats when they are in our hands, or if that would not suit [them] to commence on the town folks.

When not threatening to cut "secesh" throats, Taylor roamed the countryside with a small band, again hunting bushwhackers. This, he wrote Netta on May 17, "is just the life that suits me. . . . I know all the ranges of mountains & the places where the people reside—So I fear nothing, [and] a clear night and some food is all I ask."

But he was unable to pursue this now-familiar activity for long. On May 21, all the companies of the Forty-seventh present at Lewisburg headed back to Camp Gauley Mountain to rejoin the rest of the regiment in the still more familiar task of garrisoning it. As a consequence, Taylor and the Forty-seventh missed out on what proved to be the largest engagement of the campaign. Just two days after they left, 3,000 Confederates under Brig. Gen. Henry Heth attempted to retake Lewisburg. Despite being outnumbered nearly two to one, Crook's brigade not only repulsed but routed the attackers, most of whom consisted of reluctant conscripts who threw down their muskets and fled as soon as they came under fire. Even so, this victory soon became as strategically meaningless as it was easy. To the east, a small but potent Rebel army under Maj. Gen. Thomas J. "Stonewall" Jackson began rampaging through the Shenandoah Valley of Virginia, causing all sorts of trouble and threatening more. Hoping to trap and destroy him, Lincoln ordered Frémont to move into the valley with his 11,000 troops. This left Cox with no choice except to suspend his advance, pending the outcome of Frémont's foray. That took the form of a defeat at Cross Keys, Virginia, on June 8. Then, after roughing up another Federal force at Port Republic the following day, Jackson squeezed past Frémont to safety. His brilliant campaign upset Union plans for taking Richmond and put an end to Frémont's attempt to liberate East Tennessee. In the case of the latter, it was just as well. Owing to logistical problems and the ability of the Confederates to supply and reinforce their troops in this region via the Virginia and Tennessee Railroad, Frémont never stood a realistic chance of reaching Knoxville, much less seizing it.[7]

Taylor felt "chagrined" at having missed out on the May 23 encounter at Lewisburg. Had his company been there, he informed Netta on May 24, its location would have given it "the honor of repelling the first onslaught of the enemy." As it was, he could only write a long account of the Lewisburg expedition, one in which he figured prominently, then send it to Netta with a request that she copy it and submit it to the *Georgetown Argus*.[8]

Apart from what Taylor dubbed a "pleasure excursion" late in June deep into southern West Virginia, almost to the Kentucky line, the Forty-seventh passed the summer at Gauley Bridge, drilling, patrolling, and trying to ferret out bushwhackers.[9] Concerning the last, Taylor on June 10 informed Netta:

> We have any number of the guerrillas hanging around our camp & it is utterly impossible to beat them far back—the mountains are now covered with very dense foliage and they can conceal themselves & remain as [secure] as if they were a thousand miles [away]. Whenever one [of our men] straggles from the camp, unless very watchful he will be picked up. It is very provoking to be compelled to contend against a foe who calls in such auxiliaries to give strength to his arms. We have no mercy on them. When we catch one he hangs. Then his goods are removed from his house, his wife & children required to step out & the torch is applied & soon all that is left is a heap of smouldering ruins.[10]

Unable to fight regular Confederates in a regular way, Taylor intensified his campaign against Elliott when, early in June, the lieutenant colonel issued an order requiring all officers to obtain a pass signed by him before they could leave camp. Taylor and nineteen other officers went to Elliott's tent on the night of June 4, awakened him, and demanded that he rescind the order. Although he became, according to Taylor's account, "very pale" and "trembled slightly," Elliott refused to comply with the demand. A committee of officers thereupon went to brigade commander Crook the next day with their complaint and obtained a cancellation of the order. "It was a complete triumph," Taylor notified Netta that same day, adding that "Elliott has to leave the regiment, nothing short of this will do."

But Elliott did not leave and the "triumph" proved to be far from complete—indeed, virtually nonexistent. As Taylor wrote Netta, June 7:

> I think our present camp is almost like a penitentiary. Men can scarcely obtain a pass & it is difficult for an officer to obtain one to pass the pickets. Discipline is also strictly enforced. Officers made accountable for any improper act of his [sic] men. Consequently we have been compelled to become stricter in our rule.

In this and several subsequent letters, Taylor spoke of resigning. Only a sense of duty to the Union and his men, he declared, prevented him. No doubt he was sincere in stating this. Yet he had another and more powerful reason for remaining in the army. Should he leave it, he never would fulfill his desire to distinguish himself in combat and attain glory and higher rank. Not until then could he return to Georgetown a success and be able to laugh at those who had laughed at him when he set forth from there on July 27, 1861, with his pathetic little collection of recruits. To do otherwise would be to repeat the failure of his father, whose "life and career," he wrote revealingly to Netta on June 9, were "impressed . . . in burning characters on the tablet of burning memory."

He did not, however, wish to remain in Georgetown. He could not forget or forgive the July 27 humiliation. "The scene of my departure," he wrote Netta on April 30, "of the desertion of my friends in the hour of trial, sears my memory like a hot iron passing across my brain. How it pains me." Instead, he wanted to move beyond the Mississippi to Iowa, or Kansas, or some place in the Great Plains. Here was where the nation's future lay, and he would be a part of that future.[11]

Netta, who had been born and lived all her life in Georgetown, replied on May 7 that he was wrong to think that he had no friends there, that "Brown county is the county for you," and that he should not "let a few fellows, that do not deserve the name of men, run me away." Moreover, "It would be quite a trial to me to part from my family and friends, and all the pleasant associations that bind me to my birthplace." Yet, she added, should he persist in his desire to leave Georgetown, "I am willing to go with you wherever you think best."

This debate continued through May, June, and into July, with Taylor repeating his reasons for wishing to head west once the war ended (or he resigned) and Netta reiterating her reasons for desiring to stay in Georgetown—a desire she always took care to qualify by stating (to quote from her May 27 letter), "I am willing to go with you anywhere, and I can be happy and contented any place, if you are only with me."[12]

As Netta observed in her May 7 letter, Taylor's talk of leaving both the army and Georgetown stemmed from his being in one of his "depressing moods again." The "pleasure excursion" of the Forty-seventh Ohio into southern West Virginia late in June revived his spirits—"I like my present life," he informed Netta on July 5, "and cannot say when I shall relinquish it"—but not for long. On July 15, the mail arrived at the Gauley Mountain camp, and it contained no letter from Netta. That made ten days without a word from or about her. At once Taylor's ever-ready pen went into action. He had, he scolded Netta, looked forward to receiving "an epistle from you laden with words of love, sympathy, comfort and consolation which would infuse a new spirit, new courage and fresh hope in my mind." Instead that day's mail "had no message of cheer, no word of promise, nor anything of hope for me," and he felt "as if the ministering angel of my life had disappeared into eternity." Why, he asked, had he gone so long without "any word of intelligence from my family," while other men from Georgetown "speak of receiving letters regularly from home and in short time." Unless he heard from her soon, he threatened, he would drown his sorrows in weekly drinking "sprees."

July 16 came but not a letter from Netta. Taylor exploded. "Why in the name of heaven," he scrawled on the first of four pages addressed to "My Dear Wife," "do I not receive your letters or hear from you by some other source?"

> I hope you have not neglected to write & I also hope you have not been ill, but what is the matter—to what cause shall I attribute it? . . . If you do not wish to continue a correspondence "Speak boldly out," and though it may cost many a pang I will not trouble you hereafter. . . . I hardly believe that you are sick or else those writing me [from Georgetown] would mention [it]. So I have settled on this plan: to write again on Saturday whether I have heard from you or not. If I do not get a letter by that time you may look on it as a settled fact that I shall not write to you again this month and prob-

ably not this summer unless you can give some very satisfactory explanation. You know very well that I could never stand coquetry and
permit me to state that it is a very dangerous experiment to try on
during the existance [*sic*] of the matrimonial bonds. If you have
found anyone whom you prefer to myself, I release you from all
obligations and will render it easy for you to obtain a divorce.

No letter from Netta reached Taylor by Saturday, July 19, the deadline
he had set. He waited two more days, then wrote her that in view of his not
having received any mail from her since July 4, he could only conclude that
she no longer desired to fulfill her obligations to him as his wife and the
mother of his children and that therefore "with this letter I propose to
terminate our correspondence." The only way in which it could be resumed, he added in closing, was for her to provide "explanations of a satisfactory nature" of her failure to write him and to "request" that he again
write her.

As so often happens in such cases, the very next day brought a letter from
Netta, one dated July 15, the very day he had written her offering to "render
it easy" for her to obtain a divorce. Less than twenty minutes after reading it,
he again was at his desk, pen in hand and ink flowing. The result was six long
pages in which he described the "pain" he had suffered at not hearing from
her "for so long" and declared that the just-received letter "explains all," for
in it she informed him that both of the children had been seriously ill and
that she had been so busy nursing them that she simply had been unable to
find the time or summon the energy to write. He also told her that he had
sent her letters that would "cause you much suffering" and asked her to "view
them, for God's sake, with charity," for he regretted writing them and hoped
that she would believe him to be "your earnest, loyal and true husband and
partner."

Nine days later, July 31, Taylor received from Netta a letter, dated July 20,
that made him "supremely happy." It was, he at once wrote, "the kind of
epistle I should expect you to write—full of vivacity, buoyant, hopeful—such
a letter gives comfort to a husband." The only part that he objected to was
one in which Netta, evidently responding to his July 15 threat to engage in
weekly drinking sprees, exhorted him not to become like a Georgetown acquaintance, also a lawyer and an army officer, who had turned into a chronic
drunkard:

> Now my jewel did you really think I was serious when I spoke about one spree per week that you administered me such a lecture? My dear, it is perfectly incompatible with my future course to use ardent spirits excessively. I have a different course marked out & through the grace of heaven and the irresistible power of my little wife I will not be laid in a drunkard's grave. My future contemplates much study, hard mental labor, and I want to take with me into the contest every energy I possess unimpaired and fresh. I feel that my system is maturing; my mind is more comprehensive than it was one year ago. The free use of liquor would weaken it, render me stupid—therefore I cannot use it to any extent. Women I do not deal in at all, whiskey very little.

He then described the plain food and drink that constituted his daily fare and declared that he derived his greatest pleasure from thinking "'on the good time coming'—When we [I] shall be by the side of some 'little body' who wears crinoline and with deep drawn sighs 'go in' splendidly. Well this thinking about home is exceedingly delightful provided one has received a happy letter."

By early August sufficient time had passed for Netta to receive and reply to Taylor's July 15 and 16 letters and for the reply (or replies) to reach him. What her response was cannot be presented because the letter(s) are missing. Presumably, though, she chided him for his lack of trust in her but then forgave him, for he made no further mention of the matter in his subsequent correspondence. Not only was she well aware of his volatile temperament but also quite likely reasoned that it was better to have a husband who felt so strongly than one who lacked feeling. And feeling, feeling of the most sensuous nature, played a central role in the relationship between Tom and Netta Taylor. That is made manifest in his July 31 letter and becomes even more so in what he wrote "my incomparable little wife" on August 3 with regard to the contents of a trunk he had sent her for safekeeping; "Save that oil—for it is *pure* olive oil—[and] we may need it for certain *particular uses* you know."[13]

Meanwhile, the war had been going badly for the Union in Virginia with Jackson's stunning victories in the Shenandoah being followed by a series of battles near Richmond, which saw Lee drive back McClellan's Army of the Potomac and cause it to shelter beneath the guns of the Federal navy. As a consequence, the high command in Washington decided to abandon the attempt to seize the Confederate capital from the east and instead concentrate its forces in northern Virginia under the command of Maj. Gen. John Pope. To that end, early in August it ordered Cox to reinforce Pope with the bulk of his Kanawha Division, leaving only 5,000 troops in West Virginia to hold the central part of that region.[14]

Taylor, of course, hoped and for a while even expected that the Forty-seventh would accompany Cox. It did not. Once more it remained behind, unable to participate in what Taylor predicted would be the "final struggle" of the war, one in which "there would be so much glory won" and that "Shiloh would be as nothing compared to it."[15] Nor was this his sole or worst disappointment. Late in July, a court-martial dismissed the charges that the officers of the Forty-seventh had presented against Elliott, charges that Taylor had drafted. Since Poschner had resigned earlier in the month, this left Elliott in unchallengeable command of the regiment, a status soon confirmed by his promotion to full colonel.[16]

For a while, Taylor again entertained notions of resigning.[17] Then on the night of August 19, he had a "long talk" with Elliott. As a result, he informed Netta the next day, "he understands me and I him." Specifically, Elliott realized that "I was a prominent actor in this whole organization—and cannot be readily taken down when I start." Hence he would remain with the regiment because "I am working for the men [of my company]—to this end I am insinuating myself into the good graces" of Elliott.

Probably not even Netta credited this explanation of why her husband now desired the hitherto despised Elliott's friendship. Certainly there is no reason for us to do so, for a more candid avowal of his motives appears in an August 23 letter to Netta. In it, after reporting that Federick Hesser had been elected major of the regiment, Taylor stated that "I am glad that the place has been given to him" and that he helped him obtain it, for although Hesser was the junior captain in the Forty-seventh, it had been deemed politic to give him the post because four of the regiment's ten companies consisted of Germans. Besides, he continued, if the war lasted long enough and nothing happened to him, "I will be a field officer in this regiment." Indeed, he predicted, "The time is not far distant when I will receive a promotion."[18]

Four days after Taylor wrote what turned out to be these overly optimistic words, a portion of Cox's Kanawha Division, including Carr White's Twelfth Ohio, took part in the opening phase of the Second Battle of Bull Run. When it ended on August 29, Pope's army had been defeated and driven back to Washington, leaving the way open for Lee to advance into Maryland with the ultimate object of invading Pennsylvania. It also led to the Confederate forces in West Virginia under Maj. Gen. William Wing Loring launching an offensive of their own, one in which they intended first to clear the Federals out of the Kanawha Valley and then "liberate" the northwestern part of the state, after which they would join Lee by way of the Shenandoah Valley. In sum, the victory-flushed Confederates sought to win the war by carrying it out of Virginia and into the North.

In contrast, Maj. Gen. Henry W. Halleck, who now commanded all Union armies, thought only in terms of avoiding more defeats. Thus on September 8, after receiving word of Loring's advance, he telegraphed Col. Joseph Lightburn, whom Cox had left in charge of the remaining Federal troops in the Kanawha Valley, instructing him to fall back to the Ohio River should he deem it necessary. Lightburn, a forty-two-year-old former regular army soldier and a West Virginian, so deemed it and at once began retreating down the Kanawha toward Charleston. He believed that Loring possessed a far larger force than he did and also greatly exaggerated the menace to his rear posed by a raid into northern West Virginia by Confederate cavalry headed by Brig. Gen. Albert G. Jenkins. Had he stationed just one of his two brigades in the fortifications at Gauley Bridge, he could have, in Cox's words, "laughed at Loring," who lacked the means to attack the place and who dared not bypass it. As it was, Lightburn's panicky retreat nearly resulted in the Forty-seventh's being cut off and captured, a fate it escaped only by dint of hard cross-country marching until it caught up with the rest of the fleeing Federal forces.[19] Loring vigorously pursued Lightburn, and on September 13 overtook him at Charleston. Here, finally, the Forty-seventh Ohio engaged in a regular battle, albeit a small-scale one. Serving as the rearguard, it used recently issued Enfield rifles to repulse two Confederate infantry assaults before being compelled by artillery crossfire to withdraw, having lost three killed and five wounded. Lightburn continued his retreat, Loring following, until he reached the Ohio River, where on September 16, his troops boarded steamboats that transported them to Point Pleasant near the mouth of the Kanawha.[20]

Having thus cleared the Kanawha Valley, Loring returned to Charleston with the object of carrying out the next phase of his campaign, driving

Colonel (later Brigadier General) John Lightburn.
Francis Trevelyan Miller, ed., The Photographic History of the Civil War, *10 vols.*
(*New York: Review of Reviews, 1911*), *10: 87.*

the Federals out of northern West Virginia and then swinging over into the Shenandoah. Meanwhile, on September 17 at Sharpsburg, Maryland, along the banks of a creek called Antietam, Lee's army slugged it out with McClellan's in the bloodiest one-day battle of the war. Although Lee's outnumbered men beat back—just barely—the massive but uncoordinated Union attacks, they suffered such enormous losses that Lee had no choice other than to cross the Potomac back into Virginia, thereby aborting his attempt to carry the war into the North. Both at Antietam and at South Mountain, a sharp encounter prior to the main clash, Cox's Kanawha Division saw heavy action and incurred heavy losses, with Carr White's Twelfth Ohio sharing fully in both.[21] Also present at Antietam was Taylor's namesake cousin, Tom Taylor of the Eighth Louisiana, who was wounded and captured. Evidently his ex-congressman father still possessed influential connections in Yankeedom, for instead of being sent to a military prison hospital, the Rebel Tom Taylor went to the family's former hometown of Saratoga Springs, New York, to recuperate, then soon was exchanged, returning to his regiment and receiving a lieutenant's commission.[22]

Capt. Thomas Taylor of the Forty-seventh Ohio knew of none of these events on September 18 as he sat at a table aboard the steamer *Mary Cook* using a pencil to write Netta an account of the past week's events in West Virginia and the role of his company in them. This, after covering four pages, he summed up: "We had many narrow escapes—but I believe I lost none—I think all will turn up. I had none killed or wounded. I made my men fire and load lying down."

Ten days passed before Taylor again wrote Netta, this time from Point Pleasant. Along with being very busy with his military duties, he had fallen ill—"I have never been so weak for fifteen years as I was three days ago." But he was feeling much better and, as the letter made abundantly clear, he also felt very proud of his performance in the fight at Charleston: Elliott "says I and my boys were in the hottest fire," that if "we had stood upright instead of lying down I would not have saved a man," and that "perfect showers of balls struck all around me" when his company covered the retreat of two other companies during "a critical moment of the battle."

Elliott himself, Taylor added, "behaved most bravely at Charleston, so cooly as though he was at a dinner party." Furthermore, the colonel's "course toward me" had "changed entirely"; he was "friendly once more," and "now

The Confederate Tom Taylor.
Courtesy of The Museum of the Confederacy, Richmond, Virginia.

whenever he wishes my knowledge of the regulations on any doubtful point whatever, he sends for me and my opinion settles him."[23]

Yet, nice as it was to have Elliott's praise and to possess his friendship, still nicer would be a visit to Point Pleasant by Netta and the children: "Don't you think I have looked forward considerably to seeing your angel visage beaming over my shoulders . . . and to find clinging to each hand two bright cherubs of boys, known as our sons?"

Netta required no additional urging. On October 1, she arrived—without the children—at Point Pleasant and stayed there with Taylor until October 13.[24] And perhaps she left then only because military operations were about to resume; for on the very next day, General Cox, who had been sent back to West Virginia with his division to regain control of the Kanawha Valley, ordered Lightburn to advance on Charleston, with the rest of the Union forces to follow. The ensuing campaign was little more than, as Taylor termed it, a "peregrination." Badly outnumbered and short of supplies, the Confederates evacuated Charleston and all the other places they had occupied during their September offensive and retreated to the southeast, leaving behind only Jenkins's cavalry to delay the Federal march. On October 29, Cox occupied Charleston and then, two days later, the still-intact fortifications at Gauley Bridge.[25]

Here Cox halted. There was nothing to be gained by pushing on, even if he possessed the needed supply transport, which he did not. The truth of the matter was that southern West Virginia was a strategic dead end for both the Federals and the Confederates. Neither could move through that region with an army sufficiently large to achieve decisive results while at the same time adequately supplying it; distance, terrain, and the few, miserable roads made this effort a logistical impossibility. Hence, the most that either could realistically hope to achieve was to retain what each already possessed. In the case of the Federals, that was control of the Baltimore & Ohio Railroad and domination of northwestern Virginia. For the Confederates, it was to preserve their hold on southwestern Virginia, through which ran the Virginia & Tennessee Railroad linking Richmond with Knoxville and Chattanooga.

Made aware of these facts of strategic life by Cox, on November 8, Halleck ordered the Union forces in western Virginia to assume a strictly defensive posture and to send half their number to Middle Tennessee and the Mississippi Valley. For the remainder of the war, West Virginia would be a military backwater, with the Federals conducting antiguerrilla operations and the Confederates carrying out occasional cavalry raids.[26]

Taylor, of course, was unaware of these strategic considerations and decisions. In fact, he did not even participate in the occupation of Charleston. The day it occurred, October 29, found him in Portsmouth, Ohio, on recruiting service. What led to this assignment, his letters fail to reveal. Perhaps he owed it to his physical condition: while marching toward Charleston with Lightburn's command, he had been obliged to use a cane.[27] Certainly, he had not hitherto displayed any particular talent for inducing civilians to become soldiers; if anything, the reverse was the case.

Taylor himself had doubts. Writing Netta from Portsmouth on October 29, he declared, "How I shall succeed I know not . . . there are not many drafted men here at this time. I intend making a desperate attempt to secure a number of them for my own use. I am not very sanguine but still hopeful." (In fall 1862, Ohio began conscripting men in counties that failed to meet their troop quotas by voluntary enlistments.)

Evidently his "desperate attempt" failed, for his next letter to Netta bears the date November 14 and was written in Columbus—a sure indication that he had spent most if not all of the past two weeks in Georgetown. Moreover, at the very outset, he made it clear that his primary purpose now was not to add men to the Forty-seventh Ohio but to subtract himself from it: "I have settled on getting out of my present position by *January*. . . . I am worn out, and although the patriotic fires burn as brightly as ever in my bosom, I think that my family, my mother, and my business have claims upon me, which will not suffer themselves to remain unnoticed longer."

One cannot but suspect that these were rationalizations rather than reasons for leaving the army. By autumn 1862, Taylor had been on active duty for more than a year. Yet he remained a captain, and despite his assertions to the contrary, there was no prospect of his becoming a major so long as the regiment's German contingent needed to be appeased. As for glory, he had achieved precious little of that unless gunning down an unarmed bushwhacker and participating in a couple of minor engagements could be called glorious, something he must have realized that they were not, his long letters to Netta recounting his exploits notwithstanding. Finally, to make what was bad enough worse, the Forty-seventh seemed fated to pass another winter on Gauley Mountain, after which it no doubt would resume marching back and forth across the mountains of West Virginia while the war was being fought and won elsewhere.

Taylor's decision to quit the army—an act he described as being "a foregone conclusion"—delighted Netta. She had never ceased urging him to resign his commission and return home. "Dear," she wrote him on October 31 before receiving his letter from Portsmouth, "I am so tired living this way, so unhappy and dissatisfied living without you, indeed at times I am perfectly miserable." To her the war was a monster that had taken her husband away and that constantly threatened to take his life as well, leaving her a widow and the children fatherless. Taylor's first duty, she repeatedly told him, was to his family, not to the Union; its preservation was not worth the sacrifice of thousands of men in what probably would prove to be a futile struggle. Besides, putting down the rebellion no longer was the real purpose of the war. That now was being waged "for the equality of the Negro," and she thought it would be "a glorious thing for the country if the army would turn upon the abolishnists [*sic*] and put them out of the way."[28] In short, stalwart Unionist and army captain Thomas T. Taylor's wife was a "Copperhead," as those Northerners were commonly called who contended that the Southerners should and/or could not be forced back into the Union by military means. It was an ironic situation, and for Taylor, an awkward one. To his credit, he dealt with it tactfully, at least in his letters, wherein he never reproached Netta for her views or directly challenged them but contented himself with occasionally writing long editorial-like disquisitions on the need to preserve the Union. However, at times even his zeal flagged, as is revealed in the cynical comment he sent Netta on July 7, 1862: "Patriotism is well nigh 'played out' in the army. Pride and ambition is what keeps soldiers and officers together." By autumn 1862, his pride and his ambition had, at least for the time being, "played out."

On November 18, having failed to obtain permission from Elliott to extend his stay in Ohio beyond the allotted twenty days, Taylor headed back to West Virginia. Three days later, he reached Charleston, where he met with now Brig. Gen. George Crook, who had assumed command of the troops hitherto headed by Lightburn. Taylor's correspondence does not reveal what Crook and he said to each other, but we know the outcome of their meeting from the letter Taylor wrote Netta following it:

I think I have arranged matters so as to procure a detail for the winter. It will be necessary for the order to go to Cinti [Cincinnati] and approved [at departmental headquarters] there, [something] that will take at least two weeks but I rushed the affair here and have this for my labor. I hope it may prove true, i.e., be successful. I have no anxiety to pass the winter on Gauley Mt. again and I must say that I will be compelled to do so unless I succeed in this matter.

Thus, Taylor would remain in the army, despite his having stated that his leaving it was a "foregone conclusion"; but if he obtained the detail, which was for more recruiting duty in Ohio, he would not have to be with the Forty-seventh during the winter. In all likelihood, Crook either persuaded him not to resign or else told him that the resignation would not be accepted, and Taylor in turn induced Crook to assign him for the winter to recruiting. No doubt Taylor realized that Netta would be disappointed by his not resigning, but surely he was confident that once he explained the matter to her she would understand that he had done the best he could under the circumstances.

Taylor began his next letter to Netta on November 24 at "Camp Gauley Mountain," but after writing only a few lines, he was "ordered on duty" and so had to write "I shall discontinue." He resumed on November 27, his birthday, and used the occasion to take stock of himself and his life: "I am now twenty-six and what have I accomplished? Am I worthy of my age, do I merit these years?"

His response to these questions bore a strong, one might say uncanny, resemblance to his father's 1836 letter from Texas:

In sin I presume I am an "expert," deep in shame and disgrace and oftentimes my cheeks burn with blushes and my whole frame quivers as I indulge in a retrospect of my past life, yet something moves me irresistibly onward in the downward road. . . . I have frequently humbled myself in "sackcloth and ashes" and yet not found relief. I am the same wild, reckless, hairbraind [*sic*] person—it is inherent and I appear unable to check my spirits. My life from boyhood has been one continued course of perversity dotted and checkered on all sides by landmarks of sin and woe . . . and therefore today convinces me that I am in high disfavor with the Almighty and that I have good reason to denounce myself.

Taylor next deplored his failure to achieve more during his lifetime:

I am not satisfied with eighteen of my twenty-six years. I have improved them but poorly. True, I have enjoyed honors even younger which others envied and sought after unsuccessfully at forty but still I might have been much higher, have done much more. Now I am just wise enough to know that I am very ignorant, that I have not improved those gifts which my Creator endowed me—that I have suffered them to become paralyzed [and that] now I am a poor, feeble incompetent being and will be compelled to begin life anew—to crawl up once more.

Prompting this prolix outburst of maudlin self-excoriation was Taylor's fear that he would not secure the recruiting detail: "Well, I am in suspense— if I come out all right [with regard to the detail], I will see you before this letter does, if not it will greet you first and you will know how badly disappointed I am." Indeed, so pessimistic was he that he closed the letter by asking Netta to "give my boys a kiss each and hurry me two or three good letters."

But as it turned out, Netta did not have to kiss the boys for their father or write her husband two or three good letters. We know this because not a single letter from Netta to Taylor or from Taylor to Netta exists for all of December 1862 and most of January 1863. This means that Taylor obtained the detail and that he reached home ahead of his November 27 letter.

Perhaps this was well. Quite possibly, Netta, when the letter did arrive, asked her husband what he meant by describing himself as an "expert" in sin, and he found it necessary to explain. If so, it would be interesting to know what he told her. And how persuasively.

Thus ended 1862, with Taylor still in the army, still a captain, and still without any of the glory that he craved. On the other hand, he had a cushy assignment that enabled him to stay much, if not most, of the time at home, safely and happily ensconced, as he would have put it, in the bosom of his family. He could, and surely did, congratulate himself on his good fortune.

But good fortune often is paid for by bad, and Taylor was about to make such a payment. On December 31, the Forty-seventh Ohio left its Gauley Mountain camp and marched toward Charleston. Along with the other three regiments of its brigade, it was on the way to join Maj. Gen. Ulysses S. Grant's army on the banks of the Mississippi River above the Confederate fortress city of Vicksburg.[29] Had Taylor remained with his regiment, he would not have had to spend the winter in West Virginia after all. Yet because he was on recruiting duty in Ohio, he was being left behind while the Forty-seventh went off to participate in one of the greatest and, for the Union cause, most glorious campaigns of the Civil War.

The Almighty Will Preserve Me
January–July 1863

I T IS UNKNOWN when and by what means Taylor learned that the Forty-seventh Ohio had left Gauley Mountain and was on the way west with the rest of its brigade, headed by Brig. Gen. Hugh Ewing, to the Western theater of war. Possibly, though, he garnered the news from the Saturday, January 3, 1863 issue of the *Cincinnati Commercial*, which reported that the day before, steamboats carrying Ewing's brigade had passed down the Ohio by the city. Netta subscribed to the *Commercial* and conceivably Taylor read the news while at home in Georgetown, it being a weekend and the holiday season still in de facto existence.[1]

Taylor's reaction also must be surmised, but this can be done with reasonable certitude. Having, through great effort and with much stress, escaped from another cold, boring winter in the wilds of West Virginia, he suddenly found himself left behind in Ohio while his regiment went off to serve in the West, which had become the focal point of the war since the cessation of active operations in Virginia, following the Army of the Potomac's bloody debacle at Fredericksburg on December 13. Thus the same issue of the *Commercial* that noted the passage down the Ohio of Ewing's brigade also carried detailed descriptions of a tremendous battle on December 31 between William Rosecrans's Army of the Cumberland and Braxton Bragg's Confederate forces near Murfreesboro, Tennessee. Nor was that all. Also present in the January 3 issue was a report from Maj. Gen. William T. Sherman's army in Chickasaw Bayou north of Vicksburg, Mississippi, and a story explaining why Ulysses S. Grant had been obliged to abandon an attempt to reach Vicksburg by advancing overland because Rebel cavalry had destroyed his supply base at Holly Springs, Mississippi, December 20. Obviously, Tennessee and Mississippi were where the action was and where glory and promotion could be won. But now he, Tom Taylor, was stuck in Ohio—and stuck, too, with the rank of captain. By seeking and obtaining assignment to recruiting duty, he had, as he himself would and perhaps did put it, ended up being hoisted by his own petard.

Yet there was a curious aspect to the Forty-seventh Ohio's transfer to the West; Col. Lyman Elliott did not accompany it. Instead, Lt. Col. Augustus C. Parry assumed command of the regiment while Elliott remained at Gauley Mountain with those soldiers who had been left behind because they were too ill or otherwise unfit for active field service. Then, on January 17, Elliott resigned his commission and journeyed to Cincinnati where he met Taylor and told him what he had done. Taylor's light-blue eyes must have gleamed. If matters followed their normal course, Parry would become a colonel, Frederick Hesser lieutenant colonel, and there would be a vacancy for major. Taylor resolved to fill that vacancy.

"I shall go to Columbus," he informed Netta from Cincinnati January 22. "Col. Elliott has resigned and is here to go with me. He resigned because of private affairs. He had to attend a lawsuit or be entirely ruined thereby. The Col. & Col. Poschner will go with me."

Taylor and the two ex-colonels of the Forty-seventh went to Columbus, but they were unable so much as to talk to the recently elected new governor of Ohio, David Tod. Their only accomplishment was hardly that— a visit to the state adjutant general's office where they learned that under its regulations no officer absent from his regiment could even be considered for promotion.[2]

The obvious remedy for this frustrating situation was to rejoin the regiment. But to do so, Taylor first would have to secure a release from recruiting duty. Hence, he hastened from Columbus to Charleston, West Virginia, with the intention of securing at district headquarters a release from his present assignment and an authorization to proceed forthwith to Mississippi, where the Forty-seventh and the other regiments constituting its brigade had been sent. If he arrived there in time, he believed that he stood an excellent chance of becoming a major. If not, he would have no chance.

Before leaving Columbus and while traveling to Charleston, Taylor notified Netta of his plans and hopes. She neither cared for the former nor shared the latter, as she made clear when she wrote him on January 29:

> From the tone of your letters I fear it is your intention to return to the Regiment without visiting home. I hope not—my dear it would grieve me very much were you to do so.

I wish you would resign. You have sufficient excuse, but why do I
write this [?]—have I not asked it time and again only to be laughed
at, must the thought of a little more honor and few more dollars
supplant home, wife, and children. I trust not. You know my husband, I do not doubt your love for us, but you are led on by that wild
infatuation that ever follows the ambitious in military life. I beg of
you to break this spell, and be content to remain with us. We shall
do all in our power to make you happy, be willing to live on half if
we are only blessed with your kindly presence.

Netta need not have worried that her husband would leave for Mississippi without first visiting home. District headquarters in Charleston, Taylor
learned, lacked the authority to grant his request to be relieved of recruiting
duty and be reassigned to his regiment. That could be done only by departmental headquarters in Cincinnati. Until it acted, he would have to stay with
the remnant of the Forty-seventh at its Gauley Mountain camp.[3]

Thus, Taylor found himself in West Virginia in the winter after all. His only
consolation was, as he soon learned, that it already was too late for him to obtain the coveted promotion. Late in January, the Forty-seventh had held a re-
organization, which resulted in Parry becoming colonel, Hesser lieutenant
colonel, and Capt. John Wallace rising to the rank of major.[4] It was not consolation enough. Having soared high, once again Taylor's mercurial emotions
plunged low, as revealed in this sometimes incoherent passage from a February 27 letter to Netta bearing the all-too-familiar heading "Camp Gauley Mt.":

You know how much I dread to deviate from my original intentions.
[Yet] I now have given up all my brilliant visions of the judicial er-
mine &c. Here [however] is "the rub." I feel more like entering the
cloister, turning monk and having nothing more to do with my fellow men. . . . You know how greatly I have been deceived, misled and
maligned not only by friends, but by those nearer than friends. How,
every step, I have had to contend with unseen foes, struggle hour by
hour, in daytime, *and* dream, hour by hour, at night, while your sweet
nice and placid, serene smile have [*sic*] wooed me from all unpleas-
antness. How I have toiled and worked to make my reputation fair
& my name honored. What a bitter, bitter life this has been, how
brimful of "gall and wormwood." How often have I asked is there
no brighter day for me, no haven of rest,

"Where grows the flowers of peace—
The rose that cannot wither—
Thy fortress, and thy ease."

Soon afterward, departmental headquarters responded to Taylor's re-quests. They were denied. He would resume and remain on recruiting duty in Ohio. Only instead of recruiting he would be implementing the Con-scription Act that Lincoln had signed on March 3. Copperheads, who were notably strong in Ohio, homestate of arch antiwar Democrat Clement L. Vallandigham, threatened to defy the act, even to rise up in armed resis-tance. The act empowered the army to execute and enforce its provisions. Taylor was an army officer, he was available, and that was that.[5]

Netta, of course, was pleased that her husband would be coming back to Ohio rather than leaving for Mississippi. As for Taylor, probably he was not displeased. Why should he be? He now had nothing to gain by rejoining his regiment, neither rank nor even glory, for Grant's campaign against Vicksburg had become stalemated, with his troops, those of the Forty-seventh Ohio included, engaged in the inglorious task of removing trees from swamps and digging canals in what would prove to be a futile effort to get at the fortress city by some route other than a direct approach down the Mississippi River.[6] Drafting men for the army, which Taylor heartily favored, certainly was a more pleasant and perhaps no less useful activity than this. Besides, after suffering so much bad luck, surely he was due to enjoy some good.

He did—and lots of it. First, on returning to Ohio, he was placed in charge of a recruiting party stationed in Cincinnati, a most congenial and convenient place for him to be. Next, early in April, he received a letter from 1st Lt. Henry King, commanding Company F of the Forty-seventh Ohio in his absence, notifying him that Hesser had rejected his lieutenant colonel's commission and resigned from the service.[7] King had no need to tell Taylor what this sig-nified. It meant that Major Wallace would become a lieutenant colonel and that the post of major again was open.

Or was it? King also reported that Colonel Parry had recommended that Capt. William H. Ward be promoted to major on the grounds that Taylor was ineligible owing to his absence from the regiment. As before, it seemed that Taylor was in the wrong place at the right time. But then he had another stroke of luck—indeed, several such strokes. Returning from Lebanon, Ohio, on Sunday, April 12, to his room at the Broadway Hotel in Cincinnati, Taylor found a letter from Parry in which the colonel gave him permission to make an effort to obtain the major's commission notwithstanding his recommendation of Ward. During summer 1862, Taylor had joined with other officers of the Forty-seventh to have Parry rather than Elliott named colonel of the regiment, and Parry evidently was doing what he could to repay the favor.[8]

Taylor hastened to the home of Charles Wilstach, patron of the Forty-seventh and now mayor of Cincinnati, and procured from him a letter of introduction to Capt. W. R. Looker, Governor Tod's military aide, and also a promise to visit the governor in person and urge Taylor's promotion. Taylor then took a train to Columbus where on Monday he visited Looker and went to the state adjutant general's office where he obtained the backing of one of its clerks for the major's commission. That accomplished, he returned to Cincinnati and talked to "some friends," one of whom traveled to Columbus that night and secured the influence of two powerful Republican politicians in Taylor's behalf.

On Tuesday, April 14, Wilstach and Taylor's other Cincinnati friends called upon Tod and asked him to appoint Taylor major. At first Tod refused. Then 1st Lt. John G. Durbeck, adjutant of the Forty-seventh who was present for the purpose of being recommissioned, asked the governor who was to be the regiment's major. Ward, came the answer. Durbeck thereupon stated that he would not accept the new commission if this was the case and at the same time denounced Ward. Seizing this opportunity, Wilstach and the other Cincinnatians declared that the Forty-seventh Ohio would resent Ward, who was from Michigan, becoming major when Taylor, an Ohioan and far better qualified, was available for the post. This argument persuaded Tod. He tore up Ward's commission, placed Taylor's name on the roster of the Forty-seventh as major, and signed a commission conferring on him that rank.

None of this was known to Taylor when, on April 15, he arrived in Columbus in response to a telegram from Captain Looker to come there at once. At the capitol—the same place where, nearly two years earlier, he and the other military neophytes of the Twelfth Ohio had slept on straw in the basement—Looker ushered Taylor into the governor's office. What ensued is best, although awkwardly, described by Taylor himself:

The governor took me in[to] the next room, referred to a roster and asked my name. I told him Taylor and he ran his finger along the line [and] said that is it—you are already promoted. I was so surprised I could not speak for a few moments. I attempted to express my gratification and thanks but my words clove to the roof of my mouth and they all shook hands and then I parted. It might be termed a thunderbolt of joy and I was like Saul pursuing the Christians.

Taylor wrote this on April 17 to Netta from the Broadway Hotel. He began by explaining why he had not informed her of the good news sooner: "I know you took the 'Commercial' and would see the notice of my promotion and I thought the surprise would do you more good than any letter I might send and make you feel more like I did."[9] Possibly there is some truth to this, but one cannot help suspect that Taylor spent the remainder of April 15 in Columbus celebrating the receipts of the major's commission with Wilstach and other friends and then devoted a goodly portion of the following day recovering from the celebration before returning to Cincinnati.

There, as he also wrote, he bought a "saddle and trimming together with a sword" from former Lieutenant Colonel Hesser—as a field officer, he was entitled to ride a horse—and "will have a coat tomorrow." His rank as major, he added, dated from December 30, 1862, "for which the pay and emoluments are due." But the most satisfying aspect of his promotion was the impact it would have on certain persons in Georgetown: "What will my *quasi* friends say now or think of Tom Taylor[?] I hope I shall live to drive all opposition from me. I have some powerful friends down here and in many sections [of Ohio] and many [men] may live to regret what they have done and said to my prejudice."

For Taylor, becoming a major was more than promotion, it was vindication. This probably explains why, many years later, he would claim that Governor Tod commissioned him a major, without "solicitation" on his part, to reward him for having exposed a plot by the Knights of the Golden Circle, a Copperhead secret society, to resist the draft in "certain parts of Ohio."[10] This tale, which is contradicted by Taylor's letters, provided a more flattering explanation of his promotion than the true one; that he obtained it by a combination of wire-pulling and sheer luck.

On the other hand, it is unlikely that Netta felt "more like" Taylor did about his promotion when (or if) she read the notice of it in the *Commercial*.

Instead, her reaction probably was one of disappointment and frustration. Now there was no chance at all of her husband's resigning and returning home to his family. The most she could hope for was that he would serve out the remainder of his three-year enlistment without being killed, maimed, or captured and then leave the army.

Taylor expected to be "ordered away e're long" to join the regiment. Writing Netta on Saturday, April 18, he asked her to come to Cincinnati on Monday "prepared to visit Uncle Julius," his mother's brother, for the purpose of establishing a better acquaintance with him. "The reason," he stated, "is obvious. Vicksburg must be ours. The missiles which will fall will be large. I may, perchance, be among the unlucky and I want you to have friends outside your own family." Also, she was to "fetch my new pants," along with his revolver and old sword; the latter he planned to sell.

Presumably Netta arrived in Cincinnati on April 20 bringing the pants, revolver, and sword and then visited Uncle Julius. Almost surely, too, she stayed overnight with her husband at the Broadway Hotel. But, as it turned out, more than two months passed before Taylor set out for Mississippi. The reason for the delay was that he could not secure a release from recruiting duty until he was replaced by another officer from the Forty-seventh Ohio. Not until mid-June did this officer, Capt. Henry Sinclair, show up in Cincinnati, and not until the night of June 19 was Taylor able to board a westward-bound steamboat.[11]

On June 25, following a "tedious trip," he reached Memphis, Tennessee. "Residences fine," he wrote Netta that same day. "Town well laid out—streets lined with ornamental old shade trees." By then Grant, by marching most of his army down the west bank of the Mississippi and then crossing it over to the east side below Vicksburg on steamboats that had run past the fortress's batteries at night, had defeated the Confederate forces in Mississippi in a series of battles, cut off Vicksburg from the rest of the South, and laid siege to the town; its fall had become a mere matter of time and not much of that as its stockpile of food rapidly dwindled. Although he did not realize it yet—he anticipated more great battles—Taylor again was destined to have no chance to attain glory by treading the "path of glory."

From Memphis, Taylor traveled on the steamer *Silver Moon* down the Mississippi. Along the way, he admired the "fine large plantations with capacious one story residences surrounded by village of [slave] cabins all neatly

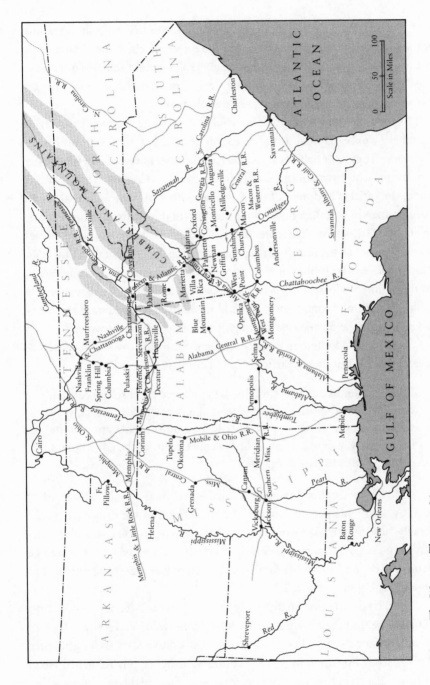

Map 2. The Western Theatre, 1864.

whitewashed and generally located in groves" that dotted both shores. Some of the places passed, however, had "felt the direct effects of the revolution & of those plantations that have sheltered guerrillas naught remains but blackened ruins." Such devastation, mused Taylor, demonstrated "how vain are the works of man! Erect one day, another destroy."

As the time drew near when he would be rejoining the regiment, Taylor must have wondered what sort of reception he would receive. Not only had he been away from it for half a year, but he had also spent most of that time either at home in Georgetown or comfortably ensconced in a Cincinnati hotel. Meanwhile, the officers and men of the Forty-seventh had been wading through swamps, marching endless hours along dusty or muddy roads, digging trenches, and fighting battles in which scores of them had been killed or wounded. Moreover, in spite of all the time he had spent recruiting, he brought with him from Ohio only a small number of new troops, not nearly enough to compensate for the regiment's losses to bullets, shells, disease, and physical exhaustion. He could do nothing more, he wrote Netta on June 28 while aboard the *Silver Moon,* than "hope for the best although I am prepared for the worst."

Taylor also adopted, in essence, the same attitude toward what he believed to be his imminent participation in combat:

> I have no doubt that the Almighty will preserve me through coming conflicts, whether disaster or success shall crown our efforts, yet I wish to say one thing to you. Should I be unfortunate and you be left a widow, you will find that I have collected from the government enough funds to pay all my debts.

As to her own debts, Taylor continued, she should be able to take care of them by selling his personal effects and his interest in the drugstore. Additionally, he estimated, she would receive a twenty-eight-dollar-a-month pension from the government. Obviously, Netta, if she were widowed, would be financially dependent on her family and Uncle Julius unless she returned to schoolteaching or remarried.

The next day, Taylor finally rejoined his regiment at its camp on Walnut Hill close behind the Union siege lines to the north of Vicksburg. Much to his delight (and perhaps surprise), no one seemed to resent his long absence or his rear-area promotion. On the contrary, as he happily informed Netta on July 2, his reception was "happy, joyous—'a real highland welcome'"—

with "congratulations and shaking of hands on every side." In particular Colonel Parry greeted him warmly, saying that he was "very glad" that he had come, and Lieutenant Colonel Wallace did and said the same. Indeed, probably most of the members of the Forty-seventh envied Taylor for his long vacation from the war and soldiering.

The regiment now belonged to Maj. Gen. Frank P. Blair Jr.'s division of Maj. Gen. William T. Sherman's XV Corps of Grant's Army of the Tennessee—quite likely no accident, for its brigade commander was Brig. Gen. Hugh Ewing, Sherman's brother-in-law. It had not participated in the battles that led to the siege of Vicksburg, Sherman's mission having been to threaten the town with a direct attack from the north so as to prevent its defenders from concentrating their full force against Grant as he advanced from the south and then the east—a role he successfully performed. Not until Grant trapped the Confederates in Vicksburg did the XV Corps join in the investment of the town. On May 19, and again three days later, Grant tried to take the place by storm; and on each occasion the Forty-seventh formed part of a column that assaulted an enemy bastion that bore the ominous and, as it turned out, appropriate name of the Cemetery Fort. Both times the regiment got within a few yards of the fort but could go no farther owing to obstructions and withering, almost point-blank fire that forced the troops to lie down or else be exterminated. The same happened all along the front, with the result that Grant settled down for a regular siege designed to starve the Confederates into surrender.

When Taylor returned to the Forty-seventh, it had become a battle-hardened, veteran regiment. It also now had the kind of commander it needed. Poschner was too old and infirm, his European military background good for the drill field but otherwise a handicap. Elliott, although brave and intelligent, lacked the personal qualities necessary for effective leadership. Tall, lanky, and thirty-five, Parry was a rough, tough warrior who liked fighting and was good at it. During the rearguard stand at Charleston, he heard the Confederates call out as he rode along the firing line, "Shoot that man on the white horse!" Whereupon he shouted back, much to the delight of his troops, "Not this load of shit, by God!" At Vicksburg, on discovering after the failure of the first assault that one of the regimental flags had been left behind to fall into enemy hands, he cursed the color bearer as a coward even though that soldier, who had been shot in the hand, declared that he had been unable to

Colonel Augustus C. Parry.
MOLLUS Collection, USAMHI

Union Siege Works at Vicksburg.
Miller, ed., Photographic History, *2: 201.*

bring back the banner because so many dead men were lying on it. And at the outset of the second assault, he had yelled, sword in hand, "Every man of the Forty-seventh Regiment follow me!" and then ordered the enlisted men to shoot any officer who hid behind a tree or stump and gave the same order to the officers with regard to enlisted men. In the charge, the Forty-seventh planted its flag on the Rebel rampart and, when forced to retreat, carried it back.[12]

Taylor moved into Lieutenant Colonel Wallace's tent. From it, he had a good view of the Confederate works and of the Federal siege operations. In his July 2 letter, he described them to Netta:

After the charge of the 22nd our men passed a little under the brow of the hill [Cemetery Hill] and as soon as the mantle of night descended . . . handled the spade and pick. In the morning the rebels beheld that they had taken up lodgings upon their hill and tried in vain to dislodge them. These works were increased and strengthened during the day and during the night "gabions" [wickerwork cylinders filled with dirt] were placed on them, loopholes made and then sand bags placed on these, forming a complete shelter. These works are constructed in an irregular, zig zag manner so as to prevent an enfilading fire from the enemy and also to give us many fronts and lines of fire so as to be able to command every approach and . . . every foot of rebel works. From the works of our saps [trenches] extend in every conceivable direction so as to shelter us in passing to the rear or to other works. Similar lines of works pass all around the city. The line for infantry at the remotest angles is not more than 150 yards from the rebels [and] our pickets . . . are posted in saps so close that they could bayonet men in the ditch of the rebels. [The forts on both sides commonly had ditches in front of them.] Every few hundred yards we have forts mounting guns of heavy caliber [and] besides our rifle pits as described we have a cordon of forts confronting theirs. . . . No man either Federal or rebel can show himself above the works safely, all have learned caution.

The firing is continuous, not so constantly artillery firing but infantry as sharpshooters.

The night I came I went on duty with our regiment and enjoyed it much, visited every point of our lines and could hear conversation with the rebels as we were not ten feet apart but its against orders and save friendly nods nothing passes except leaden messengers.

This afternoon there is considerable [artillery] firing along the line—not much damage doing I think. Sometimes the concussion is so great that although a person is very well accustomed to it, it will cause him to dodge or stumble.

Feeling the impact of exploding shells was as close to combat as Taylor came at Vicksburg. On July 4, the Confederate garrison, close to 30,000 troops, surrendered, an outcome not unexpected by the Federals, who in recent days had been told by prisoners that they were subsisting on meager rations of mule meat and food provided by the people of the town, themselves half-famished. That evening, an elated Taylor provided Netta with a long account of what he had witnessed on this "already immortal day":

This morning the affair culminated, details were arranged and at ten A.M. white flags were planted by the rebels on the counterscarps [outer slope of the ditches in front] of the forts; at half past ten they commenced marching out, stacked their arms, grounded their colors. Then away went our flag and color guard and under my immediate orders [the flag] was planted on one of their largest works in our front. The 8th Mo. desired to plant their flag there and did do so but we made them return with it. Therefore you see the 47th O. V. I. [Ohio Volunteer Infantry] had the honor of first placing their colors properly on the works they had assaulted before so frequently. This is the 47th day of the siege.

The men [of the garrison] were clothed chiefly in white cotton cloth, very dirty, [with the] greater portion [having] no coat, hats as varied as the forms of the clouds, most of them had shoes. They had lived on mule meat for a number of days (four or five) and were short in all things except ammunition. They defended the city bravely but their destruction was sure. . . .

Their works I was permitted to examine only to a limited extent as I was on duty with the regiment and could see those only which were on our immediate front. We passed out over a sap to their works to the glacis [dirt mound in front of counterscarp] on our front. They had planted stakes about five feet apart and fastened to them a network of wire, about eight feet deep, extending the whole length of the fort. The ditch is not formidable—I jumped across it. The outer works of the fort consisted entirely of earth [and] is well arranged for sharpshooting. Behind the parapet is another fort constructed of bales of cotton. There is a space in the fort inside the outer wall for artillery, their feeble pieces. In it are twelve pound field howitzers, some of which are dismantled and knocked to pieces by our shot. Behind these is a traverse forming a rifle pit, with sharpened pickets in front. On the left side is another range of pits & pickets, high & large [but] badly destroyed and injured by our shot. Inside this are the quarters of the men which consist of holes dug in the side of the hill and covered with earth [to provide] bomb proof shelters.

The works are well located in commanding positions, but in construction are very irregular and do not speak very highly of their skills in engineering. They cannot be enfiladed from any quarter—this is their chief recommendation. They are perforated with shot of all descriptions and sizes, hardly a stake is [undamaged] but is shattered & seared. On the spurs running from there [the hills on which the Confederate forts are located] are nothing but rifle pits, no heavy works, hence had we once got inside they would have been slaughtered by the hundred.

The appearance of the men was very much like that of Falstaff's guard—dirty, ragged and many, many of them lousy, their complexions sallow, countenances wan and dejected, but many of them breathe defiance.[13]

Only one thing marred Taylor's joy; Captain Ward, to whom Governor Tod first had issued the major's commission, had rejoined the regiment and was "endeavoring to persuade the Col. and others that I obtained my commission by misrepresenting him." But, so Taylor assured Netta, "I have no apprehension on that score."

Taylor's next letter was dated July 8 and written at "Camp Baker's Creek." On the night of July 4, Grant had sent the XV Corps, the XIII Corps, and two divisions of the IX Corps, all headed by Sherman, against a Confederate army of about 23,000 under Gen. Joseph E. Johnston, which had advanced toward Vicksburg from the east in a halfhearted attempt to assail the besiegers from the rear. Grant hoped to smash Johnston's force and ordered Sherman to do so; but Johnston, learning of the fall of Vicksburg, at once fell back toward Jackson, capital of Mississippi and a railroad junction. Sherman followed, his pursuit slowed by the climate and the condition of the countryside. "The weather," wrote Taylor, "has been exceedingly warm, warmer than I ever before experienced," and the "country through which we are passing is totally devastated and depopulated."

"Our present camp," he continued, "is one occupied by the rebels the night before the battle at Champion Hill [May 16, 1863, the decisive engagement of the Vicksburg Campaign] and recently by Gen'l Johnston's forces." Found there had been an order book indicating that Johnston had advanced to within a short distance of Vicksburg before turning back on learning of the surrender. He "retreated in much apparent haste, leaving sabers, guns, etc." in the camp. "Some think the rebels will make a stand at Clinton & another at Jackson, but I think they will do nothing of the kind."

As he usually did, when it came to military operations, Taylor proved to be a poor prophet. Before he could send off his letter he had to add a postscript. It read, "In front of Jackson. The city well fortified. We are well in-trenched. Heavy cannonading. Sometimes very fierce. I will write again when I can send it. It is too dark to see. I am very well."

Johnston did elect to make a stand at Jackson in the hope that a lack of drinking water in the region, caused by a prolonged drought and torrid temperatures, would compel the Federals to make a costly and futile frontal attack on the town's fortifications and then fall back toward Vicksburg. He had good cause to adopt this strategy, as can be seen from Taylor's description of the march to Jackson in a July 15 letter to Netta:

> I never saw or even read of a march more enervating in my life. The distance was nothing, but there were no creeks, no wells, no springs . . . with the only sources of water supply being cisterns and stagnant pools. Then [there was] the dust which arose in clouds so dense that frequently I could not see thirty feet in advance of me. Then at noonday the heat was very oppressive and under this condition of things, is it any wonder that men fell down in their tracks and that horses and mules reeled and fell under the saddle—sun struck was a familiar word. . . . [The] men were doctored and recovered, but who can tell how many brutes [animals] died.

The Confederate fortifications at Jackson, the main part of which was located on the west bank of the Pearl River, ran in a semicircle about the town, with each end anchored on the river. Sherman, although his army outnumbered Johnston's more than two to one, made no attempt to break through this line or to outflank it by sending a force across the Pearl, either above or below Jackson, to threaten Johnston's railroad supply line, a move that would have obliged him to beat a hasty retreat. Instead, the Federals dug in opposite the enemy works—the Forty-seventh Ohio even constructed a tunnel—and then opened up with an artillery bombardment designed to drive the Confederates from the town. The sole infantry assault was neither intended nor approved by Sherman. On July 15 Taylor described to Netta how it occurred and what happened:

> A few days ago [July 12] one of our Genl's [Brig. Gen. Jacob Lauman, a division commander in the XIII Corps] was ordered to advance his line of skirmishers; he did so, [and] meeting with no opposition he concluded that they [the Confederates] must have evacuated. There-

fore, without orders, he hurried up his brigades & when they came within good easy range of the rebels they opened with grape, canister and shrapnel. The slaughter was fearful, the Gen'l retired in disorder with a loss of from 500 to 700 killed & wounded. Shortly after he was relieved and sent to the rear. Justice follows quickly in many instances in the army and he no doubt will be severely dealt with. The slaughter was fearful and altogether unnecessary, but he was willing to make the sacrifice to procure another star. What a commentary on ambition.

Apart from Lauman's fiasco, which took place at the very beginning of the siege of Jackson, Union casualties had been few, and the main problem, as Taylor informed Netta on July 15, was water:

This now concerns us all, private & officer alike. It is apparent to us all that our supply is about exhausted. Col. Seibert [Edward Siber, commander of the Thirty-seventh Ohio, a predominantly German regiment] very expressively remarked that his cisterns are dry, that he tried to dig a well but "by tam de grownd was trier than de cistern." On the ridge between the Big Black [River] & Pearl I understand that water cannot be found by digging—hence you can imagine how lively we are exercised by the prospect.

Taylor concluded his July 15 letter with an account of a visit he made with General Ewing to the headquarters of division commander Maj. Gen. Frank Blair, who extended "'a real highland welcome' to his guests" (meaning that whiskey was served in generous quantities and presumably undiluted by water), and then to what Ewing and he thought, along with other Union soldiers, was Jefferson Davis's plantation but was in fact that of the Confederate president's brother, Joseph Davis. Here they found what they assumed were the "remains of Jeff Davis's library," the greater part of it being "scattered over the dooryard & house in the greatest confusion" along with "papers, letters, &c., &c., all exposed to the action of the weather." They took a few of the books and "brought in a quantity of letters for information." Taylor also picked up "some checks for the purposes of his [Davis's] autograph" and enclosed one of them in the letter for Netta's edification.

Ironically, in view of the Federals' precarious water situation, on July 16 Johnston decided to evacuate Jackson. Sherman had refused to make the frontal attack that he had hoped for, and he feared that his opponent would eventually execute the obvious stratagem of sending a flanking column across the Pearl to cut the Confederate line of supply and retreat. Thus he ordered his army to withdraw from Jackson on the night of July 17.

That night, Taylor, serving as brigade officer of the day, "heard the fire bells in Jackson and saw a grand old reflection of the heavens—a beautiful crimson mingled with gold and as the flakes & cinders descended it looked as if the heavens were spangled with rubies & gold."[14] He asked some soldiers of the Forty-seventh what this meant, and they told him that at about 11:00 P.M., while he had been napping, a train had chugged into Jackson, that its arrival had been accompanied by the sound of cheering and bands playing, and that shortly afterward they had seen what appeared to be an increase in the number of campfires behind the enemy lines. Johnston, they supposed, had received reinforcements.

For more than an hour, Taylor gazed at the town, watching the progress of the fire. Satisfied that it was spreading, he returned to his tent and went back to sleep. At 5:00 A.M., a messenger aroused him with the news that a white flag was flying from an enemy fort in the brigade's sector. The train, the music and cheering, and the campfires, he realized, had been a ruse to cover the evacuation of Jackson. He sent a message to Ewing with this news, then hastened to the fort where he had the Forty-seventh's color guard plant the regimental banner. Next he went into Jackson with one of Ewing's aides and the brigade color guard. A regiment from another brigade already had its flag waving from the capitol dome, and so his party had to be content with putting the brigade banner beside it.

Ewing, upon arriving in Jackson, instructed Taylor to take charge of a patrol for the purpose of maintaining order and combating the fires. This proved to be a difficult, indeed impossible, task, as Taylor's account of his endeavors vividly demonstrates:

> I posted the first guard that was posted in the town and then worked very hard. The rebels had left very large fires behind them & they were spreading, the flames cracking & snapping, paint hissing and black smoke rolling up, men whooping and yelling, furniture rattling as it would strike the pavement [when burning buildings collapsed]—all added to the confusion. Then as news [of the Confederate evacuation] spread throughout the various divisions and corps men came

straggling in, hugging, shouting & plundering. I was Asst. Pro[vost] Marshall on that day [July 18] and used all our brigade in protecting the houses of the city, but the brigade was absorbed & still I had need of more men. . . . Ammunition had to be moved, fire engines worked, [and] I was directed to do it. So down I went [into the streets] and I worked alone. Sometimes I could not see the men in the intense heat, whole blocks would thus be consumed in a very short space of time. The citizens were perfectly stupefied and appeared indifferent. Occasionally shells would explode in the burning buildings and men at work stampeded in an instant. . . . Thus the fire raged until night—extinguish it in one section of the city and it would burst out in another. It reminded me of the descriptions of the burning of Rome.

Many of the houses I regret to say were set on fire by our men and many excesses were committed by them in pillaging & plundering. The army acted more as a mob than as disciplined soldiers. Not the whole army but twenty or thirty from a regiment out of so large an army makes quite an extensive crowd and this number disgraced our entire army. In some instances I was compelled to use violence. During the day Lieut. [Charles] Dennis [of the Forty-seventh Ohio] was struck by men for attempting to check the spirit of plunder. Other officers were threatened but nothing beyond this outrageous conduct was manifested. . . .

We found any quantity of sugar, rice & molasses and in the hands of speculators flour and bacon, [but] no coffee or tea. Our men had been on quarter rations of sugar for a long time but now they supplied themselves beautifully. Vast quantities of the above articles were consumed by the fire, so much so that the earth was completely saturated with it and was redolent.

Between both parties I presume that at least $1,200,000 or $1,500,000 of property was destroyed on that day, two thirds . . . by the rebels and the remainder by our forces.

According to Taylor, once the fires subsided, hundreds of Confederate civilians and soldiers began coming into Jackson, "many of whom desired to take the oath of allegiance to the U.S." These people reported that Johnston's army was "in a demoralized condition and short of rations and its men deserting in squads." Taylor himself saw "six, eight and more perfectly armed & equipped" Rebels give themselves up to "our officers who were bathing in

Pearl River." Before long, he believed the number of prisoners in custody of Blair's division, which occupied Jackson, would reach 1,200.

Another indication of the demoralization of Johnston's army was what it left behind in the town: "enough ammunition to keep twenty pieces of artillery firing incessantly for five or six months. Empty shells and capped shells, solid shot and every other description of shot imagineable [*sic*]. Small arms in untold quantity were lying around & stored in their arsenals . . . [and] all his [Johnston's] siege guns, four in number."

Sherman did not pursue Johnston's army, even though some of the Confederate deserters declared (so stated Taylor) that if he did, all that would be necessary "to cause it to disband is to follow it up, offer to send all home who wish to take the oath of allegiance to the government . . . and a bloodless victory will be the result." Instead, Sherman, declaring that further pursuit would be "more destructive of my own command than fruitful in results" because of the intense heat and scarcity of drinking water, ordered his forces to destroy the railroads to the east, north, and south of Jackson and everything in the town that might be of use to the enemy, and then they would return to Vicksburg.

Taylor took part in the work of devastation. Placed in charge of six companies of the Forty-seventh, he used them to smash a siege cannon, tear up tracks, and burn railroad cars, bridges, and hundreds of cotton bales. Other units of Blair's division, which occupied Jackson, did the same. When, on July 22, Sherman set out from the town, he left behind "one charred mass of ruins."[15]

Blair's division followed the rest of the XV Corps as it marched back toward Vicksburg. On July 23, near Clinton, Confederate cavalry drove in the pickets of the rearguard, which Taylor commanded as brigade officer of the day. He quickly disposed of the threat by counterattacking with a company of skirmishers, but he subsequently wrote Netta, "you cannot imagine the difficulty I had with stragglers—men exhausted, sick, and footsore." Some of them he placed on his horse, and he walked until they could be transferred to wagons. By evening, when the division halted at Bolton to bivouac, he had "almost a brigade of them," so "hard the labor [of marching] was both on men and horses" in ankle-deep dust and a 110 degree temperature. Sherman, it would seem, was right in deciding not to pursue Johnston's army beyond Jackson. Mississippi's summer climate constituted a greater menace.[16]

On July 25, the XV Corps crossed the Black River and encamped at Fox's Plantation, thereby bringing the Vicksburg Campaign to a final, formal conclusion. Concluded too was Taylor's first participation in major, large-scale military operations. He rejoined his regiment too late to engage in actual combat during the siege of Vicksburg, nor was he involved in any serious fighting at Jackson. Yet he received and successfully performed important assignments, displaying as he did so an energy and enterprise that fully justified the major's oak leaves on his shoulder straps. Moreover, he was with Grant's army, the ever-victorious Army of the Tennessee, an army whose troops had come to regard themselves as invincible and that surely would go on to fight and win more great battles. With that army, and if the Almighty indeed preserved him, he would have ample opportunity to find the glory and recognition he craved. In that sense, for him that very crucial sense, Tom Taylor's Civil War at last truly had begun.

We Will Achieve Mighty Victories
July–November 1863

W HILE TAYLOR WAGED WAR in Mississippi, the war came to Netta in Ohio. It arrived with Brig. Gen. John Hunt Morgan's Rebel raiders, 2,500 of whom early in July crossed over the Ohio River from Kentucky into Indiana and then rampaged eastward through the southern counties of that state and Ohio. On July 15, about 200 of them showed up in Georgetown. The following day, Netta described to her husband what they did there:

> They robed [*sic*] our stores and groceries, took just what they wanted. Mewkirks loss is about five hundred, Galbreaths three, Adam Shane, Thies and Peter Stigler they almost broke up, taking nearly everything out of their stores. They also took a great many horses, examined every stable in town. They respected private property, entered but a few dwellings and politely asked for something to eat, did not give us a call. I saw two in the clover lot, I suppose [they] were looking for horses. From some unknown cause they took very little out of the Drug Store, they drank to your health and took George's big boots is all.[1] I think they were afraid. They were well posted in regard to some of our citizens, were very lenient toward the "butternuts" [a popular synonym for Copperheads]. Several asked where Chilt lived and if he was in town. When they went to Levi Jacobs store he threw open the doors and said "Walk in gentlemen and help yourselves," one of the fellows asked him his politics, he said a "butternut," they bowed and said they wanted nothing of him. They asked which were the abolition stores, and one of our citizens took it upon himself to show them. . . . Some Indiana, Cincinnati and the 7th Ohio Cavalry passed through today. I do hope they may be fortunate enough to capture them. . . . Well dear I believe I have given you all the particulars, though very disconnected. The children have interrupted me so often.

Taylor "had the extreme felicity" of receiving this letter and one dated July 2 on Monday, July 27, the first mail from Netta to reach him since he had left Cincinnati more than a month earlier. They arrived, moreover, while the Forty-seventh was establishing, along with the rest of Frank Blair's division, the new Camp Sherman about six miles east of the Big Black River, where Grant had instructed Sherman to deploy the XV Corps to guard against any Confederate foray, unlikely as that might be. Hence, not until July 29 did Taylor have a chance to reply. His first comment, understandably enough, dealt with the visit of Morgan's men to Georgetown:

> I well know that ladies and children would not be injured [by the raiders] although property might suffer. . . . I regret greatly they plundered our grocery so extensively, but am compelled to say that it is customary to take from them what is needed in the way of supplies. We do the same and I will add that in the future I shall go and do likewise. Our town will have an avenger to the extent of my ability.

Taylor devoted most of the remainder of the letter to denouncing Levi Jacobs for saving his store from pillage by proclaiming himself to be a butternut, to relating the march from Jackson to the Vicksburg area, and to describing the Forty-seventh's quarters at Camp Sherman, "on the side of a hill in a large grove of ancient oaks whose boughs are draped in long soft Spanish moss." The only unpleasant aspect of the camp was that Capt. William Ward had arrived there and "had a talk with Col. Parry" with the object of finding "something in my line of conduct on which to base charges against me." Taylor, however, thought, "he is impotent to harm me" because the other officers of the regiment "are my friends and would discountenance anything of the kind." Yet should "something apparently unfortunate occur, I shall not be discomfited, but accept it as some gracious interposition of Providence in my behalf, remembering that 'God moves in a mysterious way, His wonders to perform.'" To say the least, this scarcely was a characteristic attitude for Taylor to take, particularly when he felt threatened. He must have been confident that he had little to fear from Ward.

During the march to Jackson, Taylor had written Netta predicting that Sherman would keep going until he reached Chattanooga.[2] If an army could be moved on land as easily as on a map, this would have been a brilliant strategic stroke. Late in June, Rosecrans's Army of the Cumberland launched an offensive designed to take Chattanooga, the gateway to Georgia and the Carolinas. Had a large portion of Grant's army joined in the campaign, not only would the capture of Chattanooga been ensured, but also the Confederate force defending it, Gen. Braxton Bragg's Army of Tennessee, would have faced such overwhelming odds that it would have had to retreat at least as far as Atlanta to avoid being destroyed in a battle it dared not fight. This in turn would have enabled the Federals to concentrate against Robert E. Lee and Richmond. Barring a major Union blunder or a Confederate victory approaching the miraculous, the war could have been militarily won by the North by Christmas 1863.

All of this, though, is fantasy. In actuality, the absence of a usable rail line connecting the Mississippi Valley with the Chattanooga area made it logistically impossible for Grant to reinforce Rosecrans in sufficient time and with enough troops to make any substantial difference. Thus, if the Federal troops made available by the fall of Vicksburg were to be of use, it would have to be somewhere other than Middle Tennessee. Lincoln himself found a place for some of them to operate. On his orders, Grant returned to the Department of the Ohio the two divisions of the IX Corps that had participated in Sherman's Jackson expedition. They then joined an army that Maj. Gen. Ambrose Burnside led from Kentucky into East Tennessee during August, thereby at long last fulfilling Lincoln's desire—some would say obsession—to liberate that predominantly Unionist section from Confederate domination. Furthermore, after occupying Knoxville, which he did on September 2, Burnside was to reinforce Rosecrans, giving him more than adequate strength to defeat Bragg should he offer battle.[3]

Another suggestion for using the abundance of idle manpower in Mississippi came from Grant. Why not, he proposed to Henry Halleck, send a joint army-navy expedition against Mobile? Seizing it would deprive the South of its main Gulf seaport and open the way to Montgomery, Selma, and Atlanta; the loss of those cities would reduce the Confederacy in essence to Virginia and the Carolinas. Halleck, in response, did not say no, but neither did he say yes. The reason was that Lincoln, placing diplomatic ahead of military considerations, desired to counter a French takeover of Mexico by occupying eastern Texas. When finally informed of this plan, Grant obligingly provided a corps for an invasion of Texas by way of Louisiana.[4] But before this expedition could get under way, events in Georgia caused Chattanooga to become the focus of Union military operations in the West after all.

During July, August, and early September, Rosecrans, thanks to a combination of skillful maneuvers and Confederate bungling, compelled Bragg to abandon Middle Tennessee, evacuate Chattanooga, and retreat into Georgia. Rendered overconfident by his spectacular success and believing that Bragg's army was demoralized, Rosecrans pushed into Georgia, seeking to finish off the enemy. In doing so, he divided his forces, providing Bragg with an opportunity, which he seized, to strike back by concentrating superior strength against the separated Union columns. Only the incompetence and disobedience of his top generals prevented him from dealing Rosecrans a crippling, perhaps fatal, series of blows. As it was, in order to regroup, Rosecrans had to fall back toward Chattanooga, closely pressed by the Confederates, who received 20,000 reinforcements from Lee's army in Virginia and Johnston's in Mississippi, giving them an edge they rarely enjoyed—a sizable numerical advantage. In contrast, not a single soldier came to Rosecrans from Burnside's 20,000-man army in Knoxville, despite repeated orders from Halleck that Burnside go to the support of the Army of the Cumberland.

On September 19 and 20, Bragg's and Rosecrans's armies clashed south of Chattanooga along Chickamauga Creek in the bloodiest two-day battle of the war. On the first day, the Federals repulsed all Confederate attacks and were doing the same the second day until a Union division commander, by executing in absurdly literal fashion an obscurely worded order from Rosecrans without asking for a clarification, opened up a gap in the Federal defense line at the exact time of a massive enemy assault. The entire right wing of the Army of the Cumberland was swept from the field, and had it not been for the staunch stand of the left wing under Maj. Gen. George H. Thomas, "the rock of Chickamauga," the Confederates would have gained total victory and regained Chattanooga, behind the fortifications of which Rosecrans's battered forces sought refuge.

Yet it seemed that the Confederates would achieve both of these goals eventually in any case. Rightly realizing that his army was too weakened by its heavy losses at Chickamauga to storm Chattanooga, Bragg entrenched on the heights overlooking the town and interdicted all of Rosecrans's supply lines except for a wretched road that wound for sixty miles through the mountains. Since this route provided only an inadequate trickle of provisions, the

Army of the Cumberland faced the same fate that had befallen Vicksburg's garrison; being starved into surrender or else making what almost surely would be a disastrous attempt to escape.[5]

The crisis at Chattanooga called for prompt action, and Union high command took it. From Virginia, two corps of the Army of the Potomac under Maj. Gen. Joseph Hooker hastened by rail to Tennessee, and Grant received orders to send Sherman's XV Corps by steamboats to Memphis, from where it would move overland to Chattanooga. Hooker's and Sherman's mission was to rescue the Army of the Cumberland from destruction and then join it in driving back, and if possible, smashing Bragg's army, thereby securing the Federal hold on Chattanooga and opening the way for an invasion of Georgia.[6]

Resumption of active operations by the XV Corps came at an inconvenient time for Taylor. During most of the past two months, Parry had been on leave, and Wallace had gone to Ohio with Captain Ward to raise troops, leaving Taylor in acting command of the Forty-seventh. He enjoyed this de facto realization of his prediction that someday he would be its commander, and as might be expected of him, strove to improve the regiment's drill, with the result that Sherman himself praised its fine showing at a review.[7] But with the return of Parry and Wallace, he hoped, indeed expected, to take a leave also. Now that was no longer possible. Writing Netta, who was six months pregnant, on September 23, he declared with regard to coming home: "Don't expect it, don't look for it, don't desire it." Indeed, he added, "I shall . . . not be able to be with you until our term of service shall have expired. Therefore, I pray you, be strong and stout of heart [and do not] fill every letter with pleas to resign. The cause demands me as much today as it did a year ago and so let me finish my good work. The honor will be greater."

On September 27, Blair's division followed Brig. Gen. Peter J. Osterhaus's and Brig. Gen. John M. Corse's divisions of the XV Corps to Vicksburg to board steamboats bound for Memphis. The march there, Taylor wrote Netta on October 1 from the "Steamer Adams," was one of "extraordinary exhaustion—hardship is no name for it. . . . The roads were one cloud of dust, the earth actually giving way as we stepped plunging men ankle deep in it. The heat was great and we were compelled to press on regardless of the noon-day sun, as an army had to be relieved. We were all filled with dust and hoarse as though possessed by great colds." Neither Taylor nor any of the other soldiers of the XV Corps could possibly foresee that this march to Vicksburg was merely the first of many more to come, during which they would traverse nearly 2,000 miles, and that the final one would take place a year and a half hence with a parade down Pennsylvania Avenue in Washington, D.C., a parade Taylor would witness but in which he would not participate.

Taylor somehow got the notion that the XV Corps, instead of going to Chattanooga, would relieve another corps for that purpose and thus end up being assigned to outpost duty in West Tennessee. If that proved to be the case, he told Netta on October 1,

> I shall make an effort . . . to be detached from the regiment and assigned to some special duty at Memphis or some other place. I despise this outpost duty and it has always been my luck to be compelled to perform more than my share. . . . In future I shall endeavor to avoid it and by the means above stated. If detached I shall be rid of the pestiferous presence of Ward. You are aware that I have always had something to impel me to greater exertion and his very anger and the desire he manifests to have me out of the service will cause me to attain greater skill and science in military affairs and matters.

Taylor need not have fretted about being assigned to odious outpost duty. As he happily notified Netta on October 6 from a "Camp near Memphis, Tenn.," the XV Corps received "orders to be ready to move at a moments warning, to prepare for campaigning and also to take two hundred rounds of ammunition per man." All this, he continued, "looks very much like business and as though we shall have something to do." Other than knowing that the corps would march to Tuscumbia, Alabama, by way of Corinth, Mississippi, "no one ventures to predict anything," but his own belief was that "we will form a column which will be used to amaze and terrify the rebels on Rosencranz's [sic] right, making a right wing to that army and that we will sweep through the [Southern] States in conjunction with Rosencranz & Burnside. Where we will stop is anyone's guess."

The following day, Blair's division set out for Corinth on a "rough road" paralleling the Memphis & Charleston Railroad. The march took them, Taylor later informed Netta, through "a country completely worn out by cultivation" of cotton and dotted with "straggling villages" with "unattractive houses," where, in the weed-grown front yards, blacks stood "grinning at us like apes." No enemy opposition was encountered until October 11 at Collierville. Here a large force of Confederate cavalry attacked a train carrying Sherman, Hugh Ewing, and their staffs. A four-hour fight ensued during which Sherman's escort and the local garrison held the assailants at bay until Corse's division, coming from Memphis, arrived and drove them away.[8]

Blair's division, which had been too far ahead to provide assistance to Sherman's party, reached the village of Pocahontas on October 13. Here it halted while the Forty-seventh and the other Ohio regiments cast ballots for the candidates in their state's gubernatorial election. The vast majority voted for John Brough, the Republican candidate, and only a small minority for Clement L. Vallandigham, who had been nominated by the Democrats even though he was residing in Canada, where he had gone after being arrested for treason and turned over to the Confederate government. Taylor helped increase Brough's victory margin by adding "twenty tickets [ballots] in our regiment and three or four times that number in other regiments against the Val. ticket." Reporting to Netta what he had done in a letter written that same day, he cautioned her; "You need not say anything concerning this to anyone." Not only had he engaged in what in effect was ballot-box stuffing, but he also had turned against the Democratic party and voted Republican, a shift he would not have dreamed of making before the war. Like many other Northern War Democrats, especially those serving in the army, he looked upon Peace Democrats such as Vallandigham as traitors.

Two more days of marching brought Taylor and the Forty-seventh to Corinth, Mississippi, a town that had been the scene of a so-called siege in spring 1862 and of a fierce battle in fall of that year because it was bisected by two strategically important railroads, the Mobile & Ohio and the Memphis & Charleston. The latter went to Chattanooga, and Sherman had orders from Halleck to repair it as he proceeded eastward so that it could serve as a supply line to that town. There was not much left of Corinth, Taylor reported to Netta on October 16—only a hotel, a few other buildings, and some cottages. The countryside, however, was fertile and reminded him of New Jersey, with pines, chestnuts, and oaks being abundant. Moreover, the inhabitants of this region were mainly pro-Union; a Tennessee cavalry regiment serving with Sherman "secured many recruits" there.

On the way to Corinth, Taylor also saw for the first time another type of Southern recruit for the Union army: black troops. "The enlisted men," he commented, "performed their part well [when on drill], bearing themselves quite soldierly, wheeling and flanking in good shape. The white officers were at a loss in several evolutions. They make good looking soldiers and enjoy it amazingly."[9] For Taylor, the war was one to preserve the Union, and like Netta, he abhorred abolitionism. Yet nowhere in his correspondence does he criticize or even refer to Lincoln's Emancipation Proclamation, and the preceding passage seems to indicate that, unlike a great many Northern soldiers, he did not resent the enlistment of blacks. If they could help put down the rebellion, fine.

Already at Corinth, having journeyed there by rail, was Osterhaus's division of the XV Corps. With his full force thus united, Sherman made several organizational changes. One was to give Blair tactical command of two divisions, Osterhaus's and his own, which henceforth would be headed by Brig. Gen. Morgan L. Smith, a forty-one-year-old former enlisted man in the regular army with a reputation for being a rough and ready fighter. Another was to put Hugh Ewing in command of Corse's division, an act justified by Ewing's being senior in rank and age to the twenty-nine-year-old Corse, who reverted to brigade commander in that division. Finally—the change of most interest to Taylor—Joseph Lightburn, who was a brigadier general, assumed command of what had been Ewing's brigade, to which was added the Eighty-third Indiana. The new regiment, Taylor proudly notified Netta, gave the brigade five regiments, the other four being the Thirty-first, Thirty-seventh, and Forty-seventh Ohio and the Fourth [West] Virginia, and made it "by considerable the strongest brigade in the 15th A.C." Taylor also was pleased to have Lightburn back as commander: "He suits us all and he is a good officer and a gentleman."[10] Certain events on two hot July afternoons outside Atlanta later caused these words to become quite ironic.

While Sherman reorganized his army, far greater changes took place in the command structure of all Union forces in the West. At Lincoln's direction, Halleck put Grant in charge of a newly created Military Division of the Mississippi, comprising the entire area between the Appalachians and the Mississippi except Louisiana, and authorized him to replace Rosecrans with Thomas as commander of the Army of the Cumberland. This Grant promptly

Brigadier General Morgan L. Smith.
Miller, ed., Photographic History, *10: 87.*

did. Furthermore, after he saw a message from the War Department's representative in Chattanooga that the Army of the Cumberland soon would be compelled by hunger either to retreat or surrender, Grant decided to go to the Gate City and see for himself what the situation there was and what could be done about it.[11]

The same day, October 18, that Grant assumed his new command, Morgan Smith's division arrived in what Taylor described in his diary as the "pleasant" village of Iuka, Mississippi. From here, after a one-day halt, it moved into Alabama and, on October 21, camped beside Cherokee Creek where, apart from a reconnaissance to Tuscumbia, it remained for the rest of the month. The reason for this, Taylor explained to Netta on October 24, was that the Confederates had damaged the Memphis & Charleston Railroad "considerably" east of Iuka by "burning bridges, cattle guards, sleepers, etc. and bending rails." As a consequence, "repairs will delay us for a considerable period." Furthermore, "The rebels hover around us [with cavalry], making rushes on our pickets, trains, etc. but are not strong enough to do anything more than harass our movements."

More bothersome than the Confederates was the weather. No longer did Sherman's troops suffer from too much heat and too little water; now it was biting cold, with frequent rains. As usual in war, the enlisted men, who, unlike the officers, had no tents, suffered the most. If Netta, declared Taylor on October 24, "could only see all hands shivering in the rain and the cold piercing winds of autumn it would make your heart bleed for them. Each man has his oil cloth and these they unite and make shelters but are not so comfortable as tents." Yet in spite of "all their suffering & exposure you never hear a murmur," and "the fire of patriotism burns just as bright as in the first day of our troubles."

It still was raining on the night of October 30 when an order came for Morgan Smith's division to march the next day to Chickasaw, a village on the Tennessee River near Eastport. Prompting this order was a message from Grant that Sherman, who now headed the Army of the Tennessee, had received on October 27 from a courier: "Drop all work on Memphis & Charleston Railroad eastward, cross the Tennessee, and hurry with all possible dispatch toward Bridgeport, till you meet further orders from me."[12]

By coincidence, on the very day this message reached Sherman, Grant carried out an operation at Chattanooga that enabled the Army of the Cumberland to open another and much better supply line, one that not only eliminated the danger of starvation but that also could provide for Hooker's detachment and the XV Corps. Hence, as Grant evidently anticipated, restoration of the Memphis & Charleston ceased to be necessary. What he needed and therefore wanted to do was to assemble as rapidly as possible a force at Chattanooga capable of defeating, or better still smashing, Bragg's besieging army.[13]

The morning of October 31 brought an end to the rain at the camp of Morgan Smith's division and revealed the sun—but also a very muddy road. Because the wagon train, "a long one," frequently stalled in the mud, it took the division four hours to cover the first seven miles of its march. This "left us," Taylor subsequently reported to Netta, "eight miles to march after night," and "so we went slipping and stumbling along until about 10 o'clock when we came into camp at Chickasaw." Here the division remained a day and a half, during which Taylor served on a court-martial that sentenced a Confederate spy to death. The division then crossed the Tennessee in steamboats and scows and spent the next two weeks zig-zagging across northern Alabama until it reached, along with the rest of Sherman's army, Bridgeport. Writing Netta from there on November 18, Taylor boasted, "We have moved around more and had our directions changed more frequently than any other corps of the army ever had since we commenced this march. We look upon it as one of the achievements of the age and are proud that we have performed it."

Located in Alabama on the north bank of the Tennessee River, Bridgeport lay twenty-eight miles due west of Chattanooga and also was the point at which the Nashville & Chattanooga linked up with the Memphis & Charleston by a now-destroyed railroad bridge. Being there put Sherman's forces in position to participate in Grant's attempt to break Bragg's grip on Chattanooga. This, Taylor stated in his November 18 letter, would occur soon:

> We will probably cross the [Tennessee] river this afternoon [by a pontoon bridge]. We are going to the front, our Corps is expected to clear Lookout Mountain. To do this we will strike Bragg's left and will in all probability have a sharp little fight, but I have no doubt of the results. Grant will not suffer disaster to befall his favorite Army Corps, and with Sherman to direct us we will achieve mighty victories.

Again Taylor proved to be a poor military prophet. Although one of Sherman's divisions, Osterhaus's, joined the Union right wing under Hooker for an attack on Lookout Mountain, the other three divisions moved up the Tennessee to Brown's Ferry, where they recrossed the river on another pontoon bridge and then headed northward. In a November 22 letter from a "Camp on Mt. Near Chattanooga, Tenn.," Taylor described the march to that place and outlined the plan of battle, which called for the Army of the Tennessee to strike Bragg's right flank on the north end of Missionary Ridge, a long height overlooking Chattanooga from the west. "I feel," he assured Netta, "that I shall come forth from the impending conflict unharmed," but "if I should not return remember *Mother*." Then, after giving instructions regarding financial matters, he closed with these words: "Goodbye. God be with you & the children. Kiss the dears. I would like to write more."

Taylor did not have an opportunity to write more until December 20. He then produced a vivid account of Sherman's assault on the northern end of Missionary Ridge, an account derived from his diary and which, like all his descriptions of combat, is highly detailed.

We left camp near Chattanooga on the 23rd ult. at 4 P.M. and marched to a point four miles above C. [hattanooga] known as the Coalwell [Caldwell] House, at which place we laid until 12 at night. (The order was to take three days rations & a blanket or overcoat.) The first brigade [commanded by Brig. Gen. Giles A. Smith, Morgan Smith's brother] marched three miles above to West [North] Chickamauga creek where we had about 120 wooden pontoon boats concealed into which boats they embarked and floated down the

Where Sherman Crossed the Tennessee River to Attack Missionary Ridge.
Miller, ed., Photographic History, 2: 292.

[Tennessee] river capturing the pickets of the enemy as they moved down until they arrived at the mouth of the East [South] Chickamauga where they landed. Only two of the enemies [sic] pickets escaped. The boats then crossed to the opposite shore and we embarked and rowed to the south side of the mouth of [South Chickamauga] and landed on a bottom under a hill. At this point we expected to have a desperate struggle and it took strong nerves to bear up under the contemplation of this prospect. In the event of disaster we had only the boats mentioned, each of which held only twenty, to carry our division [back across the Tennessee]. We had no artillery and only the ground we stood upon. Soon we formed, advanced our skirmishers, and started forward. Judge of our surprise when we found no enemy when we expected to experience our hardest fight. As we gradually ascended and possessed ourselves of the hill and field our confidence increased. We thought when we gained the summit that if enemy then advanced we could receive him on more equal footing. We halted a few yards beyond the summit, advanced our skirmishers and put a spade in the hands of each man of the main body with instruction to "bury himself" in the shortest possible space of time. I superintended the construction of the "pits." By daylight we had a line of pits over a mile and a half long, almost four feet deep and the same wide, with good parapet capable of resisting shell and shot from ordinary sized guns. When daylight dawned how anxiously we scanned Mission[ary] Ridge which we were compelled to take that day. With my glass I examined closely and critically every stone, fence and tree, but saw no [enemy] soldiers. It was apparent that they had been outwitted. Still there was time yet for him [the enemy] to do a great deal as ours was the only division across [the Tennessee River]. The Corps was camping [on the other side of the river] all the time. About 8 A.M. Genl. Jno. E. Smith landed all of his division and secured his position in like manner, then Ewing followed. About 10 A.M. the steamer "Dunbar" came up. Her arrival announced to us that Maj. Genl. [Oliver Otis] Howard [whose XI Corps from the Army of the Potomac had been added to Sherman's command to compensate for the absence of Osterhaus's division] had driven the enemy from the river bank [to the south of the XV Corps]. Then a lively skirmish by Jno. E. Smith and we had formed connection with the main army [the Union center consisting of Thomas' s Army of the Cumberland]. The fact gave us great assurance. About the same time the battle raged fiercely in the center and on the right [of Grant's army].

Morgan Smith's division was able to advance unopposed and seize the hill mentioned by Taylor because except for a few pickets there were no Confederate troops whatsoever on the northern part of Missionary Ridge. Had the Federals pushed forward instead of stopping to entrench, they could have occupied this part of the ridge without firing a shot or losing a man.[14]

At 12 M. of the 24th [by then the Federals had laid a pontoon bridge across the Tennessee River near the mouth of South Chickamauga Creek] we got our batteries and then advanced upon the ridge. The skirmish [line] there was heavy and composed of details from each regiment of the Div. under command of Lt. Col. Wallace. Very slight opposition was made to our advance and by three P.M. we gained the summit of a spur of Mission ridge. The brigade was halted and the 47th sent to carry a hill on the main ridge. Over we marched unsupported by any adjacent force. We moved up the hill steadily— the crack of rifles now became quite frequent but by half past three we had gained the summit and advanced our skirmishers down the slope between our hill and that known as Tunnel Hill. At the same time a brigade of the rebels advanced down the slope of Tunnel Hill to drive us from the ridge. Our skirmishers met them. Col. Wallace doubled the lines and poured such a fire into them that they fell back. At the same time their batteries opened on us from Tunnel Hill with shell, shrapnel & canister. Several times the smoke of bursting shells completely shrouded us, hid us from view. They enfiladed us—we changed our front and laid down. They advanced a second time on our front and again were driven back, then they attempted to turn our flank. We doubled our skirmish line again and hurled them back once more. All the while they kept their batteries playing on us but only one man of ours was wounded.

A dense fog arose now and rendered further offensive movements impractical.

The Confederates opposing the Forty-seventh and the rest of Lightburn's brigade, which now included a sixth regiment, the Fifty-fourth Ohio, consisted of two Texas regiments. They came from Patrick Cleburne's Division, which had been sent by Bragg to defend the north end of Missionary Ridge, and were supported by only two cannons, not by "batteries" as related in Taylor's account. Given his lack of serious battle experience, it is understandable that he exaggerated the strength and firepower of the Confederates. Otherwise, though, his account of what took place on November 24 is confirmed by other sources, including Lightburn's report.[15]

> At 5 P.M. we were reinforced by the 30th O. and later by 83rd Ind. & 4th Va., the whole under the command of Col. Parry. At dark I was ordered to fortify the hill & picks and shovels were sent over. I laid off the work and soon had a couple hundred men at it. The mt. [hill] is one of the highest of the ridge & commands a view of Chattanooga, the ridge & Lookout Mt. The night was clear & "The cold moon shown brightly down," enabling me to obtain a grand view of the movements of friend and foe and of the fierce struggle which raged on Lookout until 10 P.M. It is beyond the power of pen or mind to describe it. To me it was a condensation of thunder storms without the rain—hundreds of cannons belched forth huge missiles of death, which went shrieking and ploughing through the air, raising currents & counter currents. Then the sharp rattle of thousands of muskets & the bursting of shells—clouds of fire floating through the air, clouds of smoke hovering over the plain, capping the mountains in their gossamer folds and the flashes of fire, all combined to render the scene startling and sublime beyond description. I was fascinated by it. At the same time I knew how desperate would be the struggle of the morrow and felt the necessity of pushing the work. By two A.M. of the 25th I had the pleasure of seeing it complete and the next morning I heard Genl Sherman say it was "well done and angles well taken." This day on this point Maj. Genl's Sherman, Howard, Blair, [Carl] Schurz and Brig. Genl's M. L. Smith, Lightburn, Corse, Kindle [Nathan Kimball] and a host of others.
>
> Next day [November 25] I was up at 5 A.M. In consideration of my labor at night and of the hard duty of our regiment the day and night ... preceding we were not put in the main action but had six Cos. under Lt. Col. Wallace (which had done nothing the night before) to hold the left of the attacking party which advanced on Tunnel Hill. In this position they sustained heavy fire of musketry, shell & grape. I was sent with orders to know about it. The remainder of the regiment was in reserve & supporting batteries. I had a fine view of the whole fight of every part of the line. None was more stubborn than

that of Tunnel Hill. In the morning about 8 A.M. Col. [Theodore] Jones of the 30th [Ohio] was ordered to take his regiment and take Tunnel Hill. This hill is next to the one occupied by us & has two peaks, the one toward us being the lower. On this at the apex they [the Confederates] had had a breastwork of logs. Jones advanced & without much of a struggle got on the outside of the log works, then over. The enemy massed on him & drove him back, scattering grape freely. He sheltered himself behind their logs, he on one side, they on the other. The 37th O. was then sent to his assistance & together they advanced again. They drove the rebels over the point & the 37th was swinging around to flank the hill [the higher peak of Tunnel Hill] when suddenly they received a heavy flank fire & were compelled to throw two companies around to protect their flanks. This made their line too short. The rebels pressed them heavily, the firing was ter- rific, bayonets were used, but our gallant regiments were literally pushed back. Not a man faltered [and] at the log works they stopped, rested and anon I heard the bugle sound a charge. Again they moved steadily forward and the enemy now were pushed back, back, back! Our men gained the summit and went beyond. They shouted and shouted. A little while and back they came, first one, then another and another and finally the whole line came swiftly back. At the logs they halted, dressed their lines, rested and repelled the enemy. Then Genl. Corse's brigade [of Ewing's division] reinforced them, [and] shortly Col. [John M.] Loomis's brigade [also of Ewing's division] followed them. In a few moments I saw [Col. Adolphus] Buschbeck's brigade of the XIth Corps marching up the hillside. A moment of silence as profound as death, then a motion was discovered—our line advanced (I was not five hundred feet from the line and marked dis- tinctly every movement). "Merciful Father" what a dreadful roar now broke the stillness and shook the earth. I could almost see the balls fly through the air. Still not a shot came from our brave boys, only their bayonets gleamed in the beautiful sunlight. They moved on [and] in a moment Genl. Corse shouted for "all who are brave enough, follow me" and climbed the parapet. With a loud huzzah the boys followed. The Genl. fell shot through the "calf" but not a man faltered, the bayonets then were used . . . [and] the summit of the first peak [again was occupied].

The [rest] of the line was not so successful. First I saw a few of the Buschbeck brigade come moving down the hill. Anon others and whole regiments came flying back. They were halted, redressed and again advanced torward. They went a few rods but in a moment [once] more back they came. Oh, what a stampede—each one for himself. (Sherman chewed the stump of his cigar earnestly. I was mad and uttered a few expletives. Said I was sorry any Div. of our Corps had disgraced itself by such conduct, when I was informed they were of Chancellorsville, Va. and not from the 15th A.C.) [On May 2, 1863, Stonewall Jackson's flank attack routed the XI Corps in the Battle of Chancellorsville.] The rebels followed, shrieking like fiends, to the border of a clearing. How the poor, cowardly devils [of Buschbeck's brigade] run [*sic*] over that open space. I never saw such a sight before—it was like a flock of blackbirds. The rebels's guns were spitting all around & shells rattling over head like thunder. This stampede did not disturb the operations of any other force—the 15th [Corps] still [was] at it. The 11th C[orps] were ashamed & said it was caused by want of ammunition, whereupon our Gen'l. [Smith?] ordered us to send them some. Our boys of the 15th held their own and from this time gained a few feet, but the ground was purchased with the blood of dead and wounded, not a foot of it which did not have some part of a body upon it. Rebels were found impaled on the bayonets of our men who had falled [*sic*] from gun shot wounds while in the act of bayoneting the foe—in some cases their feet were locked as an evidence of the struggle. During the course of the P.M. our forces got inside the rebel works on the second peak of Tunnel Mt. But they [the Confederates] opened such a terrible fire of grape and canister from masked batteries that we were driven to the first peak. Our wounded & dead on the other ground [peak] were left in their [the Confederates'] hands. Night approached and firing soon ceased.

Sherman, with close to 30,000 troops available, was repulsed by at most 7,000 Confederates and suffered close to 2,000 casualties (about 500 of whom were prisoners) while inflicting less than 300 on the enemy. Cleburne's position was naturally strong, he conducted his defense with great skill, and his troops fought with equally great determination. Nevertheless, Sherman probably would have seized the north end of Missionary Ridge had he made a coordinated, broad front attack on it with his full force instead of delivering a series of sporadic, piecemeal assaults solely in the Tunnel Hill sector, thereby enabling Cleburne to concentrate most of his strength there while leaving nearly a mile of Missionary Ridge to the south virtually undefended. Other sources, both Union and Confederate, support Taylor's account in all essentials, but his depiction of Buschbeck's brigade merely illustrates the contemptuous attitude Sherman's soldiers had toward those of other Federal armies, especially the Army of the Potomac. In the fighting, Buschbeck lost 263 men; the total casualties of Morgan Smith's division came to only 102 killed and wounded, 86 of whom were in Lightburn's brigade.[16]

I was detailed as Div. skirmish officer and placed in command of fifteen companies. Formed my line and waited for orders to advance. The night was cloudless, moon almost full, but no order [came]. . . .

During the night the rebels were industriously engaged retreating and stripping and robbing our dead of their clothing, money, etc. In the morning hundreds of our poor dead & dying boys were found stripped, in one or two cases of shirt and drawers. One Minnesota soldier who had both legs broken by a grapeshot, said that after they had taken his shirt and blouse, they made an effort to pull off his boots but he made such a noise because of the agony and suffering from the pulling they desisted.

My position kept me moving all night. I discovered they were retreating & reported to the Genl. After [a] time received orders to withdraw two thirds [of] my command, then another reduction of it & finally to draw in my whole line and march for the mouth of East [South] Chickamauga. I did so and when I reached the top of the ridge [where Sherman had entrenched on November 24] I found all had gone. I followed, we became lost in a wood in the dense fog and wandered around through swamps and quagmire until we reached the river bank. I had the boots on that Mr. Brunner had made. The day we crossed the river it rained and our advance was perforce made on foot, consequently they were all cut & torn, exposing my feet to the weather and the gaze of the public. When I rejoined the regt., I found we had orders to march in pursuit. We supplied ourselves with three days *half rations*, could take nothing but our ambulance, could get no clothing, send for no boots or shoes & took no tents, but without murmuring we moved off. Oh, how anxious the army was to overtake Bragg. We wanted to destroy his army believing it would have great effect on the rebellion & probably terminate the war.

Here Taylor ended his narrative of what he did and saw during what became known as the Battle of Chattanooga. In it, he offered no explanation of the Confederate retreat. There was no need. Netta, as she had informed him in a recently received letter, had read of the battle in the newspapers and so already knew how the Federals had won at Chattanooga the mighty victory he had (accurately, for a change) predicted a month ago. Besides, the explanation was rather embarrassing from the standpoint of a proud soldier of Sherman's Army of the Tennessee.

Grant's battle plan gave Sherman the main role. After taking the north end of Missionary Ridge, he was to sweep southward along it, rolling up the Confederates and cutting them off from their line of supply and retreat, a stroke that would annihilate them. But by the afternoon of November 25, Sherman, although his forces had been bolstered by Howard's XI Corps and a division from the Army of the Cumberland, had failed to perform his assigned part and showed no sign of ever succeeding. Grant thereupon sought to assist him by causing Bragg to shift troops from the north down to the center of Missionary Ridge by having the Army of the Cumberland advance and seize a line of enemy trenches at the foot of the ridge. This the Cumberlanders did. Then, finding that they were exposed to plunging fire from the Rebel artillery atop the ridge, on their own initiative they resumed their charge, rolling onward and upward in an immense dark-blue tidal wave. Their forward surge astonished, bewildered, and finally panicked many of the Confederates holding the crest of the ridge. Whole regiments and brigades broke in utter rout, leaving Bragg no choice except to retreat, which, thanks to Cleburne's stand at Tunnel Hill, he was able to do by a route that took his army to a railroad that connected with Atlanta. Cast in a supporting role by Grant, who believed it so demoralized by the defeat at Chickamauga that it was incapable of effective offensive action, the Army of the Cumberland won the battle by making the most spectacularly successful frontal assault of the war.[17]

Sherman gained no laurels on Missionary Ridge. Neither did Taylor. Through no fault of his, he was more a spectator than a participant in the fighting, as evidenced by his own account and by the casualties of the Forty-seventh Ohio: three men wounded. He did only what a soldier is expected to do—carry out his orders. Yet the nature of these orders—lay out a defense line for the entire division, fortify a hill, and take charge of fifteen companies of skirmishers—indicates that he had become known, favorably so, to Lightburn and Morgan Smith and that they regarded him as an officer who could be entrusted with important assignments and a corresponding degree of responsibility not normally given to one of his rank.[18]

Thus, although he still had not distinguished himself in the deadly turmoil of a great battle, the future boded well for Maj. Thomas Thomson Taylor of the Forty-seventh Ohio as he marched in his lacerated boots in pursuit of Bragg's fleeing army. During the past seven months, he had taken great strides forward in what to him was the most crucial battle, his battle with the world, and he had good cause to hope, as he did, that he would advance faster and farther in the future. "This is," he jotted in his diary for November 27, "the 27th birthday I have passed on this footstool. Today I enter upon my 28th year. May God prosper me and make it a year rich in results to me."

I Have Calculated, Worked and Talked
November 1863–March 1864

"I AM WELL," Taylor informed Netta on December 20 at a camp near Bridgeport. It was the first letter he had been able to write since November 22. The reason, he explained, was that he had been in a "region of no mails."[1]

He referred to East Tennessee. For two days following the breaking of the center of Braxton Bragg's line by the Army of the Cumberland, the Forty-seventh had participated in the pursuit of the Confederates, who gave every sign of being, Taylor noted in his diary for November 26, "totally demoralized." Abandoned wagons, caissons, and ambulances strewed the road; dead Rebels, wounded Rebels, and Rebels merely waiting to surrender lined it. At Chickamauga Depot, Bragg's forward supply base, Taylor beheld "three or four piles of mess pork & bacon twenty feet high & thirty or forty, perhaps more, in circumference, burning," huge pools of vinegar and molasses that had been poured onto the ground, and "ammunition in great abundance," and he rode his horse (again he was mounted) "knee deep in shelled corn." But before Sherman could overtake and try to finish off the rapidly fleeing enemy, Grant ordered him to hasten to Knoxville with Morgan Smith's and Hugh Ewing's divisions of the XV Corps and Maj. Gen. Oliver Otis Howard's XI Corps for the purpose of relieving Ambrose Burnside, who was besieged by a strong Confederate force under Lt. Gen. James B. Longstreet. Unless help came soon, Burnside had notified Grant, the exhaustion of his food supply would soon leave him no choice other than to surrender. Such an outcome would be humiliating for the North and offset much of the psychological impact on the South of the routing of Bragg's army at Missionary Ridge.[2]

Sherman moved toward Knoxville as quickly as possible, given the need to gather provisions along the way. Longstreet, having learned of Bragg's debacle, attempted to take the town by storm on November 29, only to suffer a bloody repulse. Then, aware of Sherman's approach, he abandoned the siege and on December 3 withdrew to the east. Sherman, who was disgusted to find that Burnside's troops possessed ample provisions and were in no danger of starving, thereupon returned to Chattanooga from where Smith's and Ewing's divisions proceeded to Bridgeport, arriving on December 19.[3]

What Taylor termed the "long tramp" through East Tennessee and back had been a grueling affair. Not only were rations meager, poor, and uncertain, but also the weather turned cold and rainy, causing much hardship among the troops, who had no overcoats and still were in their summer uniforms, which had become threadbare and ragged. In Smith's and Ewing's divisions, moreover, many of the men were barefoot, the consequence of having marched nearly 1,000 miles since disembarking at Memphis in September. Taylor, although he rode a horse and so did not have to walk in his torn boots, suffered a bout of "diarrhea bad" and recurrence of the rheumatism that had afflicted him during fall 1862 in West Virginia. Small wonder that his diary entry for December 20 read, "Washed & examined clothing, but found no insects, and put on clean clothes. Thought world 100% better. . . . Did not do much but stretch, talk, and rest."[4]

The next day, he "mustered old boots out of service" and, having obtained his pay for September and October ($297.70) and collected $100.00 from John Wallace and $50.00 from Capt. Henry King on loans made to them, he paid his mess bill ($56.85) and various debts of his own, purchased two undershirts and a new pair of boots, and "received appointment on Military Commission [court-martial]." The last led to his being introduced on December 22 to the new commander of the XV Corps, Maj. Gen. John A. Logan, whom he accurately described in his diary as being "of medium stature" and having "black eyes, hair, and mustache which has a fancy twirl & I think is his pride and delight; dark comp[lexion], broad brow and compactly built." A congressman from Illinois when the war began, "Black Jack" Logan was a political general but one with a knack for combat leadership and had performed so ably during the Vicksburg campaign that Grant deemed him qualified to head an army. Taylor served under him for most of the rest of his military career and became highly valued by him—too highly, from Taylor' s standpoint.[5]

On Christmas day, which he described in his diary as being "very much like Sunday," Taylor completed some paperwork for the military commis-

"Black Jack" Logan.
  Miller, ed., Photographic History, *10: 171.*

sion and then celebrated with a dinner of oysters, two drinks (presumably of whiskey), and an apple. The following day, the Forty-seventh marched to the vicinity of Stevenson, Alabama, where it established a camp in a cedar grove. Here, on December 27, Taylor took time out from composing his long account of Sherman's attack at Missionary Ridge to write Netta another short (by his standards) letter. He had not received any mail from her for more than a month, and he knew that she was expecting soon to give birth. Hence, after explaining why he had not been able to complete and send her his battle narrative—the work of the military commission, the shift of camps, and so on—he expressed his concern:

> My dear my anxiety to hear from you is very great. Your approaching illness disturbs me and I am solicitous about the result. Oh, how earnestly I hope you will be permitted to pass through that severe trial safely and easily and rise from your couch blessed with better health and stronger constitution. . . . These are hard trials within the life of a woman.

By rare but welcome coincidence, scarcely had he sent this letter off to Netta than he received one from her that very same day, dated December 21:

> I have had permission to sit up for a short time to write you a few lines. I was confined on the evening of the fifteenth and presented with another son of which I have no doubt you will feel very proud. He is the largest and finest looking babe we have had.
>
> Dear, I have not had a line from you since the reception of your letter written on the 22nd of Nov. Propose naming the baby Carr.

Taylor noted the reception of this good news in his diary entry for December 27 but was unable to respond to it until December 31, the day following the completion of a march to Bellefonte, Alabama, the "history [of which]," he wrote, "is mud, the substance mud & water and its end mud & rain."

> You cannot imagine how rejoiced I was to hear of your safe deliverance and of the new jewel given unto us. You have my consent to christen him Carr White Taylor. I don't think he can be named after a more honorable man or better soldier. May he live to become useful, honorable and respected is my earnest prayer. I had designed to [name] him Chilton White, but our sad misunderstanding has changed my mind.

The "sad misunderstanding" with Chilton evidently began with what Taylor and Netta perceived as a patronizing attitude from the congressman and his wife and then was exacerbated by Chilton making "insinuations" to Netta that her husband was "squandering" money on "dissipation and gambling." In his December 27 letter, Taylor heatedly denied that he was guilty of such conduct, pointing out to Netta that he had sent her $400.00 during the past six months, that he soon would receive back pay totaling $893.10, and that since rejoining the regiment, "I have not spent much more than fifty dollars for frivolities," with most of these consisting of "[news]papers, literature, and wine." Among the "literature" were Jane Austen's *Pride and Prejudice* and *Persuasion,* which Taylor read during the early weeks of 1864.[6]

New Year's Day 1864, brought fierce cold (it proved to be the coldest day of the entire year). To make matters worse, no rations were available for the enlisted men of the Forty-seventh, who understandably enough became (so Taylor noted in his diary) "gloomy." The officers, on the other hand, "joked, read, and smoked," and although their dinner "was plain," they were "gay" and talked of "home and pleasures of by-gone days."

Thoughts of home and its pleasures increasingly occupied the minds of soldiers of the Forty-seventh of all ranks. With few exceptions—Taylor perhaps being the outstanding one—they had not seen their homes since entering the service in summer 1861. Naturally, they yearned to visit them, especially after the hard, almost incessant campaigning that they had undergone during the past year. Moreover, there now was a means by which they could go home in the near future. If enough of them—three-fourths of the enlisted men—signed on for another three years of service, then the whole regiment (less those who did not reenlist) would be rewarded with a thirty-day furlough. Should, however, the required three-fourths not "veteranize," the regiment would remain on duty until August 27, 1864, the third anniversary of having been officially mustered into the army. Since then, it had become much reduced in size, dwindling from 830 officers and men to little more than 300, despite adding scores of recruits. Most of its losses, as was typical of Civil War infantry regiments, were the result not of combat but of illness and physical breakdown.[7]

Taylor hoped that the Forty-seventh would veteranize. He desperately desired to go home before the upcoming spring campaign into Georgia—everyone agreed that the next objective would be Atlanta—and the only way he could do it, given his frequent and extended stays in Ohio, was if the regiment did the same. But he did not intend to reenlist himself. Already he had served far longer than he had anticipated when he had volunteered in April 1861, that remote, oh-so-innocent time of naive hopes and unrealistic expectations. Yet he believed that Union victory was in sight and wished to participate in its attainment. Besides, Augustus Parry was seeking promotion to brigadier general, an endeavor Taylor heartily supported, for if it succeeded then Wallace would become colonel and he himself would take Wallace's place as lieutenant colonel of the Forty-seventh. In any event, so he informed Netta, an officer did not have to reenlist at that point in order to stay with his regiment but could wait until his time expired, which in his case, he believed, would be August 7, the date he was mustered with his company.[8]

Initially the prospect that the Forty-seventh would veteranize seemed poor, with only about 100 men having reenlisted by the first week of January. Moreover, little or no improvement occurred thereafter. In part, this was because on January 7 and 8, Morgan Smith's division moved to Larkinsville, Alabama, where it spent the better part of the next two weeks establishing winter quarters. Most of the officers and men erected log cabins, some quite large, but Taylor made do with his tent, which he heated with a stove and where he resided with his black camp servant, Ruben, and a one-eyed dog, Tickbug. By the fourth week of the month, everybody was more or less comfortably settled in. Yet no attempt to reenlist more troops took place in the Forty-seventh, for Parry had assumed command of the brigade in the absence of Joseph Lightburn, on sick leave; Wallace was serving as division provost marshal; and Taylor, who took charge of the regiment, found himself so busy with paperwork and camp routine that he lacked the time to do anything else. Then on January 29, an order arrived for Smith's division to set out the following day on an expedition through northeast Alabama in the direction of Rome, Georgia. Notifying Netta of this development, Taylor pessimistically predicted that the Forty-seventh would not "enter the service again until our [present] term shall have expired," that is, eight months hence.[9]

Nevertheless, he resolved, given the chance, to do all he could to induce the required proportion of the regiment to sign up for another three years. Word from Netta's sister Mollie, who, along with Taylor's mother, was staying at Elmwood Cottage in Georgetown, that Netta still had not recovered from giving birth to the new son intensified his desire to return home. At the same time, thanks to the back pay he had received, he had been able to pay off his debts and so once more felt "like a free man." This in turn filled him with a sense of accomplishment and bolstered his already strong self-confidence. "When necessary," he boasted to Netta on January 29, "I can match anyone opposing my schemes." His main scheme now was to obtain as soon as possible a thirty-day furlough.

The Forty-seventh returned to Larkinsville from what Taylor called the "big raid" into northwest Georgia at noon on February 6. The timing proved opportune. "Received large mails and got well-fixed," Taylor noted in his diary, then added, "Men in good humor—much hilarity prevails." Quickly, he moved to take advantage of their mood, as his diary entries reveal:

> SUNDAY 7TH. Inaugurated move to re-enlist regiment. All the Sergeants enlisted in it [the move]. Men taking hold & push it along. . . . Had payrolls made out.
>
> MONDAY 8TH. Heard reports of the progress of re-enlistment— cheering. Sent for paymaster—[he] paid me $297.25 for November–December '63. This afternoon had regiment out. [It] voted on the re-enlistment—results very encouraging.
>
> TUESDAY 9TH. Prospects brightening. Paymaster . . . came over and paid the regiment. . . . After payment had jollification until 12 at night.
>
> WEDNESDAY 10TH. Excitement increasing. Council with many officers and Sergeants today. . . . Col. Parry said a few things. I put the question—the result was very satisfying. Success—

Filled with pride, Taylor promptly wrote to Netta, from whom he had just received word that she had finally regained her full health and strength. After telling her how glad this good news made him, he described his campaign to veteranize the Forty-seventh, then declared:

> I did good—our regiment is veterans. I have received, again, many flattering assurances from men and officers. They want me along—
>
> Dear, what will my clever enemies [in Georgetown] think? Is it not a testimonial of which I may be justly proud—A whole regiment— I the prime mover . . . and I did it without designing to go into the service myself. I have triumphed—what joy the thought gives me!

Shortly after Taylor mailed this letter, his joy turned to gloom, as did that of the entire Forty-seventh. From Logan's headquarters in Huntsville came an order that the division, which now was under Parry's command as a result of Smith's being on leave, was to set out the next day for Chattanooga, where it would report to Maj. Gen. Charles L. Matthies. Since the order also specified that the troops would carry forty rounds of ammunition—the standard issue prior to battle—it seemed to mean that instead of soon heading home on a thirty-days' veterans' furlough, the Forty-seventh was about to take part in a military operation that would keep it in the field for an unknown period of time.[10] Such a prospect created a strong probability that many of the regiment's soldiers who had reenlisted would change their minds, an option they were free to choose until mustered in for a second term of service.

That probability became a virtual certainty in Taylor's mind when on the morning of February 11 he learned that only seventy men had been mustered, far short of the number needed. Again faced with frustration of his personal aspirations, as always he wasted no time in endeavoring to remedy the situation. He went to division headquarters and asked Parry to excuse the Forty-seventh from going to Chattanooga. Parry refused, saying that he could not do this. Taylor thereupon telegraphed the same request to Logan, who gave his consent provided another regiment took the Forty-seventh's place. Informed of Logan's response, Parry still refused on the grounds that he could not supply another regiment. And when Taylor told him that "if we went to Chattanooga a regiment of veterans would be lost to the service," Parry merely replied that he could not help it.[11]

At 12:30 P.M., the Forty-seventh marched out of its camp at Larkinsville with, to quote Taylor's diary for February 11, "saddened and angry hearts." The only pleasant item, from his standpoint, that he was able to add to this entry was that "Captain Ward returned home on recruiting service." Although William Ward promptly obeyed Taylor's orders as acting commander of the regiment and although Taylor had recently provided Ward with a horse after a back injury made it painful for the latter to march on foot, Taylor still deemed him a potential source of trouble.[12] Thus in his diary for January 13, he had noted that on going to the colonel's headquarters that day he had "found Ward." What might he be telling Parry? And Parry saying in response? The colonel, Taylor had concluded, was a man whose friendship depended on whether or not he deemed a person useful to him.

The Forty-seventh arrived on the outskirts of Chattanooga with the rest of the division on Sunday afternoon, February 14. As soon as it encamped, Taylor went into town, where he saw "various army officers" and "had plenty of whiskey & got quite merry" before returning to the camp after tattoo.[13]

Although Taylor liked his whiskey (and brandy and wine, too), this behavior was uncharacteristic. Probably he felt a need to unwind after the tension of the past week and to submerge, temporarily, his present woes in alcohol.

If he awoke with a hangover in the morning—a morning that saw the heavy rain that began falling during the night continue—he speedily lost it upon being visited by a large group of the regiment's officers. They were as "blue as anger blended with despair could make them" at the prospect of being denied their veterans' leave after striving so hard to achieve it. Taylor "laughed them into good spirits though my heart was beating & thundering indignantly against my ribs and secretly I thought the veteran spirit was about bleached out of them." That accomplished, in the afternoon he went to Parry and "told him what I thought of his course," which he believed to be motivated by the colonel's desire to become a brigadier general, a promotion he could not attain if his regiment went home on leave, for he then would have to accompany it. Parry, as to be expected, resented Taylor's attitude and informed him that the next day the division, the Forty-seventh included, would begin marching to Cleveland, Tennessee.

For Taylor, this was the final straw. Not only did a move to Cleveland imply proceeding from there to Knoxville, but, worse, it dashed any hope that the Forty-seventh would be able to take a furlough in the foreseeable future, even if three-fourths of its enlisted men were mustered in for another hitch, an event unlikely to happen. To Taylor, there could be no doubt that Parry and others as well "would be gratified" if the regiment refused to veteranize. That being the case, he "resolved to thwart them."[14]

Two days earlier, while on the way to Chattanooga, he had met with General Matthies, who had told him that the Forty-seventh could remain in that town as part of its garrison, provided it obtained authorization from Gen. George H. Thomas, commander of all Union forces in the vicinity, to do so. Taylor intended to make use of that information. And so he did, in a fashion dramatically (if somewhat erratically) related to Netta in a letter dated Cleveland, Tennessee, February 19, 1864:

> After dark my horse was saddled by my Negro boy, Rube, I mounted and I started to see the leaders of Isreal [*sic*]. . . . When I came to the pickets [outside of Chattanooga] I told the officer that I had business of the highest importance with Gen'l Thomas & must see him, no other one would do—so I got inside the lines. Then I went to the

Post Provost Marshal & from him to the military commander [General Matthies] from whom I got the countersign.

After I got it I rode boldly for Gen'l Thomas's quarters. When I arrived I went up the steps, a staff officer in fancy attire stood at the door and as I advanced to it wrapped completely in my blue overcoat, sword at side, he looked as much as to say you can't come in but looks could not daunt me. . . . I saw an orderly [and] told him my name, rank & desire. He returned and showed me in. The room was comfortably warm; stands and tables with all the materials for writing. At the desk sat [Brigadier] General [William D.] Whipple [Thomas's chief of staff], a middle-aged, good-looking man, black hair, fair complexion, heavy whiskers & above the medium height, who looked up as I entered. Around the table were two or three staff officers and clerks all [of whom] looked up wondering at my presumption in coming into his [Whipple's] presence. I asked for Gen'l Thomas & was answered by a person who until he spoke had escaped my notice. I looked him quietly all over, saw his two stars, [realized it was Thomas], and told him my tale of wrong and he assured me that my regiment should stop at Cleveland, that I could then [have it] mustered out [the necessary preliminary to being mustered back in] and he would forward my application [for] furlough [and] we would be on our way home in a week if we desired. He said I might pledge my men that this would be done.

I almost forgot to tell how Gen'l Thomas looks. He is apparently fifty-five years old, hale and vigorous, rather an oval face, fair complexion, hair almost white, above the medium stature and at the same time compactly built. His countenance indicates a hopeful disposition and a love of sport. Eyes are almost laughing and a pleasant expression hovers over his face all the time, voice mild; is easily approached and speaks earnestly and, I would swear, is a good liver and enjoys a "punch" as greatly as any man.[15]

From Thomas's headquarters, Taylor went back to those of Matthies, whom he presumably informed of the rock of Chickamauga's promise. Perhaps, too, he handed Matthies the order signed by Whipple:[16]

The major general commanding [Thomas] directs that you march with your division tomorrow morning for Cleveland, Tenn. Upon your arrival at that place you will designate four regiments to be stationed there, and prepare the remaining twelve regiments of your command for an expedition of ten days duration.

Taylor then returned to the Forty-seventh's camp feeling "well satisfied." Assembling the officers, he told them of what he had done. To his annoyance, instead of being pleased, they "looked gloomy and muttered." Consequently, in the morning he formed the regiment in an open square and, sitting on his horse, "made them a short speech," following which "they gave three cheers," and he "took up the line of march feeling assured that I had triumphed."[17]

The Forty-seventh reached Cleveland on February 17, and the following day Taylor resumed his reenlistment campaign. On February 20, he commented in his diary that "swearing of veterans going forward briskly" but that at nightfall he found that "veterans all at a dead stand and not enough to carry the regiment," a situation that rendered his "position very unpleasant." Then the next day another crisis occurred. Not only did he ascertain that the regiment still was thirty-two men short of the number needed to qualify for veteran status, but also shortly before noon an order arrived "to march at a moments notice." The regiment was being sent to Knoxville after all.[18]

At once, Taylor sallied forth "to combat the superior powers," as he subsequently put it in a March 5 letter to Netta.[19] Accompanied by Parry, who had reverted to acting brigade commander, he went to Matthies, who assured him that the Forty-seventh "would remain in garrison until otherwise ordered by General Thomas." Moreover, Brig. Gen. Charles Cruft, who commanded an Army of the Cumberland division stationed in the Cleveland area, told him that "General Thomas would perform and fulfill his pledge." Placated and encouraged by these assertions, he then returned to the regiment's camp where at 4:00 P.M. he had all the troops assembled in an open square. What he did, and the outcome, he described in the March 5 letter to Netta:

> I placed myself where the 4th front [of the open square] would have been and read a letter of a preacher [urging soldiers to reenlist] and based a speech upon it. Talked half an hour and then sent them to their quarters. Immediately the buzz and hum began. The effect was magical, before bed time I had more than enough—was serenaded

&c, &c. Oh, how joyous everyone was, and why? Because of our anticipated visit—a reunion of our families.

The Forty-seventh remained at Cleveland the rest of February. During the ensuing days, Taylor, in addition to his routine duties, busied himself with the enormous amount of paperwork required to veteranize the regiment according to regulations and to secure back pay. By February 29, he was able to record in his diary, "In the afternoon signed the discharges of the re-enlisted men." The only remaining task was to muster those men into the service for another three years, and the regiment would be eligible for furlough.

On March 1, the Forty-seventh headed back to Larkinsville, where it arrived on the morning of March 5. On the evening of the very next day, Taylor, no doubt with great satisfaction, entered in his diary: "At 9½ A.M. remustered the 47th into U.S. service. . . . Had the best brandy punch I ever drank." Only sixty men had refused to reenlist, which meant that they would remain behind while the rest of the regiment, except for some Alabama Unionists who had joined it, went home on furlough.[20]

Taylor sent the good news to Netta on March 9. He also told her something that would guarantee him a happy homecoming: "I see plainly that justice to myself and my family requires me to quit the service." Therefore, "when the proper period shall arrive I will tender my resignation." Another three years of service would be "a part of the flower of my life." Already the "last three years have retarded my advancement in my profession." Another three years "will make too great a difference from my original plan of action and cannot therefore be followed."

The next day, Taylor went to corps headquarters in Huntsville, where he saw the paymaster's clerk and extracted a promise that he would process the Forty-seventh's payrolls first. The clerk kept his word, and on March 11, Taylor returned to Larkinsville, where that evening he and Wallace, who had rejoined the regiment, as had Parry, "made up a wine party." Once the troops were paid, the Forty-seventh could and would at long last be able to return home.

And he, more than anyone else, had made this furlough possible. "Ask the Col., the Doctor [the Forty-seventh's surgeon] and the men," be boasted to Netta on March 13, "and each will tell you how I have calculated, worked and talked to get us home for thirty days. Yes—for that insignificant period.

It appears to me like an age and I am more impatient than any child you ever saw, I infuse the same energy into each one and if talking, writing or incessant drumming will avail anything we will embark ere many days."

Three days later, Taylor notified Netta that "on Friday afternoon we hope to be homeward bound" and—rare occurrence in an army when it comes to such matters—this hope proved justified. Taylor's diary tells the story of his and the Forty-seventh's journey back to Ohio:

FRIDAY 18TH. At quarter after three regt. Moved from camp. Went to depot and loaded. Left Larkinsville at 4½ P.M. . . . arrived at Stevenson at 6½ P.M. Took supper at soldiers home. At 9½ train made up & started for Nashville. Steam pipe burst and detained train at Cowan. At Christianville detained pulling wreck on track four miles.

SATURDAY 19TH. Put up stove—weather cold. Waiting nearly 1½ hrs. Continued to wait until six P.M. at which time engine returned from wreck and started with us. Had a twilight view of the battlefield of Stone river & the works of Murfreesboro, Tennessee. Reported that 100,000 men required to garrison them properly. . . . We reached Nashville, Tennessee at 10 P.M. Marched to barracks & bivouacked at the Seminary yard. Lt. Col., Surgeon and I obtained quarters at the Commercial Hotel.

SUNDAY 20TH. Col. P[arry] gone and forgot to leave order. Can't get transportation until it brought. Got bottle of brandy & took one drink. . . . Men behaving well. Visited the State House [capitol] and had a grand view of the City from the dome. Marched regiment to depot at 3 P.M.

MONDAY 21ST. Arrived at Louisville at 7 A.M. and marched around hunting barracks 47 was finally sent out to Park [?] barracks one & half miles from city limits. From here went into town & took my dinner. Met Adjt. [adjutant] who bro't orders to march at 1 P.M. for Jeffersonville, Ind. Retd. to Camp & found [regiment] ready to move to Jeffersonville. Crossed the river & were on board the cars at 3 P.M.—did not leave until sundown. Many officers & men drunk.

TUESDAY 22ND. Arrived in Cinti. [Cincinnati] 8 A.M. Marched to 6th Street barracks, stacked arms & while awaiting breakfast men got drunk again. At supper were sober. Met Reeves—went to National Theater.

WEDNESDAY 23. Awaiting orders. Met many friends—had a gay time. Sent horse out by R[eeves].

THURSDAY 24. Obtained orders for transportation. Regiment furloughed. Assigned to Rectg. Service at Georgetown, O. Bought some flannel, &c., &c.

FRIDAY 25TH. Took passage for home on omnibus. Left my sword at Bethel. Had a breakdown—got an odd wheel [which] was too high & caused spindle of other wheel to heat. Stopped three times to cool it. Arrived home at 11 P.M. & found every body sick.

Such was Taylor's return home—an anticlimactic one made even more so because, as he had warned Netta in his last letter to her before departing Larkinsville, "I expect to come rushing in home some night like a house afire."[21] But home he was, thanks to his cunning and perseverance, for thirty blessed days, after which he would have less than four more months to serve—time enough, if fortune smiled, to achieve higher rank and with it some measure of the glory he had sought in West Virginia, Mississippi, and Tennessee, only to have it elude him. Perhaps in the forthcoming invasion of Georgia, he would grasp it, finally and firmly holding it in his hand.

6

Once More Into the Breach
March 26–June 5, 1864

IN HIS MARCH 13 MESSAGE notifying Netta that he expected to be back in Georgetown soon, Taylor declared that while there "I am going to stay home with you and not see any strangers—won't leave Georgetown—have got no business running all over the country. If anyone wants to see Tom Taylor they will be permitted to call at my home."

Whether or not he kept that resolution cannot be known, as his diary contains only two entries following his arrival home on the night of March 25 only to find "every body sick."

SATURDAY 26. Called on a few people.
SUNDAY 27TH. Rube hired with Mrs. Hanna.

But since he evidently sent Netta no letters during the rest of March or in April, probably he did remain at home or close to it most of this period. Not until Monday, April 25, did he again open his diary, and then it was to inscribe these words, quoted from Shakespeare's *Henry V*: "Once more into the breach, dear friends."

For he was going back to the war, having left his family at 3:00 A.M. "after bidding an affectionate adieu," to report to Colonel Parry in Cincinnati, which he did at noon. Assembled at Camp Dennison, the regiment was scheduled to depart on April 27 for Alabama, where it would rejoin Sherman's army, which now consisted of three armies: Thomas's Army of the Cumberland, 60,000 strong; Maj. Gen. James B. McPherson's Army of the Tennessee, far less strong with 23,000 troops; and Maj. Gen. John M. Schofield's Army of the Ohio, which consisted only of an infantry corps (the XXIII) and a cavalry division, totaling a mere 17,000 men.

Union grand strategy called for Sherman, who in March had succeeded Grant as head of the Military Division of the Mississippi upon the latter's promotion to lieutenant general and elevation to the command of all Federal forces, to advance on Atlanta and the Confederate Army of Tennessee under Joseph E. Johnston, who had replaced Braxton Bragg. At the same time, Grant, with the Army of the Potomac, would move against Richmond and Lee's Army of Northern Virginia. Should either of these offensives succeed, it would be tantamount to a death blow to the Confederacy. On the other hand, should both fail, it was quite possible that the North would succumb to war weariness and thereby enable the South to win by not losing. To accomplish this became the last hope of the Confederates to establish an independent nation. In sum, 1864 would be a year of decision, and the Forty-seventh Ohio would play a part, albeit small, in the achievement of that decision.[1]

On the morning of April 26 Taylor went with Parry to regimental headquarters at Camp Dennison. There they discovered that the records pertaining to recruits enlisted by the Forty-seventh while on furlough were badly botched—so badly that it necessitated a prompt visit by Taylor to the adjutant general's office in Columbus. Hence, at 10:00 P.M., he boarded a train to that city despite having been "very sick this afternoon" from a "severe attack of Cholera Morbous [sic]" that caused him to vomit "incessantly" and made him "very weak."

Some medicine he had purchased stopped the vomiting, and he managed to book a compartment on a sleeping car, where he slept "tolerably well" before reaching Columbus at 4:00 A.M. He spent the rest of the night at a hotel, then in the morning, feeling much better, took care of the "business" regarding the recruits. That done, he passed the afternoon reading a book, enjoyed a supper of oysters and ale, and was preparing to board a train back to Cincinnati when a telegram from Parry came stating that he was on the way to Columbus. From this, Taylor gathered that the colonel wished to confer with him and so remained at the hotel.

In the morning, Taylor met him at the railroad station and found that Parry was "in a tremor of excitement"; two officers had brought charges of misconduct against him; he had received an order to report to the provost marshal general in Columbus that was "equivalent to an arrest"; and the day before, the regiment, under the command of John Wallace, had left Cincinnati on its way to the front. Taylor asked Parry to tell him the facts of the charges, and after he did so, "told him to be of good cheer"—that he would draw up a statement that would clear him. This he did, and that afternoon he made good on his promise at the provost marshal general's office—"I completely annihilated the prosecution," Taylor informed Netta in a May 1 letter describing the affair—and Parry was "released from further attendance and ordered to his regiment."

Nor was that all. Taking advantage of his stay in Columbus, Taylor next "went to see some old friends," among them the state adjutant general, and as a result was able to "settle all prospects of Ward over me." Small wonder that he thought that "the Lord is on my side and helping me along." No doubt William Ward would have said that a being quite different from the Lord was at Taylor's side helping him along. Shortly thereafter, he tendered his resignation from the army, had it accepted, and so ended his military career.

Taylor returned to Cincinnati with Parry on the morning of April 29 and at once plunged into a sea of paperwork. Not until midnight did he go to bed, and then he was up at 5:00 A.M. to take care of still more. Finally, in the afternoon, he completed the preparation of all the accounts, filled out the final voucher, and prepared the needed orders for Parry to sign. On Friday morning, May 1, he wrote Netta his exultant account of what he had done for Parry and to Ward while in Columbus and then added these words: "Dear, I must say that I am disgusted with this way of serving [but] not with the service. I am determined to get out [of the army] as soon as I can conveniently and will. I shall be out before the summer is over."[2]

At noon, he had lunch with Parry and his family at their Cincinnati home. Then the colonel and he took a carriage to the landing, where, along with another Forty-seventh Ohio officer, they boarded the steamer *Buell* to Louisville, arriving at 11:00 P.M. and having a "gay party" on the way. Unable to obtain railroad transportation, they remained two days in Louisville, where they joined some other stranded officers from the Forty-seventh and the colonel of the Thirty-seventh Ohio in having a "gay day" on May 2 and going "around" on the afternoon of the next day. Early on the morning of May 4, they secured the necessary papers and boarded a train to Nashville. What they did while traveling there and then after arriving can be easily deduced from Taylor's diary entry for that day: "Gay time—dinner at Carr City—Much whiskey—plenty of spirit, little wit and less sense. Reached Nashville little before sundown and stopped at City Hotel—visited College Street."[3]

The last three words are intriguing. College Street (present-day Third Street) was in Nashville's "Smokey Row," an eight-block district between the capitol and the Cumberland River where all the shacklike buildings housed brothels.[4] Perhaps Taylor went there merely to drink whiskey, but if so, why then did he not go to one of Nashville's numerous saloons? Let readers answer that question. They will anyway.

Taylor passed the following day innocently enough, the morning being devoted to a tour of the Greek temple–like capitol, the afternoon to a long nap, and the evening to "promenading." He also wrote a short letter to Netta in which he reported, "We are now travelling very leisurely along to the front, more so than I desire. The Army is moving—15th Corps included. . . . [A] battle is impending—Everything indicates it. I am glad, anxious for it to come and pass. I want the campaign ended and the fate of the country decided." He closed the letter by listing the names of his traveling companions but, for obvious reasons, made no mention of the "gay times" or the visit to College Street.

On the morning of May 6, Taylor's party left Nashville on the Alabama Central Railroad, a line that took them to Decatur, Alabama, where they transferred to the Memphis & Charleston, which brought them to Chattanooga on the evening of May 8, a journey delayed by a guerrilla attack on a preceding train, the collision of two other trains, and their own train striking a mule, causing it to "come within an ace of going over the bank down—down." Taylor checked into the Chattanooga Hotel and wrote Netta a letter stating that the campaign for Atlanta was under way, that the XV and XVI Corps of McPherson's Army of the Tennessee had moved into Georgia "about thirty miles from here," and that Lt. Col. Samuel L. Mott of the Fifty-seventh Ohio, which, like the Forty-seventh, belonged to Morgan Smith's division, had told him that on McPherson's front, "it will be either a big fight or a foot race."[5]

Anxious not to miss out on either, the next morning Taylor purchased a horse, whiskey, and some food, then set out along with Parry (who rode the horse) and two other Forty-seventh Ohio officers to join the regiment. Before long, they overtook the Fifty-seventh Ohio, also on its way to the front, and Mott loaned Taylor a wagon in which he and the other unmounted officers rode to Gordon's Mill, where they camped for the night. On the way there, they "passed over Chickamauga battlefield [and] saw numerous graves in some of which the occupants were uncovered" and also "*one* hand and arm was visable [*sic*] hanging on a tree just as blown off."

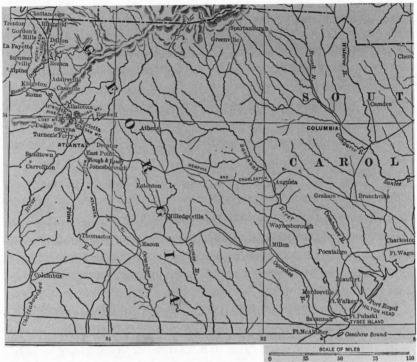

Map 3. Atlanta Campaign and March to the Sea.
Miller, ed., Photographic History, *3: frontispiece.*

Taylor rose early on May 10, breakfasted, and then astride his horse resumed the journey alone. Following the Army of the Tennessee's trail, he
passed by Gordon Springs, crossed Taylor's Ridge at Wood's Gap, and then
entered Snake Creek Gap, at the southern mouth of which he found the XV
and XVI Corps and, soon, the Forty-seventh Ohio, which "warmly greeted"
him. He discovered too that the day before the regiment had participated in
what would become one of the biggest "might-have-beens" of the Civil War.[6]

On the morning of May 9, the Army of the Tennessee emerged from
Snake Creek Gap, having marched through it unopposed and undetected, and
headed for Resaca, where a railroad bridge spanned the Oostanaula River.
Sherman's instructions to McPherson were to burn the bridge, thereby cutting Johnston's supply line to Atlanta, and then to fall back to the gap. This
would leave Johnston with no rational choice except to retreat south from

his virtually impregnable position at Dalton to Resaca in order to cross the Oostanaula. When he did so, McPherson was to pounce upon his flank while the pursuing forces of Thomas and Schofield assailed him from the rear. If all went as it should, the Confederate Army of Tennessee would be smashed, opening the way for Sherman to occupy Atlanta, send large reinforcements to assist Grant in disposing of Lee in Virginia, or both—supposing, that is, such reinforcements were required.

But all did not go as it should. On sighting Resaca, McPherson was dismayed to find more enemy troops there than he had expected, which was few if any. Furthermore, he became concerned that Johnston would send a superior force down from Dalton to overwhelm him or cut him off from Snake Creek Gap. Consequently, he fell back to the gap without attempting to take Resaca and to destroy the bridge. He did not live long enough to learn that at most only the equivalent of two brigades opposed him and that Johnston did not know of his near-approach to Resaca until after he withdrew from it.

Sherman, on being informed of McPherson's failure, sent the Army of the Cumberland's XIV and XX Corps and Schofield's XXIII Corps through Snake Creek Gap to join the Army of the Tennessee, leaving only Howard's IV Corps to confront the Confederates at Dalton. Johnston quickly perceived this obvious move and countered by pulling back his entire army to Resaca, where the arrival of two divisions from Leonidas Polk's Army of Mississippi increased its strength to approximately 60,000 to 65,000. By May 13, the Confederates were deployed along a fortified line west of Resaca that ran from the Oostanaula on its left to just beyond the main road to Dalton on its right. That same day, Sherman's forces advanced on Resaca, driving back enemy skirmishers as they did, and the first major battle of the Atlanta Campaign was under way. What Taylor did and saw during the battle he described in his diary:

> FRIDAY 13TH. 6 A.M. took up line of march for Resaca, 47th Ohio in the advance. Cos. D, E, F, H, & K were deployed as skirmishers. Advanced to the intersection of the Calhoun Ferry road [with the road from Snake Creek Gap to Dalton] where the first opposition was experienced. Skirmishers of enemy posted in dense wood. Formed lines of battle along the Calhoun Ferry road and marched down the road, the right of 2nd Brig. [Lightburn's] 2nd Div. [Morgan Smith's] resting opposite Lick Creek which rises from under the hill.

About 1½ P.M. the lines being formed Cos. E & K were sent forward
to reinforce the skirmish line. Upon reaching Lick Creek they deployed and advanced towards the Resaca road. After effecting a lodge-
ment on the road the line of battle advanced across the open field
into the woods, then across the hill to an open field when the skirmishers of [the] 47th & the right of the 2nd Brigade rec'd a heavy
fire from a stockade. Without halting the line pressed forward. Cheer
upon cheer rose and they [the Confederates] were driven from their
line. Their battle flags could be distinctly seen as they were waving
them defiantly.

At this point the 1st Brig. [Brig. Gen. Giles A. Smith's brigade of
the Second Division, XV Corps] marched by the left & the 2nd by
the right flank and thus a large gap intervened. When this was discovered the command was given to dress by the left & we advanced
by the left hunting the 1st [Brigade]. After a time we found them on
the succeeding ridge. Our skirmishers had become lost in the wood
and I was sent to hunt for them. We then waited for [Brigadier]
General [James C.] Veatch [commander of a division in the XVI
Corps, which was deployed to the right of the XV Corps] to dress
on us. Before he had joined our lines the order came to advance. The
old skirmish line was then relieved & Captain [Charles] Helmerick
sent out. In this advance we pressed forward in the face of a very heavy
fire, driving the enemy from every ridge, until we compelled them
to retire to their works. At this point the 53rd O. charged . . . & occupied a position held by the enemy. We advanced to the top of the
ridge facing the enemies [*sic*] works where we halted and laid down
much exposed to their fire. This point commands the trestle work
R.R. bridge & the village of Resaca. The enemy hold a strong defensive position & have it apparently well fortified. On this slope we remained until after nightfall when we retired beyond the crest & laid
down. . . . Casualties [of Forty-seventh Ohio] five wounded—two
severely. . . .

SATURDAY 14. Slept well. Skirmishing began at sunrise. Artillery
fire opened at 6 A.M. Loss of 2nd Brigade yesterday 60. Nothing but
heavy skirmishing during the morning. Skirmish line advanced
across Camp creek & up the hill beyond but soon returned to the
cover of the creek. About noon the firing on our left became very
heavy, our batteries were ordered to open and the [enemy] infantry
felt us and showed themselves. This demonstration brought back [to

Confederate Defenses at Resaca: Where the Forty-seventh Ohio Attacked.
Miller, ed., Photographic History, *3: 109.*

this section of the front] a [Union] column of about a brigade from
the left. About 4 P.M. the firing subsided and we stacked arms.

The heavy firing on the left heard by Taylor that started at noon and subsided at 4:00 P.M. was occasioned by two events. First, the XIV Corps and
the XXIII Corps assaulted the Confederate right center in an effort to break
through and force Johnston to retreat, whereupon Sherman hoped to rout
his army as it tried to cross the Oostanaula. The attacks, however, soon came
to a standstill, and Johnston sent two divisions from Lt. Gen. John B. Hood's
Corps swinging around the Union left flank with the intention of gaining
Sherman's rear and cutting him off from Snake Creek Gap. For a while, this
thrust threatened to overrun Howard's IV Corps, but the timely arrival on
the field of a division from Maj. Gen. Joseph Hooker's XX Corps led to the

Rebels being repelled with heavy losses. The "demonstration" described by
Taylor was designed to relieve pressure on the Union left by threatening the
Confederate left.

> After supper we received orders to be ready to fall in and move for-
> ward while the 1st Brigade . . . charged the hills beyond. . . . The first
> brigade gained [a] foothold on the opposite hills and advanced near
> the summit. In this position it was charged twice or thrice by supe-
> rior numbers sustained and returned one of the most terrific fires I
> ever heard. Oh, how I longed to rush to their support—to make part
> of that adamantine wall & assist in repelling the furious onset! At
> 7 o'clock & 10 minutes they [the First Brigade] asked for support
> on their right and the order so anxiously waited for came. Instantly
> the 2nd Brigade, 2nd Div., 15 A.C. moved out on double quick. In
> crossing the marsh and [an] open space all the artillery of the rebels
> which hitherfore maintained the profoundest silence belched forth
> and shells and shot rained all over our pathway. After crossing Camp
> creek we filed right across an open field and took a position on a knoll
> at the edge of a woods about four or five hundred yards from the
> woods bordering the river. . . . We then laid down and took the
> shelling & musketry in silence. [At] 8 & 10 o'clock the enemy
> ceased [firing] along the whole line. The silence seemed deeper
> from the contrast. Every one held his breath and listened for the
> coming storm which this deadly silence presaged. It came not, but
> was succeeded by the neighing of horses & rumbling of artillery &c
> on the bridge [a pontoon bridge east of the railroad bridge]. We then
> commenced [digging] rifle pits & [emplacements for] batteries.
>   In the march across [the open field] Captain Helmerick behaved
> most shamefully, left the head of his company on plea of keeping
> it closed up when he had three sergeants & one Lieut to 17 men. I
> ordered him forward very harshly, after crossing a small ditch he
> again came rushing back exclaiming I'm wounded! I'm wounded!
> I could see no blood. I was thus compelled to order his Lt. to take
> the Co. Many fell behind logs, trees and I never had so much diffi-
> culty in keeping the regiment closed.

The attack described by Taylor in the preceding diary entry took place
on orders from McPherson after he discovered that the enemy forces had
shifted troops from his front to bolster their right. Only two Confederate

regiments held the hill during the initial phase of the assault, but as Taylor's account makes clear, they were supported by numerous cannons. The Confederates tried to retake it with a counterattack spearheaded by Vaughan's Brigade, one of their elite units.

> SATURDAY 15TH. One A.M.—up & still [working] on rifle pits. . . . Completed pits at three. Train of cars passed down at that time [on railroad bridge]. Conversation of rebel teamsters [on the pontoon bridge] quite audible. Formed line and took place as reserves. Four & half [A.M.] firing began on our line—chiefly musketry. *During last night Helmerick returned limping* considerably. Once this morning he apparently forgot his plan and walked as nimbly as I.
>
> Coward! Coward!
>
> The skirmishers were busily engaged all the morning. Near noon [it was] reported the enemy massing in three lines upon our front. All were then called to arms and remained in position one hour. Mail was received—got letter . . . [and] copy of [Georgetown] Argus. Nothing but skirmishing all day.
>
> At 11 P.M. an assault was made by some party—very heavy cannonade and immense cheering. About an hour and all became silent.

Although McPherson's forces were in the best position to take Resaca and the railroad bridge, Sherman issued no orders for them to attack on May 15. Instead, he tried again to break through the right center of the Confederate line, with the XX Corps making the attack. It failed, and Johnston in turn attempted again to turn Sherman's left flank, only to suffer another repulse. The cannonade and cheering Taylor noted during the night was not, as he surmised, the result of an assault but was occasioned by some units of the XX Corps dragging away four cannons from an emplacement in front of the main Confederate defense line. The most important event of the day was the crossing of the Oostanaula upstream from Resaca by a division of the XVI Corps. This put the Federals in position to sever the Western & Atlanta Railroad in Johnston's rear. As a consequence, during the night, the Confederates retreated across the Oostanaula. Despite their close proximity to Resaca and the river, McPherson's troops failed to detect the enemy departure until too late, as Taylor's diary reveals:

MONDAY 16TH. Woke up about half past three [and] saw [railroad] bridge burning. Slept until near five and then got up and washed. Twenty minutes to seven moved across to the river Oostonaula [*sic*]. . . . Captured a few prisoners. . . . From river moved back to Calhoun Ferry road where we drew rations & recd. baggage. At four P.M. moved down the road, crossed the river [on a pontoon bridge] and at dark camped on a hill about two miles from the river.

May 17 and 18 saw Johnston retreat first to Adairsville and then to Cassville by way of Kingston. At Cassville on May 19 he prepared an ambush attack to be made by two of his corps (Hood's and Polk's) on one of Sherman's (the XX), but just as it was about to be delivered, Union cavalry appeared in the rear of Hood's Corps and so it had to be canceled. Johnston then withdrew to a ridge southeast of Cassville with the intention of making a defensive stand there, his army having been increased to 65–70,000 by the arrival of two more divisions from Alabama. This position, though, proved untenable, being exposed to enfilade artillery fire and flanking; thus on May 20 the Confederates retreated across the Etowah River to Allatoona, burning the railroad bridge spanning that stream once they passed over it. Sherman thereupon suspended his pursuit in order to rest and resupply. This ended the initial phase of the campaign. During it, the Federals, while muffing an opportunity to wreck or at least badly cripple Johnston's army, penetrated Georgia to within fifty miles of Atlanta while suffering little more in the way of casualties than their opponents.

Apart from a few skirmishes with Rebel rearguards, McPherson's troops engaged in no combat as they marched to Kingston and took no part at all in the operations around Cassville. For Taylor, the most important development of this period occurred on the morning of May 17. Asked by Morgan Smith to provide him with a division picket officer, Lightburn assigned the tow-haired major of the Forty-seventh Ohio to the post.

What this task entailed Taylor explained to Netta in a letter written at Kingston on May 21:

I am now detached from the regiment and holding a staff appointment as Div. Picket officer. The position is laborious and very responsible. I have charge of the guarding of our camp—have therefore to examine every foot of the ground personally, the roads, hills and watercourses and make our lines connect with others. I have continually fifteen companies and if I deem it necessary can have as many men subject to my orders as I ask for. Last night in addition I had two regiments to sleep on their arms. I don't like the position.

The reason Taylor did not "like the position" becomes clear on reading these passages from his diary:

THURSDAY 19. Here my feelings are sorely tried. The Genl. [Morgan Smith] wished two officers to go to Logan to ascertain our exact position. Lt. Davies & I started. He [Smith] said he would entrust D. with obtaining the location. I refused to have anything to do with it—said nothing but listened & when I ascertained the location I examined the ground & found location for picket. At twilight made connections with Gen'ls O[sterhaus] & H[arrow, commanders of the 1st and 4th Divisions of the XV Corps]—had a strong picket on the Rome & Kingston road & two regiments to sleep on arms to re-enforce them should it be necessary.

Genl. S[mith] gave permission to mess in my regt.

SATURDAY 21. Col. Parry made himself extremely disagreeable casting slurs &c. and finally had me marked present for duty [while Taylor was eating at the officers mess of Forty-seventh Ohio]. I said nothing but after he did his best I got an order on the subject and he could not help himself.

At supper on May 22, Parry, who obviously resented Taylor's no longer being subject to his orders, again "said many things," among them that Taylor "had no right to mess there &c." That did it for our quick-tempered hero. As soon as he finished eating, he went to Smith and requested permission to mess with him and his staff. "By all means," replied the general, whereupon Taylor had his new black camp servant (Rube remained in Georgetown) bring his baggage to division headquarters.[7]

Thus it was that Taylor, without intending to, became a staff officer and so abruptly ended, at least for the time being, his long association with the Forty-seventh Ohio, hitherto the focus and fulcrum of his ambition. Moreover, his attitude toward his new post rapidly changed as he discovered its advantages. The other members of Smith's staff tended to be better educated and more sophisticated than most of the officers of the Forty-seventh. He had the opportunity to see the army's top generals close up (the "old fellow looks pleased" he commented about Sherman in his diary entry for May 18). And the very nature of his duties enabled him to roam about the countryside seeing sights such as the one he described in the same diary entry: "Went on a highpoint where I obtained the grandest view of my whole life. Below me were the Army of the Tenn., with their ten thousand fires formed in a semi-circle around the hill, sending up a cloud of smoke of the most gorgeous hues, which floated beneath my feet."[8]

But best of all, he commanded, or had available to command, the equivalent of a brigade. Such being the case, if he could not distinguish himself in the operations to come, win the favor of his superiors, and secure promotion, it would be because he never had the chance, not because he lacked enterprise, courage, and skill. Of this he was sure; all he asked was the chance.

With regard to future operations, Taylor had mixed feelings. On the positive side, so he pointed out to Netta on May 21, "The rebels are overwhelmed—we outnumber them two to one [actually the ratio was three to two] and though they occasionally make a stand we turn their flank and they retire. In this manner they have fallen back all the way from Resaca." Yet there also was a negative aspect:

Johnston is conducting the affair on the Fabian principle. His army exhibits less demoralization than any army I ever saw that has retreated so far. We find very few stragglers, take very few prisoners. He is not destroying the railroad as much as I expected. In fact aside from an occasional bridge burned it is in as good shape as ever.
. . . In my mind [this] excites some apprehensions as to the future. Every day lengthens our line of communication ten or twelve miles and every ten miles requires at least one thousand men as guard. . . . These drippings in an hundred and twenty miles will weaken our forces considerably and mayhap Atlanta will be a story of disaster,— blood and dismay. I hope not—but cannot be convinced to the contrary at present.

The story of Atlanta would not, of course, be one of disaster, at least not for the Federals. Just as he overstated Sherman's numerical superiority, Taylor overestimated both the number of troops that had to be detached to protect the railroad and the steadfastness of Confederate morale. But in the weeks ahead, there would be much blood and much dismay, particularly for McPherson's Army of the Tennessee. To that extent, Taylor's words, though not meant to be, proved prophetic.

On May 23, the campaign resumed. Since Johnston's position at Alla-toona was, if anything, more impervious to direct assault than Dalton had been, Sherman again resorted to outflanking it, this time with his entire army, which he sent swinging off to the southwest. Sharing Taylor's belief that Johnston was pursuing a Fabian strategy and so would not offer a full-scale battle until he reached the Atlanta area, Sherman also assumed that he would retreat to and beyond the Chattahoochee River, only a few miles north of the Gate City. "We are now all in motion," the bristle-bearded commander tele-graphed his quartermaster in Nashville on May 23, "like a vast hive of bees, and expect to swarm along the Chattahoochee in a few days."

Once more the "fighting prophet," as his most eloquent biographer dubbed him with more imagination than precision, made a bad prediction. Instead of scurrying south toward Atlanta, Johnston slid off to the southwest, plac-ing his army athwart the route he correctly calculated Sherman would take in order to return to the Western & Atlantic Railroad, which served him too as a lifeline. On the afternoon of May 25, one of the Union columns, Hooker's XX Corps, suddenly encountered Rebel resistance as it turned eastward. Sherman, insisting that only a small enemy force opposed him, ordered Hooker to attack. This he did, again and again at New Hope Church, only to be repulsed each time with heavy losses. Refusing, because unwilling, to be-lieve that Johnston was doing the opposite of what he had expected him to do, Sherman thereupon looked to the south, to the village of Dallas upon which McPherson was advancing, also in an easterly direction; surely the Army of the Tennessee would open the way back to the railroad and at the same time compel Johnston to fall back toward the Chattahoochee.

The May 26 entry in Taylor's diary tells us how much success McPherson experienced in accomplishing these objectives:

> Advanced on Dallas 10 A.M. Gen'l O[sterhaus's] Division on right, 2nd Div. in the center and [Brigadier] Genl. [Grenville M.] Dodge's Divs. [of the XVI Corps] on the left. Genl. Harrow in reserve. The line was not completely formed until after 12 M. [noon]. About one P.M. Jeff C. Davis's Div. [of the XIV Corps] occupied Dallas. The 2nd Division [of the XV Corps] massed in columns of regiments in

the field west of D[allas] & remained until 4 P.M. awaiting a report of a cavalry reconnaissance. . . . In a short time orders were received to move on the cross road towards Marietta. . . . Arrived at intersection of Villa Rica and M[arietta] roads. Two companies of 116 Ill. were deployed on either side of the road and the advance continued. Had hardly got a quarter of a mile from the open ground ere the skirmish line met with opposition from the enemy. Other companies were ordered forward and finally the entire 1st Brigade was deployed, supported by the 2nd & protected by a brigade of Gen'l O on each flank. The lines advanced to the crest of the hill beyond [a] house and then were compelled to *pause*. Men were wounded quite rapidly. . . . Firing continued during the night, occasionally approaching to vollies [*sic*].

In sum, McPherson advanced against the Confederates at Dallas with the same alacrity and boldness that he displayed at Resaca on May 9—that is, he manifested the reverse of those qualities. As a consequence, all he achieved, despite having six divisions opposed by half that number of Confederate divisions, was the establishment of a fortified line one-half mile east of Dallas. Yet, in fairness, he probably could not have done more than this even had he been more aggressive. By this stage of the war both armies made it a standard practice to "dig in" whenever there was any possibility of being attacked. The product of their labor they called "rifle pits," but in fact they were highly formidable field fortifications behind which the defenders usually could repulse assailants outnumbering them two, three, and more to one, in the process inflicting heavy losses while suffering lightly themselves. Thus, Yanks and Rebs alike were reluctant to make charges and hoped that the foe would oblige them with an assault.

The alternative to a frontal assault was, of course, a flank attack. Sherman, having failed with the former at New Hope Church and then at Dallas, attempted the latter on May 27. On that day and on his orders, Howard, with two divisions, tried to turn the Confederate right flank at Pickett's Mill, and McPherson sought to do the same to the enemy's left flank at Dallas. Unfortunately for Howard, or rather for hundreds of his troops, what initially was a weakly held ridge became a killing ground when a Texas brigade occupied it before the Yankees reached it. McPherson enjoyed no greater success, but thanks to his customary caution, he lost far fewer men in an "attack" that

Taylor, who was in a good position to observe it, described in his diary for
May 27:

> During the day Gen'l. Lightburn's 2nd Brig. dug rifle pits & joined
> his brig. on the left of the 4th Div. & on the right of the M[arietta]
> road & Gen'l. Giles A. Smith's 1st Brig. [of Second Division] on the
> left [of the road]. Each of these brigades gained ground during the day
> slowly. In the P.M. [I] went over on Genl. H[arrow's] line [which along
> with a cavalry division held the extreme right of McPherson's front],
> ascended a high knob and watched the effect of Capt. [Francis]
> DeGress's [cannon] shots on a gun which was visable [sic] in their [the
> Confederates's] works 12 yds. beyond [them]. Remained there until
> after 1 P.M. when I went down to Gen'l. H H'quarters and took an
> excellent "cold punch." Saw Brig. Gen'l. [Charles] Walcutt while
> at the knob, who told us the following incident. In the morning
> when the "rebs" were about to make a charge on his brigade, one
> man wishing to raise a shout got up on the rebel works and pro-
> posed three cheers for "Southern Confederacy." Just as the words
> were uttered one of our sharpshooters shot him in the ass, where-
> upon he yelled: "Jesus! don't kill me."

Near the close of this entry, Taylor commented: "Heard very heavy firing over on our left." He referred to Howard's ill-starred assault at Pickett's
Mill. It is doubtful that Howard's troops heard any sound of battle at all from
around Dallas.

Encouraged by his defensive victory at Pickett's Mill, Johnston tried to
make a flanking movement of his own. During the night of May 27, he sent
Hood's Corps from the center of his line to the right, with orders to strike
the Union left flank, which reportedly was "in the air." In the morning, however, Hood discovered that this flank no longer was vulnerable and so wisely
canceled the operation. Next, Johnston looked to the Union right. Not only
had it been notably unaggressive, but observers atop a mountain also notified him that the Yankees in the Dallas area were pulling back. To find out if
this was true, Maj. Gen. William Bate of Hardee's Corps, acting on orders
passed down to him from Johnston, deployed his three infantry brigades and
a cavalry brigade. The latter was to charge first, dismounted. Should it encounter little or no resistance, then the infantry brigades were to attack on
hearing four rapid, successive cannon shots.

No Federal pullback had taken place at Dallas. The XV Corps's three divisions—Harrow's, Smith's, and Osterhaus's—remained in their earthworks, as did the XVI Corps on their left. But they did not expect an attack or even consider it possible. Hence, when it suddenly came at 4:00 P.M., Smith and his staff, Taylor included, literally were caught napping. Not until they heard the roar of enemy cannon and the whining of hostile shells did they wake up, rubbing their eyes and yawning. The sound of more artillery fire caused them to realize that "something was about to turn up," whereupon they mounted their horses and galloped off on the road leading to the front. What took place there Taylor recounted for Netta the next day:

> Hardly had we reached the road when a most terrific storm broke over our lines and came rolling on toward us—demonic yells were the interludes. The enemy was charging—assaulting our works. Our artillery belched forth its fierce thunders and our rifles emitted one continuous sheet of flame and lead, reserves were hurrying forward, and everything spoke the sharp notes of war. In our Division—on the 2nd Brigade the charge lasted 25 & on the 1st [Brigade] 20 minutes. The charge began on our extreme right [at] 4½ and ended on the left about six. The enemy lost I think about 1400. Our loss was not over 200. It was a fearful assault. I thank God I am still safe.

As usually happens when it comes to such matters, Taylor overstated the Confederate loss by nearly 100 percent and understated Federal casualties by almost 50 percent (they in fact totaled 379 killed, wounded, and missing). His account also implies that the enemy attacked in heavy force (Logan in his report stated that he repulsed "Hardee's entire command, estimated by prisoners to be 29,000").[9] Actually, only three Confederate brigades charged— the cavalry brigade and two of Bate's infantry brigades, altogether probably no more than 4,000 men. Furthermore, the infantry should not have charged at all, Bate having canceled their assault when it became obvious from the heavy fire that greeted the cavalry that the Federal works remained fully manned; but they went forward anyway in the mistaken belief that the attack signal had been given and they had failed to hear it. In his diary for May 28, Taylor noted, "On every hand the ground was thickly strewn with their killed & wounded" and that in "an area 40 feet square we counted 20 dead and 30 wounded."

The debacle at Pickett's Mill and the ferocious enemy onslaught at Dallas finally convinced Sherman that he had been blocked in his attempt to reach the Chattahoochee by way of Marietta and that consequently he had no viable choice except to withdraw to the railroad and reestablish his supply line before undertaking another offensive. But first he needed to reunite his army, which was divided into two groups; McPherson's XV and XVI Corps at Dallas and Thomas's and Schofield's forces in the New Hope Church–Pickett's Mill area. Accordingly, on May 29, he instructed McPherson to pull his troops out of their entrenchments at nightfall and to march north to link up with the XX Corps near New Hope Church.

Again Johnston anticipated what Sherman intended and so took measures to forestall him—measures described by Taylor in a June 2 letter to Netta that also provides an excellent insight into the role that skirmishers had come to play in both armies at this stage of the war, particularly in Georgia:

Gen'l Sherman wished to contract his lines and Sunday night [May 29] we were arranging to move out of position and march to the left. During the P.M. the rebels acted very suspiciously, moving forces to their left and opening with a cannonade towards evening. We [Smith and staff] were in the saddle most of the P.M. Just after supper they [the Confederates] dashed a line against the Division and Corps on our left [Veatch's division of the XVI Corps] and the fire became terrific—once or twice it ran down our front. Soon they were repelled and things became quiet. When we were about to return to [headquarters] we heard a shout, then a volley, and presently the artillery and small arms of the 16th Corps belched forth. Gen'l Osterhaus participated slightly and one of our batteries occasionally opened. This ceased in a short time and it soon became apparent to us that it was a "fool"—i.e. no charge had been made only [the enemy] skirmish line moved & commanded as though a column about to charge. This same thing was repeated as often as three more times during the night and in consequence thereof we were up until day light. Of course these feints prevented our leaving that night.

We remained until Wednesday when at daylight the line began moving to the left. It was considered a difficult task to withdraw from our position. My position [as division picket officer] made it necessary for me to hold the line with my skirmishers until everything had been removed and Harrow's line all out of the woods & beyond the

Marietta road, Harrow's Division having been on the extreme right and deployed across the Villa Rica road. If I was driven from the road to M[arietta] they might have been cut off. One hour after the column passed out of the works the bugle sounded "forward" at which call I marched my line "in retreat," passed over the works and in the dense undergrowth near the open field where I remained until Harrow's skirmishers had passed the road to M., assembled their companies and moved towards the division. I then resumed the march in retreat and with my line covered our entire front until within short range. When I assembled my command and sent them to their regiments the Gen'l [Morgan Smith] spoke highly of the style in which I had withdrawn.

In the afternoon the XV Corps reached New Hope Church, four miles north of Dallas, and relieved the XX Corps, which then leap-frogged the XIV and IV Corps to join the XXIII Corps on the Union left at Pickett's Mill. Using the same tactic, Sherman continued to shift toward the Western & Atlantic. Johnston made no serious effort to stop him and on the night of June 4 also withdrew toward the railroad. Early on the morning of June 5, Taylor and his skirmishers moved forward around New Hope Church through the Confederate fortifications and found that they consisted of three lines of elaborate trenches, each running along a commanding ridge. "Naturally and artificially" it was "the strongest position I ever beheld," he subsequently informed Netta, adding that "an attack in front would only have resulted in the most disastrous repulse. Thousands might have been slaughtered and still the enemy mocked at our efforts and laughed at our calamity."[10]

So ended the second phase of the campaign. During it, Johnston foiled Sherman's attempt to reach the Chattahoochee in one long, quick bound, inflicted some severe losses on his army, and kept him pinned down for two weeks in what the Union troops called "the hell hole" around New Hope Church. Yet Sherman again succeeded by means of a flanking maneuver in compelling Johnston to relinquish a strong defensive position (Allatoona) without a fight. And now at Acworth, with his supply line restored, Sherman stood a mere thirty miles from Atlanta, whose residents—those who had not fled the city—could hear the sound of the cannon fire to the north. Taylor surely spoke for the great majority of Sherman's army when he assured Netta in his June 2 letter, "We are all in good spirits and have no doubt of our ability to reach Atlanta."

7

Oh, Jerusalem, Jerusalem
June 6–July 9, 1864

THE XV CORPS bivouacked near Acworth on June 6, completing the consolidation of Sherman's forces at that point. Two days later, the XVII Corps of the Army of the Tennessee also arrived at Acworth. Consisting of 9,000 veteran troops organized into two divisions and headed by Frank Blair Jr., it more than made good Sherman's battle losses and raised the strength of McPherson's command to approximately 30,000.

On June 10 the Union army began advancing southward, with McPherson on the left astride the Western & Atlantic, Thomas in the center, and Schofield on the right. The XV Corps, which marched on a road paralleling the railroad, encountered only token resistance from enemy pickets, yet after covering a mere four miles halted and entrenched at a railroad station called Big Shanty (present-day Kennesaw). Taylor was disgusted by this lack of aggressiveness, a disgust he vented in his diary entry for the day:

> I can't divine the cause of this procrastination—to me it appears inexcusable—some call it caution. This is a great mistake. We are perfectly stationary—not feeling with skirmishers, not even reconnoitering. Everything is at a dead lock. No one can tell where the enemy is. An earthwork in the distance or an hundred pickets of nerve check the column for hours. When a line of battle is formed [we] intrench the first line. Rifle pits, redoubts, bastions and almost every other thing which requires delay must be built. Men, I fear, will soon conclude they cannot stand fire except behind works. . . . A little dash, a cautious, rapid pursuit and a few encounters will soon demoralize Johnston's army.

Unknown to Taylor, who on June 7 had written Netta that he thought "Johnston's main force now is on the banks of the Chattahoochee river," there was a reason for McPherson's halting so soon other than his habitual caution. Thomas had come up against a formidable Confederate position atop Pine Mountain, with the result that should the Army of the Tennessee continue forward it soon would lose contact with the Army of the Cumberland, thereby creating a potentially dangerous gap in the Union front. Furthermore, Sherman's signal officers reported that from Big Shanty they could see through their telescopes large numbers of gray-clad troops fortifying two other mountains—Brush to the southeast and to the southwest, rising high above the others, Kennesaw.

Although Taylor grumbled in his diary entry for June 11 that he did not "believe there is an enemy within a mile of us" and asked "why stand we here all the day idle?" he was confident that "Sherman knows his business" and on June 12 predicted to Netta that the army would go to Atlanta "beyond all doubt in about a month—perhaps earlier" and do it "by another flank movement." No doubt his more optimistic attitude stemmed from a circumstance he recorded in his diary for June 11: "Gen'l Sherman moved down near the skirmish line and remained until after 2 P.M." In his letter to Netta the following day, he stated that the red-haired commander "looked cheerful and spoke confidently as to results. To look at him you would think he had no important cares upon his mind than when [he was] our Division and Corps Commander, except occasionally he leans his head upon his hands."

By June 14, despite frequent rains that turned roads and fields into morasses, McPherson's skirmishers had managed to reach the northern slope of Brush Mountain and work their way around to its eastern end. At the same time, Thomas's IV and XX Corps pushed in so close to Pine Mountain that Gen. Joseph Johnston ordered it evacuated during the night, but not before a cannon shot killed Gen. Leonidas Polk while he was observing the Federals from atop the mountain. Maj. Gen. William Loring, the Forty-seventh Ohio's former antagonist in West Virginia, temporarily replaced him.

The Confederate withdrawal from Pine Mountain caused Sherman again to conclude that Johnston was doing what he wanted him to do—retreat all along his front. Believing that this provided an opportunity to catch the enemy in the open, he ordered Thomas to push forward rapidly and "break" Johnston's center while McPherson and Schofield carried out "demonstrations" against his right and center. Thomas, advancing, soon discovered that the Confederates had merely pulled back to another and very strong fortified line and so wisely halted to bring up his artillery. McPherson's demonstration, on the other hand, achieved what had been rare in this campaign—a successful, albeit small-scale, frontal assault on entrenched infantry. Taylor described it two days afterward to Netta:

> At 12 M. [noon] Harrow with the 4th Division moved down the Big Shanty & Marietta road to the woods in front of the enemy line and under its cover moved out on our extreme left, formed line in a valley and moved rapidly forward through an open [field] to an isolated wood in and along which the rebels were posted in small rifle pits &c as sharpshooters. The advance was so rapid & unexpected that they were unable to leave their shelters and consequently as the [Union] line swept on [they] were compelled to surrender. In this maneuver in [a] short space of time the 4th Division captured over three hundred prisoners and lost in killed and wounded only forty. This move gave the rebels great alarm and immediately they began signaling and moving troops to their right.[1]

Taylor began his next letter to Netta, dated June 21, with an accurate description of the weather and its effect, but a less-than-accurate opinion as to the condition of the Confederates: "It is still raining here. The roads are cut up, the country is cut up and the rebels are disconcerted." Then, following a lengthy and, frankly, rather tedious account of his recent operations as division picket officer, he concluded by trying to reassure his wife about the two matters of most concern to her—his personal safety and his leaving the army upon the expiration of his term of service:

> As a matter of course I had [while directing his skirmishers] some narrow escape & close shots, but who has not had in this army. I shall endeavor to take care of myself and by the mercy of the great Jehovah hope to pass through this campaign safely. . . . You need give yourself no apprehension about the government holding me beyond the 21st day of August. [Taylor should have written "27th day of August; perhaps his pen slipped.] If I remained in the service longer than that time I would have to be remustered under orders from the War Department in order to be competent to hold office in a veteran regiment.

By June 21 the Confederates had either been pressed back or voluntarily fallen back to Kennesaw Mountain, the highest and also the last peak north of Atlanta. Here their heavily fortified line ran for seven miles, beginning to the southeast of Big Kennesaw, 691 feet in elevation, and then curving around to the southwest along Little Kennesaw, Pigeon Hill, and a chain of hills and ridges extending to the Chattahoochee. It was a strong position—stronger than Dalton or New Hope Church—and Sherman, who before setting out from Acworth had promised Henry Halleck that he would not "run hot-headed against any works prepared for us," accordingly decided to do what Taylor had predicted he would do in his June 12 letter to Netta: "make them [the Confederates] leave by another flank movement."

Only this time instead of entrusting the flanking maneuver to the Army of the Tennessee, he would employ Hooker's XX Corps and Schofield's XXIII Corps. Schofield, whose corps was on the extreme Union right, had notified Sherman that there was "no material force" of Confederates between him and Marietta. Sherman at once ordered Schofield and Hooker, whose XX Corps was to the left of the XXIII, to combine on June 22 in a thrust toward Marietta, which, if as successful as it should be, would place them in Johnston's rear, cut him off from Atlanta, and at the very least compel him to retreat from his Kennesaw stronghold.

Unfortunately for Sherman's plan, Johnston anticipated this move and on the night of June 21 sent Hood's Corps from his right to his left. As a consequence, when on June 22 Hooker and Schofield linked up at Kolb's Farm on the road leading to Marietta, they found themselves faced by Hood's three divisions, a very "material force" indeed. Moreover Hood, not content to stand on the defensive, launched an attack in the hope of flanking the would-be flankers. Hooker's and Schofield's troops easily repulsed this assault, which was poorly executed, but the path to Marietta had been blocked again.

At this juncture, Sherman lost his temper and with it his patience. For a month, he had been trying in vain to reach Marietta and the river beyond. Unless he somehow managed to end this stalemate and soon, he feared that Johnston would detach troops from his army to reinforce Lee against Grant. Hence, he decided to do what he told Halleck he would not do—strike head-on against Johnston's defensive works. Johnston's front, he rightly believed, was stretched thin. Somewhere he should be able to break through it, and when he did, he would force Johnston to retreat south of the Chattahoochee, if not rout his entire army.

Kennesaw Mountain as Seen from the Union Lines.
Miller, ed., Photographic History, *3: 117.*

Of course, he could carry out another flanking maneuver. The only way he could see to do that, however, was to withdraw McPherson's corps from Kennesaw on his left and send them once again around Johnston's left. But he deemed this too risky because it would uncover his advance supply base at Big Shanty and open the way for Johnston to seize it, thereby cutting him off from the railroad and obliging him to retreat in order to avoid disaster. No, a frontal attack was the best alternative—and the safest. Besides, Johnston no doubt was anticipating another flanking movement to his left and thus a direct assault on his front would be unexpected, increasing its chance of success.

Was Sherman correct in his choice of options? In due course we shall see, but for the present let us turn to a potential answer, one that is found in the letter that Taylor wrote Netta on June 29. In it he recounts what he and his skirmishers did on June 24 on the slopes of Big Kennesaw:

Last Friday quite early in the morning I received orders to advance my line. An examination of the ground in my front convinced me that only a portion of it [the skirmish line] could be moved. This I reported and immediately was ordered to take three companies and ascend the mountain if possible, regardless of connections with other Divisions.

The reason for this order was the profound silence & the non-appearance of the usual force of the rebels upon the Mt. I rode over [to] the line and ordered three companies to deploy, one in front and one on each flank and await orders. In a short time I had [a] reserve brought over from another post and ordered an advance—caused the command to left half-wheel. This brought the command in a position to move diagonally across the side of the mountain . . . [which] enabled me to pass all the batteries while under the protection of the almost precipitous side of the mountain without a shot [being fired].

After advancing [my men] an hundred yards, Genl Osterhaus sent word he would have his line [of skirmishers] join mine and wait. When the connection was completed I advanced and deployed some companies on my left flank to make an entire line and with these connecting pushed forward in a triangular line as before. . . . At 12 M. I moved forward; at 2 P.M. was within 150 yards of the top of the Mt. and had the rebels in full retreat. My line was so close to theirs that my men fought from behind the same rocks they [the Confederates] sheltered themselves. All went merry as a wedding bell—two of the men of the 6th Mo. saw some rebels in the chasm of a rock firing [and] believing they could drive them out they fixed bayonets and charged. One of them was killed, the other ran back and reported to me. The 17th A[rmy] C[orps], which was to the left of the XV C[orps] had not advanced any, therefore . . . I had got so far up the Mt. [that] from a point in their [the XVII Corps'] front held by the rebels I received such a heavy cross and flank fire that my left broke. I halted them [his skirmishers] immediately, sent up support, put in fresh men and strengthened my entire line until I had fifteen companies deployed. Again I gave the order forward and again we moved up. The rebels had witnessed the break in my line, halted, reformed . . . [and] contested every inch of the ground—how viciously they shot! Yet I gradually pressed them back—my gain was slow but sure. At 5 P.M. I got an order to place my line in command of the ranking Officer and report to Gen'l Smith. As my orderly raised up to go for the ranking Officer he was killed. I waited until two other companies I had ordered up paused and attracted the rebels attention and [then] went myself. Gen'l Smith said others had not advanced with me and I must halt and re-establish my old line. This I did very unwillingly. My loss was four killed and fifteen wounded [but] only eleven of which required medical treatment. I was complimented for my conduct and rearrangement and the entire company was satisfied that had we made a charge up the same ground we could have taken the mountain. Indeed the most of them say that had I been supported on the left my own skirmisher line would have taken it.

If Taylor was correct in thinking that Big Kennesaw was so weakly defended that his skirmishers could have gained the crest with the support of the XVII Corps, then Sherman did have a viable alternative to a frontal assault, i.e., directing the XV and XVII Corps to make a full-fledged attack on the mountain; its seizure would have rendered Johnston's entire position untenable and led to his hasty retreat. But no one notified Sherman of what Taylor's skirmishers came so close to accomplishing, and even if he had received that information, it is most unlikely that he would have acted on it. He had resolved to break through the center of the Confederate fortifications; and on June 24 he issued the orders that three days later resulted in the XV, IV, and XIV Corps endeavoring to do exactly that.[2]

In his June 29 letter to Netta, Taylor described the XV Corps' attack, which was delivered by Walcutt's brigade of Harrow's division and both brigades of Morgan Smith's division:

At 8 [A.M.] . . . the Division and one brigade from the 4th Division formed and charged in three columns, brigade in each, upon Little Kennesaw. We drove the enemy from position after position and through one of the densest growth of saplings, &c and morasses I ever saw. By the time we emerged from this our lines were badly deranged and broken yet we received such a heavy fire that we could not halt to reform. Lightburn's brigade came upon the rebels in a rifle pit at the edge of a swamp. . . . A volley was fired by each [side] and without bayonets the men "went in" clubbing. . . . The rebels finally broke and we followed. At length we got where it was necessary to stop—some were killed within ten feet of the works, one [of them a] Colonel. But dear, we got back in the swamp and hill just beyond, left our line of skirmishers in the open field and dug rifle pits. Then we went back and subsequently we received the heaviest fire of the whole campaign.

Batteries of every description swept our position in every possible direction—men's heads, arms etc. were blown off & scattered over the earth. Our men charged gallantly—rebel fire did not break them but it was the character of the ground traversed—the morasses, the swamps. They had not the moral support of "the touch of elbows." . . . This it was that made us halt so soon, but it was better thus, had we gone farther, two thirds of our Div. would have been dead on the field. As it was the 1st Brig. lost 154 killed and wounded & the 2nd 172. The other brigade [Walcutt's] lost over two hundred. I did hard duty and so did all of us as staff officers in carrying orders and as a matter of course all had many narrow escapes.[3]

The assaults by the IV and XIV Corps were no more successful and en-tailed much heavier casualties because the terrain permitted larger numbers of their troops to get closer to the enemy works before being blasted away. Altogether the Federals lost about 3,000 men as opposed to approximately 700 Confederates put out of action and gained nothing, unless an increased reluctance to charge entrenched foes could be considered a gain. Among the Union casualties was Col. Parry with a leg wound. Lt. Col. Wallace took com-mand of the Forty-seventh in his place.

Sherman reacted to the failure of the attack, which he privately blamed on his troops displaying insufficient "vigor," by asking Thomas whether a renewal of it might succeed. Thomas replied with an emphatic no. If Sherman, he added, wished to break through the Confederate defenses, it would have to be done by a regular siege operation—saps, parallels, mines, and so on. The prospect of that, as Thomas must have anticipated, appalled Sherman. His army would be bogged down at Kennesaw for weeks, perhaps months, during which Johnston could reinforce Lee. There had to be some other way— but what? The answer came in a dispatch from Schofield. One of his divi-sions, that of Brig. Gen. Jacob D. Cox, who had commanded the Kanawha Division in West Virginia during 1861 and 1862, had found a place where the enemy left could be flanked, providing a sufficient force was sent to do it; the small XXIII Corps already was stretched dangerously thin. At first, Sherman reacted negatively to this message, but after pondering the matter further, he concluded that he would do what he hitherto had feared doing—use the Army of the Tennessee to turn Johnston's left flank, but not all of it at once. Instead, Morgan Smith's division would set out first to join the XXIII Corps, with Brig. Gen. Mortimer Leggett's division of the XVII Corps behind it and with the rest of McPherson's divisions to follow during the next several days. That way Big Shanty and the railroad would remain protected against a Confederate thrust until Johnston's own railroad supply line was so imperiled by the flanking movement that he would not dare attempt any offensive action.

The march of Smith's division to the Union right took place on July 2. Two days later, Taylor described it and what happened afterward to Netta:

> The Division moved at 4 A.M. and immediately upon arriving at the 23rd [Corps], instead of acting as support were ordered to the front and relieved two of their brigades by 11 A.M., having marched eleven miles in one of the hottest mornings of the summer. I soon had my pickets posted and at 12 M. came in to rest. I could not sleep, therefore I spent the time in sprinkling all in my quarters and wound up by binding their sleeping forms in their cots &c. At 2 A.M. of the third I was called up and sent on the line to repel an attack, but none came. At daylight I came in to breakfast & thought I would sleep but each attempt was futile—one tickled me—another would call Oh, Major! Finally an order came for us to advance. At 8½ A.M. brigades moved at right angles and therefore I had nothing to do as the Div. was separated, except to act as aide. The 1st Brigade met slight opposition, the 2nd met considerable, consequently we were near them [the Confederates]. Lightburn's brigade acted in fine style—advanced splendidly and after a heavy skirmish and a lively cannonade charged across the open field & drove the enemy beyond Nickajack Creek and occupied their works at 4 P.M. It requires considerable time to feel or develop an enemies [*sic*] lines and ascertain his force—the position of his guns and whether he has works. When this is learned the movements are directed accordingly and a short fight of an hour or two determines the question of victory. Sharp, steady, uninterrupted fighting, set it down as false. Fights are connected by skirmishes the same as wrist bands by buttons. I have seen

as high as three or four heavy fights per day in this way but never a days continuous heavy fighting.

On July 2, Johnston, as soon as he learned from his observers atop Big Kennesaw that long columns of troops were moving from the Union left to the Union right, ordered his army to retreat during the night, which it did. To remain was to risk Sherman's cutting the railroad below Marietta or else crossing the Chattahoochee southwest of that town and moving against a defenseless Atlanta—or both. The Confederates encountered by Smith's division at Nickajack Creek were merely a rearguard conducting a delaying action while Johnston established a new defense line at Smyrna Camp Ground.

July 4 found Taylor at Ruff's Mill on Nickajack Creek. Smith's division being in reserve, he had little to do on the fourth and, he was confident, last Independence Day of his military service. In the morning (so he recorded in his diary) he

> drank, read & wrote a letter to wife. At noon rec'd orders to sup-
> port 16th A.C. [which faced the Confederates at Smyrna Camp
> Ground] & at 1 P.M. moved across the Creek and over to Ruff's
> House. Gen'l Smith reported to [Brig. Gen. Grenville M.] Dodge
> [commander of the XVI Corps] for orders. . . . At about 6 P.M. [Brig.
> Gen. John W.] Fuller's brigade [of Brig. Gen. Thomas Sweeny's di-
> vision, XVI Corps] charged and captured the enemy's line of skir-
> mish pits & took several prisoners. . . . Took a big swim. After night
> heard of imperfections in the picket line & went to ascertain. Found
> the space covered & came home & laid down to pleasant dreams
> with blankets loosely wrapped. Every body very sober today. Cause:
> Supply of whiskey exhausted.

That night, Johnston abandoned his Smyrna Camp Ground line, it being too easily flanked to hold for long, and withdrew to the north bank of the Chattahoochee, where he posted his army behind immensely strong fortifi-cations that covered the railroad bridge and the direct route to Atlanta, a mere six miles to the south. Sherman, as he had at Resaca, initially believed that Johnston would not make a stand with his back to a river but, after making a personal reconnaissance, saw that such indeed was the case. More important, he also realized that any attempt to storm Johnston's new position merely would produce a bloodier fiasco than the June 27 attack at Kennesaw. There-fore, he deployed Thomas's forces opposite the Confederates and then pon-dered how best to use McPherson's and Schofield's troops to get across the Chattahoochee at some other place.

Smith's division remained at Ruff's Mill until July 8, when it moved for-ward and occupied a ridge along the bank of Nickajack Creek. From the ridge, Taylor "enjoyed a birdseye view of Atlanta," which he estimated to be eight to ten miles distant from where he stood, and on the following day related to Netta what he saw and his reaction:

> . . . tall white spires, glittering domes and [the] black, towering chim-neys of its scores of factories, vomiting forth dense clouds of smoke. The city appears to cover as much ground as Columbus but its pub-lic buildings show clearer and better in the sunlight of evening than those of that city. It appears to be situated in a gently ascending plain, covered with orchards and beautiful forests, in form an amphi-theater, in the background is a range of high hills or mountains. It is a glorious scene and most forcibly reminded me of Christ's behold-ing Jerusalem from the mount and his most fearful curse:
>
> Oh Jerusalem, Jerusalem, thou that killest the prophets and stoned them which are sent unto thee, how often I would have gathered thy children together, even as a hen gathereth her chickens under her wings and ye would not! Behold, your house is left with you desolate.

Atlanta's "offense—rebellion," continued Taylor, "is exactly the counter-part of the crimes" of Jerusalem and "how deserving are the citizens of the city of such punishment—desolate their homes, raze their city to the ground, pull down their temples and hang their traitors. God's most fearful curse is not too hard for them to bear and not an improper punishment for their offense."

That Atlanta would fall, Taylor was certain. All signs indicated that even the Confederates expected this to happen—"Georgia has moved all her pub-lic institutions [in the city] to Macon"—and he doubted that Johnston would make a serious effort to defend the place but again would retreat. Yet a long time might pass before the Federals occupied Atlanta.

> Our movements hinge upon the Richmond campaign. Sherman does not push Johnston too hard for fear of a general engagement and

decisive victory for us. If Johnston suffers some reverses here, the supposition is that he will send a considerable portion of his forces to reinforce Lee and abandon this country. This is one of the reasons alleged for our advancing so slowly. Our movements are regulated by Grant's campaign. Indeed it is a question among those high in command whether Sherman will take Atlanta until Grant gains something decisive. The struggle is to entertain the rebel armies— Sherman to prevent Johnston from reinforcing Lee and Grant to prevent Lee from reinforcing Johnston. It appears to be the settled conviction of military minds that the rebels are unable to hold both sections of the country and [if] they are pushed so hard in either section as to bring them to a realization of this fact they will at once abandon the least important point and move rapidly for the other and strive to crush our army ere it can be reinforced. Sherman . . . is considered [to have] the easier task to accomplish though more delicate position to maintain and therefore it is deemed highly injudicious for him to push forward until Grant is so finely fixed that he can withstand all attack of and overcome all reinforcements which may be sent to Lee.

Sherman, then, had not yet defeated Johnston and taken Atlanta and might do neither in the near future because he feared the consequences for Grant.[4] There was some truth in that explanation, for Sherman regarded his campaign as supplementary to Grant's, thus attacking frontally at Kennesaw in order to forestall Johnston's sending reinforcements to Lee, but it suffered from two major flaws. First, those "high in command" who expounded it were not high enough to know that on the night of June 27, Sherman received a telegram from Halleck, which, had it arrived the previous night, possibly would have caused him to cancel the Kennesaw attack. In the telegram Halleck stated, "Lieutenant General Grant directs me to say that the movements of your army may be made independent of any desire to retain Johnston's forces where they are. He does not think that Lee will bring any additional troops to Richmond, on account of the difficulty of feeding them."

And the second flaw was that Confederate president Jefferson Davis had not the slightest intention of reinforcing Lee by drawing units from Johnston's army. He was rightly confident that Lee would continue to hold Grant at bay outside Richmond with his present forces until the North's presidential election in the fall. Yet he was increasingly alarmed by the situation in Georgia, coming ever closer to the conclusion that Johnston could not be trusted to make a determined effort to hold Atlanta but would again retreat after a mere token attempt to defend it.

Following his disquisition on what "military minds" believed to be the true nature of Union grand strategy, Taylor closed his July 9 letter on a personal note:

> I have very easy duty now and my promptness, perseverance and dash has [sic] secured the good opinion of General Smith. Yesterday he told me he had several times been afraid that I would be hit and didn't see how I escaped even a wound. Dear I think the prayers of a little wife, an aged mother and a good sister has [sic] as much to do with my preservation as anything. Then I think about such matters sometimes myself.

Perhaps even as Taylor enscribed these lines, Cox's division of the XXIII Corps crossed the Chattahoochee at Soap Creek and established a bridgehead whereby Sherman could turn Johnston's right flank and advance on Atlanta from the east. This move took Johnston by surprise. He had assumed that Sherman again would seek to outflank him on his left and so deployed his forces accordingly; thus Cox was able to make his crossing virtually unopposed. As soon as he learned of the bridgehead, Johnston ordered a retreat, and that night his troops passed over to the south bank of the river, then burned the railroad bridge. At long last, Sherman's army could swarm along the Chattahoochee like bees.

Atlanta now was only a couple of hours march away. As did Jefferson Davis, most of the Federals (as noted in Taylor's July 9 letter) doubted that Johnston would fight hard to hold it, that after a few skirmishes he would evacuate the city, and that they soon would occupy it. They could not foresee that the hardest, bloodiest battles of the campaign lay ahead and that nearly two months would pass before they could reach their goal.

Likewise, Maj. Thomas Thomson Taylor, picket commander of the Second Division, XV Corps, presently enjoying "very easy duty," had no way of knowing that soon he would take part in combats where he would have dire need of his wife's and mother's prayers—and lots of luck besides.

Hell, Stranger, This Is No Place for Me to Halt!
July 9–22, 1864

UNLIKE GRANT AND LEE, William Tecumseh Sherman as a matter of policy—a policy that reflected his temperament—never sought to destroy enemy armies by engaging them in titanic offensive battles with his full available strength. Instead, he preferred and hence endeavored to achieve lesser results at lesser risk by means of maneuvers designed to cut or that threatened to cut his opponent's line of communications. Thus he put into effect, following Johnston's withdrawal to the south side of the Chattahoochee, a plan that envisioned no heavy fighting unless the Confederates were so obliging as to attack, an event he considered highly unlikely.

In accordance with this plan, McPherson's Army of the Tennessee switched from the Union right to the left by moving up the Chattahoochee to Roswell, crossed the river there on July 17, and in conjunction with Schofield's XXIII Corps, advanced on the town of Decatur with the objective of destroying the Georgia Railroad, Atlanta's direct link to the Carolinas and Virginia, and thereby preventing any reinforcements from Lee reaching Johnston except by a long, roundabout route. That accomplished, McPherson, supported by Schofield on his right flank, was to move against Atlanta from the east while Thomas descended on it from the north and cavalry severed the Atlanta & West Point Railroad, the city's rail connection to the west. Sherman expected that Johnston, after making a pro forma defense of Atlanta, would then evacuate the city and retreat southward to protect what would be his sole remaining supply line, the Atlanta & Macon Railroad.

It was a good plan and probably would have achieved the outcome Sherman anticipated had it not been for an occurrence that he could not have foreseen. On July 17, Jefferson Davis, having failed to obtain from Johnston a convincing assurance that he intended to make a determined effort to defeat Sherman, replaced him as commander of the Confederate Army of Tennessee with John Hood, who could be counted on to fight, and fight hard, to hold the city.

This Hood did. On July 20, he threw two-thirds of his infantry against Hooker's XX Corps and a division of Howard's IV Corps along the south bank of Peachtree Creek, a tributary of the Chattahoochee into which he hoped to drive them. The attack caught the Federals off guard and for the most part unentrenched. Assuming, as did Sherman, that the Confederates had concentrated most of their forces east of Atlanta to ward off McPherson, the Union generals had not expected to encounter any serious resistance, much less a fierce onslaught. Only by desperate fighting, and thanks to the failure of Hardee's Corps to make a coordinated assault in full strength, were they able to beat off their assailants, inflicting heavy casualties but not suffering lightly themselves.

Meanwhile, McPherson advanced from Decatur toward Atlanta. He had at least 25,000 troops; at most 5,000 Confederate cavalry, fighting dismounted, opposed him. He believed, though, that Hood's infantry lurked behind the cavalry, ready to pounce on him—a belief shared by Sherman, who, during the height of the fighting at Peachtree Creek (the sound of which did not carry to him), sent a message to Thomas, advising him to have "all your troops push toward Atlanta, sweeping everything before them." As a consequence, McPherson repeated his May 9 performance outside of Resaca, which Taylor described and rightly judged in his diary entry for July 20:

Up at 4 A.M. By Special Order 2nd Div. 15 A.C. advanced on the main road from Decatur to Atlanta. One mile from Decatur encountered the enemy's skirmishers and drove [them] from ridge to ridge capturing one line of light works. Here much precious time was lost waiting for the A.C. to close up. One section [of artillery] was placed in position & fired a few rounds. Finally advanced skirmish line past Clandson's house up the ridge beyond & advanced skirmishers to the ridge next the one on which the brick house stands & which is occupied by the rebs. Here the line was halted for Blair to come up [on the left of the XV Corps] & for some one to join on the right. The precious time passed swiftly away and Oh! the golden opportunity to take the ridge commanding the City glided by all unused because forsooth, some one who had the power, had not the nerve, the *spirit & dash* to order *forward-march!* How long o Lord! will our leaders continue to let such opportunities slip through their fingers & afterwards sacrifice hundreds of lives in vain efforts to take the same position they let the enemy fortify & occupy under their very noses?

Not until late evening did McPherson realize, as he admitted in a dispatch to Sherman, that there was not "much of anything but cavalry in front of us." By the same token, not until midnight did Sherman learn that the biggest and bloodiest battle yet of the campaign had taken place during the afternoon along the south bank of Peachtree Creek. Once again a combination of an erroneous assumption by Sherman and of excessive caution by McPherson had, as Taylor observed, wasted a "golden opportunity." Had McPherson pushed forward vigorously, not only could he have taken Atlanta but also could have cut off the bulk of Hood's forces from their wagon train and exposed them to attack in front and rear.

As it was, during the night, Hood reinforced the cavalry opposing McPherson with Cleburne's Division, which occupied and fortified the ridge that Taylor believed should have been seized during the day. On the morning of July 21 the XVII Corps did succeed in capturing a tactically advantageous hill south of the XV Corps' position, but an attempt to advance beyond it was driven back by Cleburne's troops. This convinced Sherman and McPherson that a large portion, if not most, of Hood's army faced them east of Atlanta. Hence they made no further attacks and contented themselves with raking the Confederate lines with artillery fire and lobbing some shells into the city until it became too dark to aim cannons accurately.

Toward dawn on July 22, Schofield, whose corps was on the Army of the Tennessee's right, notified Sherman that the Confederates on his front "have abandoned their lines." At the same time, McPherson reported that large enemy contingents had been observed marching southward. Immediately Sherman sprang to the conclusion that Hood was evacuating Atlanta and so ordered Thomas and McPherson to pursue him and Schofield to occupy the city.

Once more Sherman assumed too much too soon. Far from evacuating Atlanta, Hood was putting into effect an attack plan that in scope and audacity surpassed the Lee-Jackson flanking maneuver at Chancellorsville. Under it Lt. Gen. Alexander P. Stewart's Corps (formerly Leonidas Polk's, then William Loring's) was to hold Thomas in check south of Atlanta, and Maj. Gen. Benjamin F. Cheatham, acting commander of what had been Hood's Corps, would do the same against the Union forces east of the City. In the meantime, during the night of July 21, Hardee's Corps and Maj. Gen. Joseph Wheeler's cavalry corps would circle around and behind Sherman's left (southern) flank to Decatur and at daylight on July 22 strike McPherson's forces in the rear, crushing them; then Hardee and Cheatham would combine to roll up the entire Federal army, either destroying it or so badly crippling it that it would be obliged to retreat back across the Chattahoochee.

Thus when McPherson's and Schofield's troops moved forward to pursue Hood and to occupy Atlanta, they quickly found themselves faced by formidable fortifications filled with gray-clad soldiers busily engaged in rendering these fortifications more formidable still. Obviously, Hood had not evacuated Atlanta, at least not yet. Sherman perforce issued new orders. McPherson, Schofield, and Thomas were to deploy their forces in a line paralleling that of the Confederates but refrain from attacking. Meanwhile, John Fuller's division of the XVI Corps was to destroy the Georgia Railroad all the way to Decatur. Then during the night, McPherson would march his three corps to the Union right, where he would be in position to strike and cut the Macon Railroad. The threat of this action, Sherman believed, would compel Hood to leave Atlanta so as to safeguard his sole supply line.

McPherson disliked these orders. First, his troops already had obliterated a thirteen-mile section of the Georgia Railroad to the east of Decatur, and a cavalry division that hitherto had been covering his left flank had gone to tear up still more track in that direction, leaving that flank exposed. Second, and worse, the enemy works opposite him extended southward beyond his own line of entrenchments. Last, and worst, enemy columns continued to be seen moving to the south. To him, these circumstances added up to a strong possibility, in fact the probability, of a large-scale attack on his left flank, which at present was protected only by a single brigade of Fuller's division of the XVI Corps facing southward at a right angle to the XVII Corps. Since Fuller's only other brigade already was at Decatur guarding the wagon train, a strong Confederate force could turn McPherson's left flank and attack him from the rear—which of course was precisely what Hood hoped to do.

Accordingly, McPherson directed Thomas Sweeny's XVI Corps division, presently in reserve behind the XV Corps, to move over to the left and join

Fuller's troops in guarding that flank. He then went to Sherman and asked him to withdraw the order concerning Fuller. Sherman agreed, but with the proviso that if no enemy assault took place on the left by 1 P.M., then all of Fuller's men would go to work on the railroad. Privately, he was confident that there was virtually no danger of the Confederates attacking on the left or anywhere else and that their construction of a new line of fortifications around Atlanta merely masked an impending departure from the city.

Sherman's attitude communicated itself to some of his division and brigade commanders, among them Morgan Smith and Lightburn. We learn this from Taylor's account, written for Netta on July 26, of what he saw and did on "the most eventful day of this campaign":

> In the morning as usual at daylight I went down to the skirmish line to learn the condition of things. Soon Gen'l Morgan L. Smith sent an order to move forward my line and feel the enemy. I pushed forward and soon began driving his [the enemy's skirmish] line. At his skirmish pits I redressed it [his own line] and advanced on his main works and soon drove his skirmishers in, but without giving them time to form I hurried forward with a shout and a volley which set the rebels skedaddling and a regiment of reserves in full and rapid retreat. In the main [outlying] works I again dressed the line and pursued them, capturing a few prisoners and two lines of skirmish pits and drove them square into their [main] works and occupied with my line a portion of the corporation of Atlanta, not more than 600 yards from their forts. Here they served us with "minnies" [rifle bullets called Minié balls], case and solid shot and shells. I soon discovered where their skirmish pits were and made my line crawl forward in some places within 20 yards of them and build rail barricades. I found one set [of his own skirmishers] timid and awkward and I had to crawl up to a point where I wished a post, show them the bearings and range and help them build it. By this method I got my line so close to theirs that they were afraid to burst shells and case shot the proper distance in front for fear of killing their own men and consequently were compelled to fire solid shot or burst their other shot so close to us that the fragments would fly clear over us. Hence I had only three wounded by their continuous cannon fire.
>
> Their skirmishers were kept so close [to the ground] that I had only two wounded by musket balls. One solid shot knocked down a rail

pile and buried the men under it. A Captain thought destruction had come and wished to retire but I make it a point never to give up my ground if my flanks are protected [and] so they rebuilt it. I sent back for shovels to dig good pits but our Division General was not at liberty to send them to us. Our men in authority appeared to think the enemy were evacuating Atlanta because they were moving columns to the left. About 9 or 10 A.M. Logan's Senior Aide came out and I showed him how earnestly they [the Confederates] were working in town upon their fortifications and asked if it looked like an evacuation. He said no. I then asked him for tools, but they came not. Our Commanders appeared infatuated with the thought of evacuation of Atlanta.

After a time two regiments of infantry and a section of artillery were sent out as a second reserve. I laid down and got a good nap and awoke about 12½ M. Just after I got up Lieut. [Adolph] Ahlers [of the Forty-seventh Ohio] and two men were wounded near me and I was struck with dirt, bark or something and Ahlers reported me wounded. My negro went to the rear with the horses, but came back. About 1 P.M. I moved to a high point in the line and sat down. Firing soon commenced and became very heavy on the extreme left and in the rear. The enemy appeared to be doubling our lines up.

Doubling up the Union left was exactly what the Confederates were attempting and, to a degree, accomplishing. Hood's attack plan, it will be remembered, called for Hardee's Corps and Wheeler's cavalry to march during the night to Decatur, then at daylight to slam into McPherson's rear. This, however, had proved to be an impossibility. Hardee's troops, after forty-eight hours of almost constant marching and fighting, simply were too weary to move so far so fast. Consequently, Hood modified his plan: Hardee, once he got beyond the Federal left, was to strike it in the flank and rear while Wheeler's troopers were to go to Decatur to destroy the Union wagon train gathered there and then join in the assault on McPherson. That plan still remained scheduled to begin at daybreak, but it also turned out to be overly optimistic. Not until noon did two of Hardee's four divisions reach the desired position and, as Taylor's account notes, not until 1 P.M. did they begin attacking. One of them, William Bate's Division, was quickly repulsed by Thomas Sweeny's division, which by sheer good luck (for the Federals) had deployed at exactly the right place to do this. The other division, Maj. Gen.

W. H. T. Walker's, suffered the same fate as it ran smack into the brigade of Fuller's division, the one that Sherman intended to send off to tear up track.[1]

Cleburne's Division, however, was more fortunate. It passed through the gap in the Union line between the XVI and XVII Corps and in conjunction with Cheatham's Division (commanded by Brig. Gen. George Maney) assailed the southernmost division of the XVII Corps in both front and rear, inflicting heavy casualties, taking many prisoners, and forcing it back until it faced south instead of west. Moreover, while advancing through the gap, Cleburne's men came upon a mounted Union officer obviously of high rank, called on him to surrender, and when he tried to flee, shot and killed him. Their victim was McPherson, on the way to investigate the situation of his left.

Taylor also felt great concern about what was happening there:

> Oh! how anxiously I listened and waited, how anxious for the cheers! The enemy cheered before [his] charges, our men cheered after repulsing [them]. For two hours they appeared to drive our line back until it was at almost right angles with my [the XV Corps'] line. Can you imagine how my heart throbbed, every pulsation grew more rapid. There I sat under a big oak tree . . . only 600 yards from the main line of [enemy] works, from which solid shot was being thrown and case & shells, too, with fearful rapidity at and over us. I was anxious not from fear, but dread that we might lose our advantage, the ground we had gained and again be compelled to retake it by charges. At three o'clock the tide of war seemed rolling back. I could not mistake those cheers and that firing—the enemy at last were checked and being driven oh, how rapidly. At 4 P.M. we had regained our old lines and the fighting on the left had subsided like a fierce rain & wind storm, [and] only gusts and sobs sounded in the ear.

Taylor was mistaken in surmising that the XVII Corps had reestablished its former position; it had not. But it had succeeded in stemming the Confederate onslaught, being aided in that endeavor by reinforcements sent from Smith's division of the XV Corps. Hood thereupon ordered two of Cheatham's divisions to attack that sector of the Union front held by Smith's division, which by then had come under the command of Lightburn as a consequence of Smith's taking charge of the XV Corps in place of John Logan, who, as its senior major general, now headed the Army of the Tennessee owing to McPherson's death. Taylor vividly describes what happened next as the largest, fiercest battle of the entire Atlanta Campaign roared to a climax:

My attention was called from this [the subsiding of combat on the Union left] by a Captain saying: "Look, Major, look!" What a grand sight—I was almost entranced by it. The enemy's Hindman's Division of 25 regiments [commanded by Maj. Gen. John C. Brown] were moving out of the works and deploying in line of battle. How well they moved, how perfectly and how grandly did the first line advance with the beautiful "battle flags" waving in the breeze [and] not an unsteady step nor a waver was perceptible in it. Anon they moved by the right flank, then halted and fronted and a second line was formed. I saw them complete it and an Officer rode a short distance from us to advance their skirmish line & [I] ordered several of the men to shoot him but they failed. I then saw the 4th Div [skirmish] line [to the left] break and run, called my line to attention and remained until I saw their line of battle approach within 250 yards of us.

By the retreat of the 4th Div. [skirmishers], my left was exposed and I marched back to my first reserve. Here I shall tell you that as soon as I saw the 2nd [Confederate battle] line form and the advance toward us begin, I sent back word. At the reserve we halted and again opened [fire] on the enemy, drove in his skirmishers and, when the [Confederate battle] line flanked us on the left and was within about fifty yards [I] rallied on the 2nd reserve. Here we made a fine little fight and broke their [skirmish] lines but being outflanked we were compelled to fall back. In making this distance part of the time I moved leisurely and part lively—picked up a canteen of coffee and moved for the [Union] works when some miserable [Southern] traitor with murder stamped on his countenance deliberately shot at me. But I was a little too far away & his bullet almost spent struck me a glancing blow in the muscles of my left thigh as I was lifting my leg to run. I knew if I was hurt it would bleed in my boot so I went on as rapidly as I could as other bullets were dropping too close to make it at all pleasant.

The rebels reformed and advanced upon our main line in three columns. Two columns moved up on our right . . . and were both after a heavy fire severely repulsed and took refuge behind some outbuildings and a large house where they reformed. About twenty yards from our works on the left of the rail and wagon roads is a ravine which at the railroad was so thick [with] undergrowth as to completely screen as well as protect an advancing column. The railway through our lines is built in a cut about 15 feet deep. On the left of the railway was a section of artillery occupying three rods [about 50 feet]. [The] width of cut at top [is] 3 rods [and] between cut & wagon road on right of railroad is a space four rods wide [65 feet], protected by a log earthwork terminating a few feet from the railway. The wagon road is almost two rods [33 feet] wide and on the right of this road was a section of artillery [two cannons] occupying about three rods more and all of this space of 15 rods had only one company in position [and only] one platoon [of] 16 men . . . was between the [artillery] section in the space between the wagon and rail roads. The cut was open and clear, nowhere was it occupied by troops nor blockaded, the wagon road was likewise open and unoccupied by works or troops. When Col. [Wells S.] Jones, 53rd Ohio, came for the reserve, he suggested to Genl's Smith & Lightburn the propriety of burning said outbuildings & placing his regiment in rear of this artillery to support it and shut the gaps, yet they disdained the proffer and they were not filled.

Concealed by the dense smoke of the artillery the first we saw of the third [enemy] column it was rushing in the gap in the wagon road around the low works between the rail & wagon roads and over the parapet at the guns. Every one was surprised but none thought of moving, the platoon between the guns fired and fought with bayonets & butts of their muskets, the other platoon lying down in the rear of it could not fire without killing their comrades and artillerists in their front. Some of the men [in the platoon] were bleeding at the ears and nose from the concussion, yet fought until all were killed, wounded and captured except four. I started across the road to move the other platoon to make it effective when I happened to look at the upper end of the cut and saw a column of rebels *deploying* from it. This 2nd [Union] platoon was shut in by a line of fire on every side and to avoid capture retired. Simultaneously the whole line began to fall back. Gen'l Smith moved over to the right & Lightburn went off on a run. I heard no order given and after vainly trying to rally the men dashed into the woods, where on a small ridge I halted a few men and again tried to form [a line]. Then, hearing someone shouting *halt,* I went to the road supposing it was one of our officers trying to form the line. I came within five feet of a rebel officer on a white horse with a flag in his hand and a revolver in the other. I took this in at a glance, he said "Halt! we'll treat you like men." I said, "Hell, stranger, this is no place for me to halt!" and went for the bushes. I told a man at my elbow to shoot him. [In his diary for July 22, Taylor stated that the Confederate officer shot at him as he fled.] When I got out of his reach I went slow and got some men of the 47th to go down and run off two caissons which the artillery had abandoned. I then went down to the works. Lt. Col. Wallace & Capt. [Hananiah D.] Pugh [of the Forty-seventh Ohio] while striving vainly to form a line were captured, [Capt. Charles] Haltentof wounded and Adjt. [John W.] Duecherman wounded. Only four officers [of the Forty-seventh Ohio] were left.

I was relieved as Div. Picket Officer to take command of the regiment and reformed it very quickly and then was ordered forward and marched up the road some distance by the flank. . . . I [then] was ordered into line [and] to fix bayonets and to retake the works [with] one small company and [some men] from other regiments [who] joined me. . . . I advanced on the "double quick" and got within a few feet of the works, when such was the hail storm of fire and bullets which swept over us that both flag staffs were shot off, the regiment's standard was torn from the staff by the fragment of a shell, one color bearer killed, and a color corporal wounded, [and] others as a matter of course fell. Finding I was completely flanked [I] withdrew to avoid capture.

On account of an entanglement and the dense undergrowth in my rear, the command became separated. Meeting a line upon a ridge in the rear advancing I halted and with them made a second assault. A portion of the regiment under Capt. [Joseph L.] Pinkerton went to the right of the railroad. I kept on the left, we reached the point I reached in the first assault but were again compelled to fall back. This time we went to an open field when reforming as best we could, [then] again advanced. Upon reaching the crest of the first ridge the men halted and laid down to avoid the sheet of bullets which swept over. I could not urge them forward. Then I determined to do by example what entreaty, orders and discipline had failed to do. I pushed through the line, dashed ahead, shouting, cheering and exhorting [but] only one man followed. I went fifty yards in this manner and finally halted and gave three lusty cheers, [then] without waiting I pushed on and in a moment had the pleasure to see that the line was hurrying [forward]. I soon struck another line [of Federal troops] on the left which had halted. I sent Capt. Pinkerton & Lieut. [William] Brachman with a portion of the regiment again on the right, while I with the rest of it and the remainder of [the men from other regiments] pushed up immediately on the left, pouring a continuous and deadly fire upon the enemy, driving them from their works and recapturing a section of artillery upon the left of the railway which the [Rebels] had turned upon us and which with the assistance of [a number of enlisted men] I turned and served with considerable effect upon them until they withdrew from range. . . .

Lightburn said we had disgraced ourselves. I told him "that was enough of that! I would show him whether we had." I had no idea that I had such determination, such stubbornness or strength. I was almost frantic, yet perfectly sane—directed the entire line. *All* the officers obeyed me and ran to me for advice and directions. I saw men perform prodigies, display the most unparalleled valor. One man, Joseph Bedol [Bedall] of Co. "D", was surrounded and knocked by rebels, he came to, jumped up & wounded them and knocked a fourth down with his fist and escaped.

Dear, I would not write this to any other one as it seems egotistical, but is nevertheless true. The men of the Division give me credit for much more.

Taylor ended his battle narrative by stating that "our loss was large . . . in killed, wounded & prisoners." The Second Division suffered 678 casualties, of which 103 came from the Forty-seventh Ohio, whose number was reduced to a mere 150. But he also declared that the "enemy loss much heavier as we buried two of them for every one of our own and picked up almost as many wounded of their forces as of ours after they had one hour to carry off their dead and wounded." Hence, the "result of the affair . . . was a glorious victory to us. They attempted to crush the left wing of the army composed of the Army of the Tennessee but most signally failed [and] in the whole affair lost three to one."[2]

In essence, Taylor's description of what occurred on that part of the Union front held by the Second Division of the XV Corps is accurate, being supported by other accounts, both official and unofficial, Confederate as well as Federal.[3] Thus Morgan Smith and Lightburn did ignore Col. Wells Jones's proposal to block the railroad cut and burn the nearby buildings; and Light-burn in his report (Smith filed none) tried to conceal this blunder by blaming the enemy breakthrough on his own men, whom he accused of becoming "panic-stricken" when "one regiment" (meaning the Forty-seventh Ohio) was routed.[4] Yet because he could not view the battlefield as a whole or know of actions taken by the top commanders, Taylor exaggerated the role of his scratch force in driving back the Confederates. This was accomplished mainly by the devastating artillery barrage organized by Sherman himself and by a strong counterattack carried out by troops brought over from the XVI Corps' sector by Logan, who led them in person. Finally, contrary to Taylor's estimate, the Confederates did not lose three times as many men as the Federals, their casualties having totaled approximately 5,500; those of the Army of the Tennessee came to 3,722, nearly 2,000 of whom were in the XVII Corps.[5]

Even so, Taylor was correct in stating that the battle was a "glorious victory," for never before and never afterward during the campaign did the Confederates have a better chance of inflicting a major, perhaps decisive, defeat on Sherman's army than they did on July 22 outside Atlanta. And in helping win this victory, Taylor displayed, in this his first experience of large-scale combat, valor, presence of mind, and above all indefatigable determination. He had every right to feel proud of his performance and to express his pride when writing Netta on July 26.

As his pen rapidly—sometimes too rapidly—filled with words page after page of what he termed in his diary for July 26 a "long letter," he had no way of knowing that just six days later he and the Forty-seventh would find themselves engaged in another desperate struggle, their opponents being many of the same Southern soldiers whom they had fought on July 22. As a consequence this warning, which he conveyed in a letter to Netta written at Rossville shortly before the Army of the Tennessee crossed the Chattahoochee, came close to being realized: "Dear, I beseech you not to build your hopes of the future and my return too strongly. I have seen men's hopes dashed to ground and blighted by one cannon shot or musket ball. I may suffer the same calamity."

9

We Had Another Big Fight
July 23–30, 1864

THE ARMY of the Tennessee on July 22 had foiled Hood's bold, in some ways brilliant, but overly ambitious and ill-executed attempt to crush it, at the same time punishing the Confederates severely. But it had paid a high price for the victory and come close to disaster—in the cases of the XV and XVII Corps, very close. Hood, manifestly, liked to attack, and when he did, he hit hard. He also could be counted on to strike again; the sole uncertainty was when and where. Consequently, the veteran soldiers of the Army of the Tennessee resolved to be ready for him the next time and not to be caught off guard again. Taylor's diary entries for July 23 through 26 convey their attitude and the wariness it engendered:

> SATURDAY 23RD. Fixed the works. . . . Reported twice that the rebels are coming. Under arms but no one came. . . . Gen'l Sherman came around, talked with the boys & I and gave me some useful hints. Borrowed axes from 23rd A. C. & fell timber in front of works.
>
> SUNDAY 24. Again fixing works—making abatis [sharpened stakes made from tree limbs and planted in ground with pointed ends facing enemy] & sitting a [barrier] in front.
>
> MONDAY 25TH. Am building head logs & completing works whenever can procure tools. Our new & most excellent brigade commander [Col. Wells Jones] has had the gaps filled & fortified and the house & out buildings in our front destroyed.
>
> TUESDAY 26TH. Worked on Cheauvrau de friste [chevaux de frise: logs through which crisscrossed and sharpened stakes had been driven] and commenced placing head logs upon them and otherwise perfecting the works.

When not "perfecting" their works, Taylor's men spent much of their time destroying more of the Georgia Railroad. This was, commented Taylor in his diary for July 24, "hard work [with] no tools, but at last [we] succeeded in turning it [a section of the track] over and then pryed the ties up, laid them in piles & placed the rails on the top. The most effectual way to destroy a road is by placing [burning] wood upon the rails at the joints and in the center & kinking it by expansion. This destroys rails and ties simultaneously."

The tearing up of the railroad provided a preparatory prelude to Sherman's next effort to extract the Confederates from Atlanta. In essence, this consisted of doing what he had planned to do prior to Hood's July 22 onslaught—transfer the Army of the Tennessee to his right with the object of having it secure a lodgment on the Macon railroad. The Confederates would then be left with three choices; attacking to regain control of the railroad, evacuating Atlanta, or remaining there to starve. That they would choose the second alternative Sherman doubted not. What he failed to foresee was that presenting them with these alternatives would prove far more difficult and take much longer than he anticipated.

The Army of the Tennessee began its move to the right during the early hours of July 27. Commanding it was thirty-three-year-old one-armed Gen. Oliver Otis Howard, named to that post the day before by Sherman. His appointment angered Joe Hooker, who believed he was entitled to the command as the senior major general in Sherman's army and who resigned as head of the XX Corps in protest. It was also bitterly resented by Logan, who felt with some cause that he was being displaced solely because he was not a West Pointer, as was Howard. In truth, both Hooker and Logan were better fighting generals than Howard; yet in favoring Howard, Sherman did the right thing if for the wrong reasons. The Army of the Tennessee had become accustomed to a cautious leader under McPherson, and Howard gave it another such leader—which soon proved fortunate.

On reaching the right, Howard began slowly deploying his forces southward along a ridge west of Atlanta. By nightfall, only two of his seven divisions, both from the XVII Corps, occupied the ridge, where they entrenched. The other five—the XVI Corps two and the XV Corps three—remained in reserve, ready to repel a Confederate flanking attack. As he saw it, Sherman doubted that Hood would be so foolish as to make another sally. Howard, who had known Hood at West Point, thought otherwise.

Sherman was mistaken, Howard correct. Expecting, then detecting the Federal move to his right early on, Hood on the evening of July 27 instructed Lt. Gen. Stephen D. Lee, who had assumed command of Hood's former corps in place of Benjamin Cheatham, to block the move by deploying two of his divisions in a defensive position covering the Lick Skillet Road, which ran northwest from Atlanta to the Chattahoochee. This done, then Alexander Stewart's Corps was to use the road to swing around Howard's right flank and, at dawn on July 29, strike and smash the Army of the Tennessee from the rear. In essence, Hood sought to do west of Atlanta what he had failed to do east of the city the week before.

Like his plans for Peachtree Creek and the July 22 battle, his strategy was a good one in conception and might have succeeded in execution had all gone as he both desired and ordered. Probably it is unnecessary to say that it did not. When, on the morning of July 28, Lee reached the Lick Skillet Road near a small wood building called Ezra Church, he decided to attack instead of defend, believing on the basis of reports from his skirmishers that he had a golden opportunity to hit the advancing Yankees by surprise while they were out in the open. Toward noon his troops swarmed forward, sounding what one Northern soldier dubbed "the cornbread yelp."

The assault fell on the XV Corps, which was deployed with the First Division, headed by Brig. Gen. Charles R. Woods, in place of the ailing Peter Osterhaus, on the left; William Harrow's division in the center; and Morgan Smith's division on the right. It came, however, as no surprise except to Sherman, who had just left Howard after scoffing at his prediction that he soon would be attacked. Furthermore, it found most of the XV Corps behind makeshift but effective fortifications of rails, logs, and, in the case of some of Woods's troops, pews from Ezra Church.

The main exception was the Second Brigade of Smith's division. Now that Logan had resumed command of the corps and Smith of the division, it again was headed by Lightburn, concerning whom Taylor had developed, understandably enough, a low opinion as a result of the July 22 battle. That opinion did not grow any higher when, earlier in the morning and just after the Forty-seventh had occupied a ridge and constructed a "light rail work," Lightburn had come to him and asked if his regiment could "take a battery and drive the enemy from the next ridge."

"Who," responded Taylor, "will support me on the left?"

"Oh, you will go over by that fence and deploy."

Taylor said nothing but thought to himself that this meant he was not to have any support. His silence caused Lightburn to change his mind. "Oh," he said, "I guess your regiment is hardly large enough." He then ordered both Taylor and Col. Wells Jones of the Fifty-third Ohio to deliver the attack, the former acting as support. What followed Taylor describes in a letter to Netta written two days later:

Well dear, on the 28th of July we had another big fight. . . . After moving forward and occupying a part of the ridge, the enemy were discovered moving around the right. To check this I was ordered over on the right and deployed. This extension of the line only made them [the Confederates] move further to the right but we dashed over an open field and position on a road. Presently I saw a column of the enemy move from a wood a short distance in front, [then] pass up a ravine near my left and between the 53rd Ohio and the 47th. To prevent them from cutting me off, I moved out of the road & half way across the field behind the crest [of the ridge]. This movement thwarted their designs and after a heavy fire the column retired to the woods [beyond the ridge].

Again I advanced but shortened my line by moving obliquely to the left and connecting with the 53rd. We first took position about 10 A.M. and from that time had very lively work. After advancing to the fence [along the Lick Skillet Road] I placed men on posts of observation who discovered the enemy still moving to the right and likewise massing in our front. Of this I sent word to the Division Commander who said "Now I know it is so when Major Taylor sends word." After a short time the enemy made his appearance, this time moving from the woods, in line of battle and then moving by the flank in three or four columns. We held our position, firing heavily and doing much execution but finding them too heavy to check we retired to the crest of the hill or ridge before mentioned where we made a stubborn stand from which we were driven by another forward movement of the enemy. This time they were moving by right of Co[mpanies] to the front, in columns of regiments, followed by a line of battle with bayonets fixed. This meant work and again we were compelled to retire. In the meantime we had been reinforced by one regiment [the Fifty-fourth Ohio] but it was impossible to withstand this avalanche of bayonets and again we retired.

I halted behind a fence in the skirt of the woods and gave one shot [volley]. [Then] Col. [name illegible] hollored to look out or I would be cut off as they [the Confederates] were rushing up a hollow passing in our rear. At the same time I received notice from the right and beheld a [Confederate] column . . . both on the left and right, the enemy converging [and] leaving us a gap only about two or three hundred yards in width to escape through. All three regiments hurried through this and escaped the enemy [by] only about 50 yards. . . .

Our [new] line was formed upon [a ridge] at least half a mile from the line [just abandoned] and as it afterwards turned out this move of ours saved the day. Immediately upon gaining this ridge we reformed . . . as best we could behind the yard and garden fences [of a house on the ridge] and fought the enemy as they charged our position. We maintained our ground until they moved right up to us and pressed us over the hill by superiority of numbers but we were not yet defeated. I never run because my command is scattered but take the material [troops] at hand and improvise one [a force]. Every officer and man in the Division knows me and will fight under my orders, therefore, I began rallying men and officers and started after a gallant Captain of the 53rd Ohio up the hill, leading a varied lot of men and shouting and cheering to the best of my ability and having every one do likewise. Our noise almost enveloped the rebel line of battle which was formed upon the hill we had just abandoned and believing we were trying to surround and capture them, they retired without firing a volley.

We took possession of the hill and I got a color bearer of the 54th & one of [the] 53rd Ohio and rushed to the garden fence through a perfect storm of bullets and exhorted but only three or four ventured to follow, as the rebels, deeply chagrined to think so small a force had made them yield such a position gave us volley after volley which made us move from the garden fence to a less exposed position. Here we soon mobilized our regiments and took position [for] driving the rebels back.

The Confederate troops who captured the hill and then in turn were driven from it "more by noise than numbers," as Taylor put it in his report, belonged to Brig. Gen. William F. Brantly's Brigade of a division of Lee's Corps that was under the acting command of Brig. Gen. John C. Brown—the same division that broke through Lightburn's line in the July 22 battle. Brantly in his report explained the poor showing of his men, all of whom were Mississippians, by stating that after taking the hill, "being greatly weakened by the killed and wounded and the innumerable cases of utter exhaustion among the best men of my command, as well as by the absence of a goodly number who had no legitimate excuse, I was unable to hold the works [on the hill]." Ordered to retake the hill, Brantly's Brigade tried to do so, as Taylor's account indicates, with volley fire but made no further attempts to charge. After a while, it was relieved by units from Maj. Gen. Edward C. Walthall's Division of Stewart's Corps, which had joined Lee's Corps on the Lick Skillet Road and at Lee's behest joined in the fighting. It was troops from this division, almost all of them Arkansans and Tennesseans, who next attacked the hill.[1] And so back to Taylor's narrative:

> We then had a little independent fight of our own—four regiments under Col. Jones, 53rd Ohio [the fourth regiment was the 37th Ohio]. He arranged our lines so as to give us complete cross fire over every part of the ground in our front. This we had to do as our four regiments were compelled to hold over a mile of space and we had many gaps and this was the only way by which we could defend them, [because] across these gaps we had only small skirmish lines. This occurred about noon [according to Confederate reports it was much later than that]. After this time the enemy made four successive assaults; my men fought from open ground, almost as clear as our yard except [for] a few brush [heaps] which I [had] piled up in front of the lines to offer some slight obstacle to their approach. One charge was made after dark but I think only for the purpose of recovering their dead and wounded.
>
> At half past three we were relieved by the 81st Ohio and at 5 P.M. again went on duty. [In his diary for July 28, Taylor wrote that during the Forty-seventh's respite from combat its men cleaned the badly fouled muzzles of their rifles "by urinating & pouring water into them & shooting it out."] We lost ten wounded and three captured. The Commander of the III Division [Harrow's] thanked me and said he believed my fire had saved him twice.
>
> I never saw more stubborn assaults & more bloody repulses. Three times they were compelled to go back and leave colors standing on the field. We soon learned that the same Division [Brown's] was in our front that charged us a few days ago and we did our best to repay them for the heavy loss which was inflicted upon us by them on that occasion. How well we accomplished this you can judge when I tell

Colonel Wells S. Jones.
MOLLUS Collection, USAMHI

you they left 300 dead in our front, [and] altogether we buried 900 of them in front of the 15th A. C. after they had been most of the night engaged in removing their killed and wounded. The loss of the enemy is estimated at 9,000. I think that number is an overestimate, but cannot say as I have not ever heard how much of the army was engaged.

The 53rd & 47th Ohio brought on the whole affair. [If] I can, the General [Smith] said, be recommended for Colonel, he will do so and he says the Generals above him will take pleasure in recommending me.

. . . A rebel officer, a prisoner taken on the 28th inst. said "Hood has about enough [men] left to make two more killings." Co. "F" [Taylor's former company] had William Weber [from Georgetown] slightly wounded by an explosion of his load by ramming. I can't give you any more particulars. Wait until I get home.

So ends Taylor's description of and reflections on what became known as the Battle of Ezra Church. Although hastily written with numerous missing words, clumsy wording, and at times confused and confusing, it basically is accurate with respect to what his regiment and the three other Ohio regiments that fought beside it accomplished, which was to hold the extreme right of the Union line against repeated attacks by stronger Confederate forces. Most of the errors in his account are ones of omission and stem from Taylor's not being in a position to know all the facts. Thus Howard, when he realized the danger to his right, reinforced it with troops from the XVI and XVII Corps—the Eighty-first Ohio, which relieved the Forty-seventh, came from the XVI Corps. He also massed his artillery in a position so that, even if the Confederates had succeeded in capturing the hill so skillfully and valiantly defended by Colonel Jones's de facto brigade and thus had turned the Army of the Tennessee's flank, the Rebels would have been met by a devastating barrage backed by strong reserves from the XVI and XVII Corps, neither of which was engaged. Likewise, Taylor was unaware that the second series of assaults delivered by the enemy came not from Brown's Division but from Walthall's Division, the consequence probably of not having taken any prisoners from the latter. Finally, and as usual when it comes to such matters, he again greatly overestimated the Confederate losses, although to his credit he did express skepticism about the 9,000 figure. Actual casualties in

Lee's and Stewart's Corps came to about 3,000, with nearly 1,200 of them being in Walthall's Division, testimony to both the persistency with which it attacked and the effectiveness of the stand made by Jones's Buckeyes and the troops that came to their relief. In contrast, Howard's total loss was 632 killed, wounded, and missing, all but 70 being, for obvious reasons, in the XV Corps where, again for obvious reasons, Smith's division suffered the most, as Lightburn's brigade alone had 71 casualties. For the Confederates, Ezra Church was a total, one-sided defeat for which Hood received the blame, blame that should have gone to Stephen Lee, whose impulsiveness in attacking despite having orders to defend brought on the battle. Hood did not even know that a major engagement was taking place until the fighting was nearly over.[2]

With regard to Taylor's role in that fighting, there is no reason to doubt that he wrote the truth, boastful as it seemed and boastful as it was, when in his next letter to Netta, dated August 5, he declared that "I must say that there are few, very few if any, of my rank in this entire army [the Army of the Tennessee] who enjoy a more enviable reputation for skill, courage and determination than I." This, he added, "is highly gratifying to me," albeit it brought some disadvantages, the main one being that "it makes me labor, study, &c. to maintain my superiority."

Thus it was that after three-plus years of military service, Tom Taylor achieved an abundant measure of the glory he craved and at the same time had an excellent prospect of promotion to colonel, supposing (as he presumably did) that Morgan Smith told him the truth about his intention to recommend him for that rank and about the higher generals (Logan? Howard? Sherman?) being ready to do the same. In any event, he could return triumphantly home to Georgetown, which he expected to do in little more than a month at the most, knowing that he had vindicated himself in the eyes of the townspeople, particularly those who had laughed and jeered at him when on that terrible July morning in 1861 he had set forth with his handful of recruits.

What he did not know, as July 1864 gave way to August, was that Netta would have to wait much longer than she or he anticipated for him to "get home" and relate the "particulars" of the fighting on July 28 and that when he did it would be under circumstances far different from those either of them desired. Nor could he foresee that promotion, seemingly nigh as well as deserved, would not come until he had marched many more miles, fought more battles, and acquired more glory at the price of his blood.

I Am an American Slave!
July 31–August 25, 1864

HOOD'S THIRD ATTEMPT to reverse the tide of war in Georgia by driving Sherman back from Atlanta did succeed, at the price of excessive and avoidable casualties, in stemming that tide. For nearly a month following the clash at Ezra Church, Sherman, rendered wary by Hood's sorties, all three of which had taken him by surprise, attempted no more major offensive operations. Instead, he endeavored to force the Confederates out of Atlanta by bombarding the city with artillery and launching cavalry raids on their sole supply line, the railroad to Macon. Both devices proved to be exercises in futility, the latter resulting in a series of fiascoes that cost Sherman one-half of his mounted forces. As for Hood, he remained willing to attack again if Sherman gave him another opportunity, but since that did not happen, he had no other choice except to hold on in Atlanta while sending his own cavalry against the Western & Atlantic Railroad in hopes of forcing the Federals to retreat by depriving them of sufficient food and other necessities to remain at the city's gates. Like Sherman's, his only achievement was to lose half his troopers as they rode off into Tennessee and out of the campaign after doing negligible damage to the railroad.

Meanwhile, the opposing armies settled into a semisiege warfare reminiscent of what they had experienced around New Hope Church and at Kennesaw. Spades and picks became as important as rifles; fighting took mainly the form of sniping and cannonading; and while the Federals occasionally sought to extend their right wing south toward the Macon railroad, they did so by short hops rather than long bounds, each hop being matched by an equivalent Confederate one. Unlike at New Hope Church and Kennesaw, though, no large-scale frontal assaults occurred. In fact, the commanding generals did not so much as contemplate making them, much less order them. They knew full well that their soldiers either would refuse to advance or at most merely go forward a few steps and then flop down on the ground. Yank and Reb, veterans all, had learned the hard way that charging the elaborate fortifications, obstructions, and entanglements that both sides had erected "did not pay"—unless ending up in a hole called a grave be considered payment.

Yet the generals worried about their men losing the "offensive spirit," as they termed it, and thus being unable, because unwilling, to charge when there was a good chance of success or when military necessity required it. Hence, in the name of preserving that spirit, or to "improve our position," or to "eliminate an enemy advantage," they from time to time ordered "limited attacks" of the kind that in future wars would be known as "trench raids." And so it was that on the morning of August 3, such an order came to Maj. Thomas T. Taylor, acting commander of the Forty-seventh Ohio. How he reacted to it and with what results, he described in his August 5 letter to Netta for the purpose of demonstrating to her the truth of what he had written to her before this description: "If anything requiring extra nerve, skill and considerable daring is required Taylor is sent for and told what is desired and that I will receive all the men I want and ask for, with whom to accomplish the object."

> Wednesday morning [August 3] our skirmish line advanced and drove the enemy from their skirmish pits. About an hour afterward the enemy charged the line & retook the pits. At noon a Staff Officer came up and informed me that I would have my regiment ready to move at 2 P.M. and retake the pits. I protested against taking the regiment up and went and saw the Brigade & Division Commanders. I knew the reception we would get and told them that the regiment was already small and instead of running it alone into the jaws of death I preferred a detail from the brigade so that the loss would be equalized. I told them that I would go wherever directed, regardless . . . but if I could avoid it, my men should not. The regiment was excused and a detail made of thirty-two or -three companies. I was instructed as to the signals—three shots in rapid succession from [Capt. Henry H.] Griffiths's 4th Div. battery. The 4th Div. on the left were to cooperate. I had charge of our brigade & Lt. Col. [Frank S.] Curtis of the 1st brigade. The hour set was three. I had my lines arranged—the assaulting line, the first support and fortifying line, the 2nd, third, 4th and 5th supporting lines and a line in the old pits to halt stragglers from the front.

I passed down the lines & gave the instructions & showed them the ground and the best way to advance and told them the signal and then made them lie down. But could I be still? could I lie down? No! The anxiety of my mind was so intense that I could not rest, but step after step and pace after pace wore away the minutes and I was listening for the signal when I got word that it [the attack] had been postponed one hour. Another hour of painful suspense, made more disagreeable by a severe thunderstorm, dragged slowly by. Presently the quick boom! boom! boom! burst upon our ear and instantly the loud forward double quick, march! resounded through the woods and that line of brave men dashed forward and hurled themselves upon the enemy who made a stubborn stand. . . . [On] seeing the first line falter a little, the second moved [up] with tools and these [two lines] combined broke the line of rebels and our men went rushing down in their rear. They [the Confederates] attempted to rally and away went my third line. This completed the rout and capture of most of them in our front.

Word came to me that the first brigade had not advanced and [that] my right would not go forward on account of a furious cross fire. Away I went, exhorting, driving, pulling and pushing, shaming them &c. until I took them clear up and over the point of a hill. Men groaned with fear, some supplicated, begged &c., but the Officers helped finely and I brought them up, but the 1st brigade did not advance and I had not men enough to drive the rebels from their front. I then massed three of four companies and endeavored to take their line and charge them by the flank, but on each flank we had a hollow to cross and a hill to ascend. These I found by actual experiment to be perfectly raked by their batteries and the enemy line of skirmishers and reserve on the right of our brigade. I tried and tried again but it was killing men in vain and I sent a report up stating what I had done and what I could not do. I then received an order to fortify but I had already laid out my line and had very good works up. I passed over the whole line and examined its strength and capacity for resistance. I went back [and] sent up the other two lines of reserves and constructed my works so that both reserve and main [lines] could fire at once.

Anon the enemy came in very heavy skirmish lines almost amounting to a line of battle and three lines deep. As they always do they came bravely and handsomely up, but Oh! such a withering fire as greeted them. On my left was the 4th Div., with a skirmish line supported by 900 men, the whole commanded by Major [William] Brown of the 70th O.V.I. In the beginning of the war this would have been called a big battle. Poor Brown—gallant officer and most excellent gentleman, fell mortally wounded. The first enemy line broke and moved off [to] the right flank, the second came up and [then] third. But how nobly our boys stood up to the work and repelled them. Then I had three loud, defiant cheers given and each man felt glad. Again I passed along the lines, made details for work, instructed officers, and encouraged men. Dear, I was almost every where. I was so anxious—the point taken is of great importance and I was determined to hold it. When I got it safe and saw the assaults of the rebels repulsed, I went up to report [to Smith] in person [and] was warmly greeted, thanked, &c. . . .

Dear, Logan told me yesterday that if that other brigade had advanced our success would have been complete. Before I thought, I spoke and said yes, and [that] I thought they [skirmishers of the other brigade] could have moved in the wood on their [the Confederates'] right, broke the [enemy skirmish] line by a charge and then swept down in the rear of it. He said "yes, yes, if I had a regiment I would have done it." Morgan L. [Smith] was not pleased with them [presumably Lightburn and the commander of the other brigade] and said he ought to place all seniors under arrest and place Col. [Wells] Jones in command of one brigade and Major Taylor in command of the other and then they would have brigades. If I had the rank I would not be an hour without a brigade. My reputation is too good and I am afraid for it.

Taylor's narrative reveals the important role being performed by skirmishers in both armies by this stage of the Civil War and the complexity of their tactics. It also makes it clear that the Confederates, despite their recent defeats, remained formidable, and that barring a brilliant strategic stroke by Sherman there was a strong likelihood of more hard fighting, as Taylor had assured Netta at the end of the letter, before "Atlanta will surely fall." Yet for him personally, the Rebel army was ceasing to be the only foe. More and more, with each passing day, it was being joined in his mind as an antagonist by his own army, its generals, and by the North's political leaders—above all, by President Lincoln. The first signs of this transformation appear in his diary entries starting with July 29, the day after Ezra Church. By an unfortuitous coincidence, July 29 happened to be the date in 1861 when Companies A, B, and I of the Forty-seventh had been mustered, and consequently the members of those units who had not reenlisted—the "nonveterans"—believed that they had fulfilled their military obligation and so acted accordingly:

> FRIDAY 29TH/64. Today time of many of the regiment expired. One Lieut. [Jacob] Wetterer came to me and said he did not like to do any duty as his time expired today. This fellow acted in a very cowardly manner yesterday & I feel like having him dismissed dishonorably. These non-veterans should be sent away forthwith. They straggle, play off and do many other contemptible acts for which they should be most severely punished and yet the campaign for us is so active that I cannot have them fired.

> MONDAY AUGUST 1, 1864. Non-veterans of Co. "A" refused to do duty. Co. moved out and they were placed under strong guard. . . . Division Adjutant General came in and had long talk with [me] about the boys. . . . [I] spoke with the non vets. as to their course [and] they "came down" and went cheerfully to duty.

> FRIDAY 5TH. Forwarded recommendation for acceptance of Lt. Wetterer's resignation.
> SATURDAY 6TH. Twelve o'clock at night my three years term according to the muster of my company will have expired yet the non-veterans will not be mustered out until the 20th inst. This most unjust act on the part of the government grates harshly on the mind of every patriot.

Certainly it grated harshly on the mind of a patriot named Thomas Thomson Taylor. Acting on the assumption that he would be discharged on or shortly after August 7, he had concluded his July 30 account of Ezra Church by informing Netta that "I can't give you any more particulars. Wait until I get home." That, according to his August 5 letter, he had expected to be, ironically enough, by August 20. Why, though, he expected this is difficult to understand. On July 15, just before Sherman made what he thought would be the final lunge to Atlanta, Logan issued a special order:

No officer who shall have accompanied his organization on veteran furlough shall be entitled to be mustered out of service by means of the expiration of the original term of his enlistment and any officer applying to be mustered out for such reason will unequivocally state that he did not accompany his Regiment or organization home on such furlough.

The date of Taylor's mustering in thus made no difference. Having not reenlisted and having accompanied his regiment on its veteran furlough, Taylor could not resign his commission simply because he had served out his time. Moreover, in securing a leave by inducing a sufficient percentage of the Forty-seventh to veteranize without doing the same, he had ended up being a victim of his own cleverness and persistence. Quite likely this was the real reason why Logan's order, which Taylor surely realized was an implementation of a War Department policy designed to retain experienced officers in the army, grated on his mind—indeed, grated so sharply that he engaged in frantic and ultimately fantastic efforts to circumscribe it.

First, soon after learning of the order (to quote from subsequent correspondence with Netta), he "prepared an application to the Secretary of War," but just as he completed it "a short letter dated July 8th, 1864 was received" from Logan, which, for reasons not given by Taylor, "compelled [me] to lay it aside and devise some other plan." What that plan was he also did not reveal, but probably it consisted of resorting to his old ploy of asking to be assigned to recruiting duty, a plausible option, given the Forty-seventh's small size. In any case, all "went fine through Brigade and Division and I got the Adjutant General of the Division to try it at Corps, but Logan thought he detected my scheme and told the Adjutant that he appreciated my services highly and did not wish to lose me this campaign and therefore would take charge of the document."[1]

Neither Taylor's letters nor his diary indicates when this exchange occurred, but a good guess would be on or about August 10. If so, that would account for the sudden and drastic change both of content and tone in a letter to Netta that he started on that day but that, according to his diary, he was "prevented by business" from completing until the following day. It began with a response to a letter dated August 4 from Netta that he had received on August 9 in which she described her reaction to his "long and interesting" account of the July 22 battle: "How desperate the struggle, and how thankful I am to think that you escaped with only a slight wound. I wonder you were not killed. I shuddered and my very blood ran cold in my veins as I read of your many narrow escapes. . . . Oh will you not soon hasten home. I am so fearful that another shot may snatch you from me forever."

Taylor began by endeavoring to allay his wife's fears with calm words and logic:

> Dear, I regret that you give yourself so much uneasiness in regard to my safety. You may rest assured that I am both cautious and careful and only expose myself when I think I can gain some more than ordinary advantage or when duty requires. I always think of my family, my little wife and innocent babes, and if these thoughts are not incentive to caution, I am hardly able to say what would be so considered.

At this point he probably ceased writing because of "business." The next day, when he took up his pen again, what he put down on the paper soon became the reverse of calm and logical as pent-up frustration and resentment against the persons he deemed responsible for his being unable to leave the army to go home gushed forth like a torrent bursting through a dam. These persons were Lincoln and his generals:

> When I saw how matters were shaping themselves I wrote you not to calculate too strongly on my return by the 20th August. [Here he referred to his August 5 letter wherein he had stated that "I can't get home on the 20th" but gave as the reason being unable to "get a resignation accepted" until Parry resumed command of the regiment, a reason he knew to be false.] I then was uncertain, and merely gave this as a light note of admonition as I know well the effect of such grievous disappointment [on you]. Now, however, I can say to a certainty that I am a "conscript," held to service against my will. How long I shall be so held I know not, but I assure you that I shall retire from the service as quickly as it is possible to do so. Our government is a success—our rulers are despots—the administration the most despotic of any in the world at the present age—the most reckless and corrupt. As an executive officer Lincoln has proved a miserable failure. His vacillating policy besides prolonging the war and pervert-

ing it from its original course and design has cost the nation thousands of lives and millions of treasure. His tyrannical treatment and unwarranted course of action has alienated thousands of the best population in the Union from the support of the government. If Lincoln were the government, the embodiment of American freedom & independence, I would curse it, damn the whole institution and shaking the dust from my feet, emigrate to Brazil or some other Empire where an intelligent and just man governs.

Taylor continued in this vein for several more pages but added little of substance other than to assert that the policy of retaining nonveteran officers in service despite their being legally entitled to discharges was having a demoralizing effect on them:

They appear to have no regard for honor, for their reputation hereafter and are eager to welcome any event, however disgraceful to themselves, which takes them from this service. Sometimes this very course of their making makes me do more than I otherwise would, [for] I am determined to save the regiment from dishonor and disgrace. My future standing is too intimately committed with it to suffer it to disgrace itself while I am connected with it. There are only a few officers in whom I can place any reliance. Unless under my immediate observation they will sneak off like whipped curs and take refuge in Hospitals and behind Surgeons certificates.

Yet immediately after writing these words, he in effect contradicted them by admitting that many of these disgruntled officers long ago had shown themselves to be unworthy of their posts:

Parry never did his duty or they would over one year ago have been dismissed from the service. I made one of them [probably Wetterer] tender his resignation and indorsed it so that it certainly would go but it is still hanging fire at the Department [headquarters]. Then I would dismiss or recommend for dismissal men [even if] their time was not up.

The one circumstance that might have reconciled Taylor to remaining in the army was promotion to a higher rank and a better assignment than acting commander of a unit that had declined greatly in quality as well as size.

Furthermore, at the time he wrote the preceding tirade, his prospects for this outcome seemed excellent, for on August 5, both Morgan Smith and Joseph Lightburn had provided him with copies of a "flattering recommendation" that each had written, asking that he be given the "Colonelcy of a regiment."[2] But then on August 13, Taylor learned (so he recorded in his diary for that date) that Logan had been heard to say that "'he valued my services highly and fully appreciated them but would not sign any recommendation [for promotion] for me during this campaign as it probably would take me from this field.'"

If Taylor felt that he was being penalized rather than rewarded for his outstanding bravery, enterprise, and skill, and surely he must have, then he had good and just cause so to feel. In his diary, after quoting Logan's remark, he wrote, "All in your own eyes," a Civil War slang phrase for which the modern equivalent is "screw you too."

In this mood, on August 14 he wrote Netta another letter. Its subject was the same but the language more vehement:

> Were I to meet your expectations six days from this delightful Sunday morning would carry my feet across your threshold. But alas, such is not to be the case. Dear I am held by the stern decrees of the inexorable Moloch who, at Washington, presides over the destinies of this nation and ministers his gracious will. Nor am I alone in this condition of servitude. Many there are to be beheld on all sides of me who, two weeks ago cherished fond hopes of speedily seeing home and its happy inmates, still bound to bloodshed and to "the games of death" by military edicts and a gorgeous array of a circle of glittering—*bayonets*. These men have served their full term honorably to themselves and their country, yet, because of having three long years of war in which to supply their place, through neglect of those high in authority, no step had been taken to insure able successors to them. Their immediate rulers [the generals of Sherman's army] cry out "You cannot resign now in the face of the enemy, I will not accept your resignation. You will be dishonorably dismissed from the service for resigning in front of the enemy." Perchance you forward it in order to be dismissed and then be relieved from this disgraceful thraldom. Understanding this full well, they make your application travel through every foot of this circumlocution office, timing its rest so nicely that it will scarcely reach the goal ere the

campaign is ended and yet will come down to you with disgrace and dishonor stamped upon it. Thus recommended they will send you forth to struggle in the fierce battle of the world and endure the jeers and taunts of those who abide in the country round about.

A lieutenant in my regiment on the evening of the 5th August was in my quarters gaily laughing over "the times" that we would have when at home and occasionally discussing this question of the imprisonment of the officers. A detail came, he went on duty. Fifteen minutes and from blooming youth and health—a perfect man—he lies wounded, crippled, marred for life—one leg shot away. And now he goes back to his mother bearing this indisputable evidence of the despotism of our military rulers. That man's time had expired on the 29th July 1864. . . .

Oh, how I loath such a system to see brave men weaned from the government by the tyranny of its administrative officers. Yet such is the case and I assure you that it is something fearful to hear the imprecations which these thoughtless men use against the government. [Yet] I, even I, must confess that occasionally I confound the two and frequently find myself inveighing most strongly against the entire concern. I never was an admirer of Lincoln and now I enjoy a good hearty laugh almost daily at my original Lincoln "Conscript Officers."

As great as it was, the bitterness of this outburst was far exceeded by that in his next letter, dated August 17. Triggering it was an August 9 letter from Netta who, obviously still unaware that he would be unable to come home any time soon, took it for granted that her husband would arrive before long in Georgetown and no longer be a soldier: "Oh how thankful I shall be to see you safe at home. You will come soon, let nothing prolong your stay [in the army]. I am so impatient."

Taylor began his reply to these words with a touch of sarcasm: "Well my dear, you want me to come home soon. I reciprocate that wish; desire to leave the service and come home." Then suddenly he broke into another angry tirade, angrier than the previous ones:

Yet I cannot—I am an *American Slave* of Anglo-Saxon I descent. Abraham Lincoln is my *master* and John A. Logan the man with the *lash,* standing o'er us and letting it fall with all its horrid force when we swerve either to the right or left or hesitate in marching to the altar of sacrifice. I cannot form any estimate of the term of service to which I shall be held, and cannot therefore bid you hope for my speedy arrival or give you any satisfaction as to when I shall be permitted to come. I am Abraham Lincoln's *thing,* [a] *machine* and my only hope is that the Great God will endow me with strength to endure all, suffer all and accomplish all that I may be required to perform and bring me forth from this strife unto my family unhurt and unharmed.

After a couple of paragraphs of the same kind in which he again referred to himself as an *"American Slave,"* Taylor concluded with a de facto apology to Netta for his outburst and an exhortation to be brave during this time of tribulation:

This style of writing will probably have a tendency to depress your spirits, but dear, do not become discouraged, you know the darkest hour is just before the day and the silver lining to this most ominous cloud will anon appear and shed the most glorious effulgence around our hearthstone and family circle. A just God rules over all and trust in his mercy and saving power. I think when the campaign is o'er I will be permitted to come home. That may be in a short time. I intend to demean myself to come out honorably, uprightly and proudly so that you and our offspring will hereafter feel a just pride in referring to it.

Meanwhile, although he did not mention them in his correspondence with Netta, events had been transpiring in the command structure of the Second Division, XV Corps, that did nothing to lessen Taylor's dissatisfaction with his situation but only increased it. First, on August 5, Morgan Smith went on sick leave, the consequence of an old wound. This made little difference; Lightburn again took command of the division, and the highly competent Col. Wells Jones once more headed the Second Brigade. But then on August 17, Howard, who for good reason did not deem Lightburn qualified to lead a division, replaced him with Brig. Gen. William B. Hazen of the IV Corps, thereby causing Lightburn again to revert to his brigade command, in which capacity he was put out of action two days afterward when a Confederate bullet plowed a furrow along the side of his head.[3]

General William B. Hazen.
Miller, ed., Photographic History, *10: 89.*

Howard could not have made a better choice than Hazen. Only thirty-three and a West Pointer, he possessed a stalwart physique, a brilliant intellect, and a superb combat record, beginning with Shiloh and including Perryville, Stone's River, and Missionary Ridge. He was the ablest young general in Sherman's entire army and long overdue for a division command.

Given Lightburn's less-than-sparkling performances on July 22 and 28, it might be assumed that Taylor welcomed having such an accomplished professional placed in command of his division. Not so. He knew nothing about Hazen other than that he came from the Army of the Cumberland and was a West Point product, neither of which impressed the soldiers of the Army of the Tennessee, for they regarded themselves as superior fighters to the Cumberlanders and were proud of the fact that none of their corps or, hitherto, division commanders hailed from the military academy.[4] Thus when Hazen, who found the division in "wretched condition" with disproportionate numbers of its troops performing rear area duties or simply malingering, issued a series of orders designed to return them to the fighting ranks,[5] Taylor reacted with scorn in his diary:

> WEDNESDAY 24TH/64. Gen'l. Hazen attempting to institute reform and increase his effective strength, by arming all Clerks, Company Cooks, & Servants. Also ordering regimental smiths, armorers and butchers to their regiments. This is a big thing on paper, but in great measure impracticable. His wagon train is a humbug. It requires as many, if not more, men now, as before.

Actually, Hazen's reforms increased the Second Division's combat strength from a paltry 1,700—little more than that of an average brigade at this stage of the war—to 2,200, and in only one week.[6] Moreover, no one should have appreciated the improvement more than Taylor, who in his August 22 diary entry commented sarcastically about continuing to perform the "farce" of commanding fifty-nine privates, sixteen corporals, and fourteen sergeants "as a regiment." But not only was he blinded by prejudice to what Hazen was doing, he also remained obsessed by his "imprisonment" in the army. On the same day that he waxed sarcastic about being at the head of a regiment numbering only eighty-nine enlisted men, he began compiling what with one possible exception was the longest communication he sent Netta throughout the entire war.

It began with a letter addressed to her and dated August 22 in which he recounted his futile efforts to obtain a discharge or else resign. Next he addressed a long and formally worded appeal, bearing the date of August 24, to his congressman brother-in-law, Chilton White, for his aid in obtaining release from the army and with which he enclosed the relevant documents, among them a copy of Logan's July 15 order. His purpose, he explained in the letter to Netta, whom he asked to pass these materials on to Chilton, was to set the stage for a final, desperate effort to escape the clutches of Lincoln's military minions: "I have determined as soon as opportunity shall offer to obtain a leave of absence and when once within the State of Ohio make application for a writ of habeas corpus and let the legality of the position of the government be tested in the courts. It is rather a novel way to reach the matter but it appears to be the only remedy I have left."

Last, he enclosed what in effect was a new will, plus instructions to Netta to destroy his former will. The essential part read: "I want you to enjoy everything I may leave until you marry again. . . . Then as you will have someone to take care of you, let *our* children have the benefit of the remainder—this request is but reasonable."[7]

On August 25, Taylor mailed what he accurately described in his diary for that day as a "huge letter" to Netta. By then, he knew, from orders received and preparations under way, that Sherman was about to launch a major offensive movement, one that surely would lead to a final, decisive battle for Atlanta—and also quite possibly to his death. Either way, or both ways, the campaign would end for Tom Taylor, conscript officer in the Union army.

11

The Enemy Charged Upon Our Lines
August 26–September 8, 1864

A FTER ALMOST A MONTH of vainly attempting to get Hood out and him-self into Atlanta "on the cheap," so to speak, Sherman on August 23 decided to do what he could and should have done at any time during that period: conduct a large-scale flanking movement against the Macon railroad with the object of forcing the Confederates either to come out and fight or else evacuate the city once their supply line had been severed. Curiously enough, despite Hood's previous sorties, Sherman expected not the former but the latter. Hence, he planned to have the bulk of his army circle around Atlanta, in the process cutting not only the railroad to Macon but also break-ing the Atlanta & West Point Railroad to Montgomery and the already much-wrecked Georgia Railroad. Only the XX Corps would be left behind to guard the rebuilt railroad bridge and the other crossings over the Chatta-hoochee. Moreover, because he believed that Hood would remain behind his fortifications during this peregrination, he saw no need for haste. The impor-tant point, that which took precedence over all else, was to destroy these rail lines so thoroughly and extensively that the Confederates could not possibly put any of them back into service before Hood's army began to starve, thereby compelling it to leave Atlanta, which then would be occupied by his forces. It would be a brilliant victory, made even more so by being won without a battle.

As always, Sherman assigned the star role to the Army of the Tennessee. It would lead the swing around Atlanta, followed by the IV and XIV Corps of the Army of the Cumberland, with the Army of the Ohio's XXIII Corps bringing up the rear. Accordingly, as soon as it became dark on the night of August 26, the XV, XVI, and XVII Corps withdrew, in that order, from their trenches and began marching southward. What they did, saw, and experi-enced during the next ten days is described, to the extent that he was able, in Taylor's diary:

SATURDAY 27. Marched slowly with fatiguing halts during the entire night. Not so many wagons from the 47th as I expected. During night crossed Utoy creek and at daylight the North & South fork of Utoy. Raised up & took canteen off & passed to the Adjutant to drink. He tasted and smiled and exclaimed "by God, the whiskey's left under the bed, this is only water." How badly fooled—I had taken most excellent care to carry it without losing any & lo, it was only water. After breakfast resumed march, crossed Camp Creek & formed line one mile beyond where we put up light barracade [sic] of rails and then slept; at night Gen'l. Hazen required us to intrench ourselves & construct an abattis [sic]. Are going to stay only during the night. A wise general, I think, would prefer to take chances of a fight and give his soldiers a nights good repose, than exhaust their strength in constructing works to repel an imaginary foe. Traveled on a neighborhood road—country poor—improvements worthless—inhabitants appear quite ignorant. Soil thin—in most cases almost wholly exhausted. Found some good green corn. Plenty of forage for our horses. Stood to grass all night. Not [a] hostile gun. Heard cannon on the left [to the east] a long distance. Marched 15 miles.

Obviously, William Hazen, unlike Sherman and evidently Taylor, believed that there was a strong possibility that the Confederates would attack in an attempt to parry the Union thrust toward their lifeline, the Macon railroad. Events soon demonstrated that he was correct, but for the time being no danger of a Confederate attack existed. Hood, upon learning that the Federals had pulled out of their trenches, at first hoped (though did not conclude) that they were retreating but soon realized that they were moving against his left flank. Not until he obtained more and better information about their intentions, however, could he initiate countermeasures. The idea of remaining passively in his fortifications while Sherman paraded around Atlanta never entered his mind.

SUNDAY 28. Up at 5 A.M.; woke up by a Staff Officer inquiring if any of Brig[ade] had been around and why we were not in line—answered we were on the march & had guard—was letting men sleep. [Staff officer] said it was expected that we would be in line & stand to arms half an hour just before daylight which I do not intend to do if I can avoid it. At sunrise had roll call and at 6 read orders to march at 7 A.M. At 7 A.M. move out following 1st Brig. Regt. [the Forty-seventh] stretching out. Gen'l Hazen sent an Aid [*sic*] or Orderly or something directing me to ride on the flank & keep files dressed. Marched very slow. Near noon 1st Division felt enemy & halted and began building works. At noon skirmishers succeeded driving enemy and at 1:30 P.M. resumed the advance and at 3 P.M. struck the Railway to Montgomery 18 miles from Atlanta. 1st Division engaged in tearing it up. 2nd Div. put in position on the left flank. Built temporary works and cut entanglements. Marched four miles.

The only Confederates opposing, or to be more accurate, confronting the Union advance were a small brigade of Texas cavalry belonging to Brig. Gen. William H. "Red" Jackson's division, a part of the force Leonidas Polk had brought with him to Georgia in May. That the XV Corps—indeed, the entire Army of the Tennessee—halted after marching only four miles to tear up track on the Atlanta & West Point Railroad illustrates the absolute priority that Sherman gave during this operation to destroying Atlanta's rail connections. According to Hazen's official report, the point reached by his division on the Atlanta & West Point was thirty, not eighteen, miles from Atlanta, and in his personal journal, he stated that it was William Harrow's Forth Division that tore up the track, not the First Division, which again was under Peter Osterhaus's command."[1]

MONDAY 29TH. Delightful morning. Drew rations for three days. Ordered beef for night. No orders to move. About 10 A.M. Capt. King, Lieut. [Obed B.] Sherwin & [Adj. Henry] Bremfoerder & self began a game of whist and continued throughout the day and until half past nine P.M., having entertained ourselves ten hours and a half at cards. Sherwin and myself are the best beat men [at playing whist] I ever saw. Waterloo or First Bull Run don't begin to express it. Gen'l Hazen published as his own effusion & invention in the form of an order portions of the regulations concerning marches. Miserable plagiarist! Vain man "Drest in little brief authority / Play such fantastic tricks before his heaven / As makes the angels weep."

Again Taylor's ignorance of and prejudice toward Hazen, along with his current grudge against all generals, arising from being "enslaved," adversely affected his judgment. On August 28, Hazen, as a consequence of seeing so many of his regiments "stretching out" in the manner of the Forty-seventh, issued an order designed to prevent straggling and to keep units compact. He did not pretend that its contents were original; but for the first time in the history of the Second Division of the XV Corps he enforced the order, as Taylor's diary entry for that day indicates. The result, Hazen claimed in his memoirs, was that henceforth there were "no stragglers" in the division.[2]

TUESDAY 30TH. At 7 a.m. took up the line of march upon the Shoals road. At the intersection of the Fayettevile and Jonesboro road [with the Shoals road] we moved upon the latter. Three times in the course of the morning the 2nd Brigade was compelled to form line of battle. The brigade was in the advance. At noon the 47th Ohio & the 37th, O[hio] were placed under my command. The 47th O relieved the 111th Ill. and immediately began the advance and pushed steadily forward through the heaviest undergrowth about seven miles crossing Plain creek and Flint river, driving the enemy steadily before us. Whenever they would halt and make a stand the regiment raised a shout and cheer and the rebels executed the "Southern quickstep" to a charm. During the afternoon we had two men wounded, captured two horses and a servant and one rebel of the 9th Ky. Got within three-eighths of a mile of the [Macon] railway and within 350 yds of enemy's line of battle and 100 yds of their skirmish pits. At 9 p.m. the regiment was relieved by the 127 Ill. & 30th O. Roll call at half past nine before breaking ranks showed 5 absent. Regiment is in reserve.

Sherman's instructions to Howard for August 30 called for the Army of the Tennessee to march to Renfoe Place and halt there for the night, four miles west of Jonesboro. Howard reached Renfoe Place at midafternoon, only to discover that the locale lacked adequate sources of drinking water. Hence, he moved on to and across the Flint River, then to within easy artillery range of Jonesboro and the Macon railroad. He could have easily seized the village and then placed his forces astride the railroad—only Jackson's cavalry and the badly understrength Kentucky "Orphan Brigade" opposed him—but like McPherson at Resaca on May 9, he preferred prudence to risk. After all, most of Hood's army might be in the woods about Jonesboro or close by.[3]

It was not but soon would be. Late in the evening, Hood finally determined that Jonesboro was Sherman's primary target. Acting true to form, he at once directed Hardee to march to Jonesboro that night with his and Stephen Lee's Corps, attack and drive the Yankees back across the Flint River, and then join with Stewart's Corps in assailing the remainder of the Federal forces southwest of Atlanta. As before, his object was not merely to block Sherman but to defeat him.

Taylor's August 31 diary entry describes the ensuing battle:

> WEDNESDAY 31ST. Mounted Sergt. Major [Hiram W.] Durrell on a captured mule. At 10 A.M. began mustering the regiment for pay, [but] before had completed was ordered to move into line, then halted again. Continued the muster and again interrupted by being ordered into position on the left of the 2nd Brig, when [after which] I completed the muster. Laid in line until 3 & ¼ P.M. when the enemy charged upon our lines. Saw the columns dabouche [*sic*] from the wood in fine order—let them come until they moved by the left flank which, in our front, brot [*sic*] them in line when I ordered fire and a sheeted volume of fire and lead carrying confusion with it swept o'er them like a fierce monsoon—from the road in front their advance was the march of an enfuriated mob. It was scarcely respectable in numbers as a mob in the open field . . .—was wholly disorganized. Colors advancing after some stragglers with hardly a guard and the remainder of the line straggling after. The second [enemy] line stopped by the road side. It was a perfect slaughter to them and . . . most gladly did those who [had] advanced drop into the bottom of a ravine in the middle of the field. The assault lasted about one hour, during which period the Confederate officers, Generals & Staffs, bravely but vainly strove to render it more effective. Many say the charging column was driven on by [Confederate] cavalry—some prisoners assert this, but it was not the case in our front. We occupied a commanding position & could have seen it if such were the case. The assault altogether was the least determined of any I ever saw them make, whether our fire was more effective than usual or they were astonished at finding so large a force. The [enemy] loss though large I cannot estimate. Many place it from 4,000 to 6,000—this is very wild. The loss of the 47th O. is two killed and two wounded. Lieut. Sherwin accidentally shot himself.

The Confederate attack was foredoomed. On the basis of reports from "Red" Jackson's cavalry, Hood believed that only two Federal corps threatened to cut the railroad at Jonesboro. Howard, of course, possessed three corps, which, along with a division from the XIV Corps that he held in reserve, gave him a total force that equaled if not surpassed Hardee's in strength. Moreover, his troops were well-fed, well-rested, and above all well-entrenched, having had all the time they needed to prepare strong defensive works; the Confederates were hungry and weary from marching all night, and in the case of Lee's Corps, most of the morning as well. But far more important, most of the troops of Hardee's and Lee's Corps no longer were willing to charge a fortified foe, having concluded from the July battles that doing so led only to large losses and little or no gain. Taylor's account accurately describes the consequent conduct of Lee's Corps, which for the third battle in a row assailed the XV Corps. Hardee's Corps, which faced the XVI Corps, performed even worse. Thus Cleburne's famed division swerved away from its assigned objective to chase some Union cavalry, another division did not engage at all, and the third one took refuge in a gully as soon as it came under fire. Altogether, Confederate casualties came to about 2,200, a mere 10 percent of the infantry force employed. Yet they were huge in comparison to Howard's loss, a paltry 172. What became known as the First Battle of Jonesboro was on a ratio basis perhaps the most one-sided slaughter of the war involving army-sized opponents.

This easy victory put Sherman in position to finish off Hood's army. He had on hand the Army of the Tennessee's three corps and a division of the XIV Corps, the rest of that corps was only two-and-one-half miles away, and the IV and XXIII Corps, both of which had reached the railroad north of Jonesboro, as had elements of the XIV Corps, were only a few hours' march from that village. Sherman needed only to concentrate these units, then on the morning of September 1 overpower the Confederates at Jonesboro, who by then would consist solely of Hardee's Corps, as a result of Lee's Corps withdrawing during the night of August 31, on orders from Hood, to the south side of Atlanta to guard against a Federal thrust on the city from that direction. Once Hardee was crushed, it then would be a simple matter to do the same to Lee's and Stewart's Corps, neither of which could have aided the other because they were so widely separated.

But Sherman's mind remained focused on destroying railroad track, and if he gave any thought to destroying the enemy army, it was in the form of an afterthought. Consequently, his orders for September 1 to Maj. Gen.

David Stanley, who had succeeded Howard as commander of the IV Corps, and to Schofield of the XXIII Corps directed them to move south along the railroad, tearing up track and rendering it useless as they proceeded, until they reached the vicinity of Jonesboro, where they would join the XIV Corps in attacking the Confederate right while the Army of the Tennessee pinned down the left by demonstrating against it. He calculated that Stanley would link up with the XIV Corps at noon and that Schofield would be close behind.

Taylor's diary describes how realistic this calculation proved:

THURSDAY SEPTEMBER 1ST. Up at daylight. Enjoyed [Capt. Francis] DeGress' fine firing [by a battery attached to the Second Division of the XV Corps] on a body of rebels passing along and across an opening on our front. [The Rebels were troops from Hardee's Corps moving over to occupy positions previously held by Lee's Corps, a redeployment that left Hardee's line extremely thin.] Heard rebel loss in our front estimated at 1500, but believe from the most reliable data I can gather that their loss in front of the second division will not exceed 1,000. During the morning received information that the 4th & 23rd A.C.'s struck the railway yesterday two miles south of Rough & Ready and are now engaged tearing it up. Played game of whist. About 2 P.M. went up near the regiment and saw Gen'l. Sherman, Blair, presently Thomas and Howard on the left of the regiment [where they were viewing], with our national colors [serving] as a guide, the [movements of] the 17th and 14th A.C.'s which were massing about half a mile away on our left.[4] After a little the 17th A.C. moved to the right and we made diversion or a feint [against the left wing of Hardee's Corps]. Half past three the 14th A.C. charged the rebels on the left of our line and after a terrific fight captured a line of works, the 5th, 6th Regts and the 8th & 9th Consolidated regts. of Arkansas infantry, two stand [sic] of colors, one battery [actually two batteries] and Brig. Gen'l. [Daniel] Govan [of Cleburne's Division]. The [XIV] Corps then pressed on and soon gained the crest of the hill. The sun went down leaving a heavy fight raging both on the right and the left. [In fact, little if any fighting took place on the Union right. Although Howard sent Blair's XVII Corps to turn Hardee's left flank and thus block his direct line of retreat southward, that corps halted and entrenched on reaching the Flint

River. So traumatic had been its experience and so heavy its losses in the July 22 battle that it now thought and fought solely in a defensive fashion.] Never before did I so fully feel the force of that command: "Sun stand thou still upon Giborth and thou moon upon Ajalon," [for with] but one hour more of sun and Hood [Hardee] would have been totally demoralized and routed. Smoke and darkness brought quiet. About half after eleven or 12 at night I was aroused by heavy cannonade and musketry upon our left which continued until near 3 A.M. of Friday. It appeared to me as though Hood had massed his army on our left and was making an effort to drive back our left and form a junction with his force in Atlanta.

What Taylor thought to be a "heavy cannonade and musketry upon our left" actually was the reverberation of munitions trains being blown up in Atlanta by the Confederates while evacuating the city, as ordered by Hood when he learned during the night of August 31 of the failure of Hardee's attack that day at Jonesboro. The XIV Corps assault overran a vulnerable section of Hardee's line on the right, but he quickly sealed off the penetration with reinforcements from his left (the Army of the Tennessee's "diversion" accomplished nothing), and then during the night he withdrew undetected and unmolested six miles south to Lovejoy's Station. Blame for his escape rests with Sherman. First, he did not employ the Army of the Tennessee in the assault on Hardee but let it sit by as little more than spectators of the battle waged by the XIV Corps. And, making what was bad worse, he waited until midafternoon before directing Thomas to order the IV Corps to hasten to Jonesboro, with the result that when it arrived, the XIV Corps already had attacked, and it soon became too dark to carry out further offensive operations. Nominally, the Second Battle of Jonesboro was a Union victory, yet in reality it was a monumental case of wasted opportunities.[5]

How successful Hardee was in slipping away from Sherman and how obsessed Sherman remained with wrecking a railroad that had ceased to be of any conceivable use to the Confederates are revealed by the next entry in Taylor's diary:

> FRIDAY, 2ND SEPTEMBER. Up and in line at daylight. Skirmishers advanced and rebels gone. Jonesboro occupied. Wounded [Confederates] all captured. [This is erroneous; Hardee managed to evacuate many of his wounded before withdrawing.] Town occupied by 4th

division [Harrow's]. Marched 8 A.M. from Camp, passed through Jonesboro—a long straggling village—and on the road to Griffin in pursuit of the enemy. After marching about five and a half miles from Jonesboro depot struck the enemy intrenched and laid down until about 5 P.M. when we moved into Camp and furnished details, to destroy the railroad. Other troops [from the IV Corps] were engaged in pressing the enemy. Prisoners report a loss of 5,000 on the 31st August. They suffered more severely than in the fight of the 1st inst. [Taylor obviously did not realize that Hardee's Corps alone opposed the Federals on September 1 but believed, as indicated by his references to Hood in his diary entry for that day, that most of the Confederate army was at Jonesboro.] There is a report that Atlanta is taken. [troops from the XX Corps entered the city late on the morning of September 2 after learning that Hood had evacuated it during the night]. Country [around Lovejoy's Station] level, land though badly worn is strong, possessing all the carbonates. It is settled that the heavy firing last night was not done by the 4th & 23rd A.C. Saw a rebel flag [the Confederate battle flag] made of red & blue serge and white muslin. The blue bound by white, contains the stars, passing diagonally from corner to corner, intersecting each other in the center. While the space between the corners is filled with red. The flag belonged to 7th Miss and had inscribed upon it Shiloh, Murfreesboro and Chickamauga.

Taylor had no way of knowing, but the Seventh Mississippi Battalion belonged to Stewart's Corps, and thus its evident presence at Lovejoy's Station meant that this corps, which had remained in Atlanta during the fighting at Jonesboro and then evacuated the city on the night of September 1, had joined, or was in the process of joining, Hardee's Corps along with Lee's Corps. Sherman possessed more than ample means not only to prevent the reuniting of Hood's army but also to destroy its separated components, yet he made no serious effort to do so. His chief concern was the XX Corps, which he feared had been pounced on by the main part of Hood's army and crushed during the previous night. Not until early on the morning of September 3 did he receive definite, reliable word that the Confederates were gone from Atlanta and that the city was held by the XX Corps. He thereupon announced the capture of Atlanta to his troops at Lovejoy's Station, and that evening Taylor penciled the following into his diary:

SATURDAY 3RD. Slept until breakfast. About 4 P.M. had a heavy shower. This morning a congratulatory order was published by Gen'l. Sherman stating that the enemy evacuated Atlanta on the night of the first, had destroyed eighty car loads of ammunition, several arsenals and an abundance of other stores. That the primary object of the campaign having been attained the destruction of the railroads &c would cease. The firing heard the night of the 1st was caused by the destruction of the ammunition &c at Atlanta.

The most, indeed only, interesting aspect of this entry is the absence of any exultation over the capture of Atlanta. Perhaps that was because Sherman's announcement merely confirmed what already had been widely reported. Or possibly it reflected the fact that although the "primary object" of the campaign, the taking of Atlanta, had been achieved, Hood's army remained in the field and, at least when fighting on the defensive, still was a dangerous foe. Would Sherman continue to operate against it in an attempt to accomplish what he had failed, one might even say neglected, to do during the past four months—totally to defeat it or at least cripple it so badly that it no longer would be a significant factor in the war? Until there was an answer to this question, and unless the answer was no, Taylor and all of Sherman's soldiers could not help but wonder whether they would have to keep on marching, fighting, and exposing themselves to death.

The answer came soon, and it was most welcomed by the vast majority of Sherman's battle-weary men who, like him, believed that the "primary object" of the campaign had been achieved with the fall of Atlanta and that therefore they were entitled to a much-needed and well-deserved respite from the war. Taylor's diary relates its coming and what ensued:

MONDAY 5TH. After breakfast took up Rienzi [a novel by Edward Bulwer-Lytton] and read until about 10 A.M. when I recd. orders to make out a detailed report of the operations of the 47th O.V.V.I. [Ohio Veteran Volunteer Infantry] since May 3. Sent word that I could not do this as all my journals &c were back in my desk. . . . About 11 A.M. at the solicitation of party took hand in game of "Old Sledge"—then whist. At 3 P.M. ordered to move—broke up our establishment, fell in and marched into the line of works constructed yesterday.

TUESDAY 6TH. Moved from Camp about twelve o'clock at night. Was quite dark. 1st Brigade standing on the wagon road cut our Brigade in two parts and it was some time before we got together again. Reached Jonesboro and encamped in our old position at 5 A.M. Made bed and slept. At 8 A.M. breakfast. Put up shantie [*sic*]. Played whist all day. In P.M. rebels followed and in their eagerness to find us were drawn into a trap by the 4th Div. 14th A.C. and the entire body 300 captured. Remained in Camp all day. Whisky issued—two fights.

WEDNESDAY 7TH. Marched at 7 A.M. 1st Brigade in advance— progress slow. Moved from Jonesboro via Haine's house and Hughy's saw mill to Morris mill—flour—and went into Camp about noon having marched 8 miles. Camped one mile beyond the mill. Afternoon completed "Rienzi" and played Whist and old sledge. At night [army] received order of thanks from Lincoln & from Lieut. Gen'l. Grant.

THURSDAY 8TH. Moved from Camp at 8 A.M. 2nd Brigade in advance —everything sent ahead. Reached East Point and camped beyond on the road to Atlanta. About 1 P.M. Capt. [Webster] Thomas laid out Camp and by sun down every one located tolerably comfortable.

And so, anticlimactically, the Atlanta Campaign ended. For Taylor, though, it merely meant that now he could resume the campaign that had preoccupied him for the past month: getting himself out of the army and back home. But before he resumed it, he first lashed out at the person he had so often told was his main reason for wanting to do these things: Netta.

I'm One Big Halo
September 8–November 9, 1864

WHILE THE FORTY-SEVENTH established its camp near East Point, on September 8 mail arrived. It contained no letter from Netta. Taylor thus had gone almost two weeks without seeing his name inscribed in her neat petite script upon an envelope. Furthermore, in the last letter he had received from her, one dated August 14, she had adopted a sharp tone: "I know," she complained, "you can get out of the service if you wish," and then declared that "I shall not write until I hear from you, and if you do not think enough of us to come to us now it will make very little difference whether you hear from me or not." To Taylor, the nonreceipt of mail from Netta seemed to signify that she was making good on this threat; not only did he resent her giving him a taste of the same bitter epistolary medicine that he had administered to her in the past, but to make it even more bitter, it came after he had sent her a series of long letters explaining why he was unable to leave the army and return home. Hurt and angry, he sat down at his desk and filled three pages with lamentations laced with poetic quotations and concluding with some threats of his own:

> My Dear One:
> Today I was grievously disappointed. When I returned from an expedition and some hard fought fields and after an absence of thirteen days from the mails, [I] received no letter from her whom my heart delights in loving. Oh, thou incomparable one, image of my dreams, con of my heart why, why, so tardy?
>
> > "Yes there is a silent sorrow,
> > Which can find not vent in speech—
> > Which dare not shape itself in language!"
>
> Exposed outwardly to the enemy's balls and missels [sic] and the dangers incident to a stern and earnest war, I must receive, suffer and

indure the most painful shocks and sudden attacks within, almost severing my heart's most delicate chord, uprooting my happiness and destroying my peace of mind, hope and contentment.

> "Such the cold and sickening feeling
> Thou hast caused this heart to know,
> Stabbed the deeper from concealing
> From the world its bitter woe."

This is the 8th inst. [and] on the 14th ult. you said: "It will make very little difference whether you hear from us or not." Since that time I have written letter after letter and sent order after order home explaining the cause of my staying so long here, but it seems all these attempts at explanation have been disregarded and you are still acting upon your idea that it "makes very little difference whether we (I) hear from us (you) or not."

> "The spell is broke, the charm is flown!
> Thus it is, with Life's fitful fever:
> We madly smile when we should groan."

There it is, words doubted, faith questioned, confidence abused. I have been, it seems feeding myself with false hopes and vain delusions: there is now no home for me, no place where I can repose, no bosom on which to pillow my head when exhausted by fatigue or worn by the cares of the world. . . . I can have no home if my conduct is misconstrued, my word doubted and my faith abused. Rather let me enjoy the tented field and the rough fare of the warrior. Here, at least, my sword will command respect and my word is accepted without question or doubt. . . . When doubt succeeds confidence between the heads of a family the peace of that family is gone, destroyed. If you wish to be silent and cease writing, be it so—doubtless you have analyzed your feelings and know exactly what state of affairs you wish to produce. Hereafter I shall not trouble you, will not break your unnatural silence & believe I can survive the shock.

> "My heart has been all weakness, is so yet,
> But still I think I can collect my mind."

And shall seek for pleasures here which I expected to enjoy at home. The army affords excitement and I can soon drown or smother the thoughts which will struggle and will [rise] up from the innermost recesses of [my] heart. All I ask is that you cause the children occasionally to think of their father. Do this and I shall be as silent as you can possibly wish or desire.

One cannot help but suspect that Taylor composed this pretentious screed as much to display his verbal virtuosity (and his knowledge of Lord Byron's poetry) as he did to express his indignation at what he deemed to be Netta's unfair and callous attitude. In any case, it was the same situation, producing the same reaction from him, as before, and inevitably the resolution to this tiff with his wife also proved identical to previous ones. On September 11, a letter from Netta arrived. Its date, August 18, demonstrated that she had not stopped writing, and its contents revealed that the last letter she had received from him was his of August 5, one in which he had for the first time informed her that "I can't get home on the 20th inst." But he had offered no reason beyond asserting that the only way he could "get out" of the army was by resigning and that this would be impossible until Augustus Parry resumed command of the regiment. All of this was true (more or less) yet scarcely offered the full explanation. Obviously, mail had traveled very slowly between Ohio and Georgia during the past month. Just as obviously, Netta had not read his August 5 letter, much less his subsequent ones describing his "enslavement," when she had written to him on August 14 that "if you do not think enough of us to come to us now it will make very little difference whether you hear from me or not." Relieved, and also ashamed, he at once responded to this new letter with words of affection and a portrayal of his personal plight designed to secure Netta's forgiveness for his September 8 outburst.

Three days later, a "large mail" arrived containing four letters from Netta. One, dated August 21, stated: "I've received yours of the 10th last evening and was much gratified to learn that you were not remaining in the service with your own free will." Another and the most recent, having been written on September 4, declared that "I have received yours of the 24th containing orders and letters to Chilt, have read them carefully and understand fully why you cannot come home to us. I hope my dear that you will forgive any light remark I have made on the subject in former letters, for I did not understand things as I do now."

Then, having in turn apologized for her own angry words, she went on to "proffer a little advice":

Be cautious how you act and what you say, remember there are men higher in authority and there is no telling what they might do with you, and another thing dear do not ask me to put these orders [regarding the discharge of officers] in the hands of Chilt. It would not be a week until the whole thing would be published to the world. It would be grand capital for him. How he and Fanny [Chilt's wife] and his followers would exult over it. They would say I told Tom Taylor so and so—predicted such things, but he would not listen to us [but] now they have come to pass he is glad to come to us for aid and assistance. Oh my dear do not do it, let him be the *last* man instead of the first. Dear you enjoy an enviable reputation in the Army and also in the county, and it would ruin you forever. You know Chilt is not popular and never will be again, and it would be his delight to drag you down with him. Remember how he has treated you and your family on former occasions, and let me beg you of you to ask no favor at his hands. I know you have been basely and shamefully treated, and I do not excuse the tyrants in power, or think that these things should be smuggled up and not be exposed but I cannot bear the idea of your giving yourself soul and body to Chilt and his party. You were driven to write thus by oppression and wrong, your mind was wrought with excitement, [but] when you look at the thing cool [*sic*] and calmly, I believe that you will rejoice that you sent these documents to me first and be glad they went no further.

These words reveal a Netta who possessed a mind of her own and one that could be as sharp, determined, and in this instance more realistic than that of her husband. To his credit, Taylor recognized this, as demonstrated by his prompt reply, in which he again expressed regret, but more explicitly, for having doubted Netta's love and loyalty:[1]

How near, oh, how near in a moment of desperation did I come to folding to my breast the viper now gnawing at my entrails and once more take upon myself another, newer and fresher obligation to become a victim of this irksome thraldom! But dear the opportune arrival of your letters, four in number, averted the doom and I repented "in sackcloth and ashes." . . .

Dear I know I was vexed, angry and determined at the time to strike as deep as I could against the ignoble despotism which has enslaved me. Occasionally a gleam of my better self would flash through the dismal portals of my mind and my conscience hesitated . . . but my temper and my pride impelled me and sent them [the letter and documents for Chilt] forward. Through you because I knew you would be calm and perhaps dispassionate and would therefore examine and understand the cause of my detention. . . . Yet I was anxious to have Chilt's opinion.

However, you have shown to my mind conclusively that it is impolitic at present to place them in his hands. His views have undergone a modification—he endorses McClellan [recently nominated by the Democrats for president with a platform branding the attempt to restore the Union by war a failure] and McClellan is our *man* in this division. I never was, can or will be a supporter of "honest old Abe."[2]

This morning I was inspired by your letter to tender my resignation while I yet had command of the regiment. I scarcely believed that Parry would approve it [on resuming command]—he said as much once, hence I determined to act before he arrived.

My heart is filled with forebodings. Logan will I fear disapprove of it.

Two days later, having received another "incomparable letter" from Netta, Taylor again wrote. After praising her for "asserting your authority as my wife quite effectively" in settling some financial matters pertaining to his half-ownership of the drugstore, he went on to state that "I have not yet heard from my resignation and won't for nearly a week. Parry [who had resumed command of the Forty-seventh] wants me to accept a leave of absence. I won't do so until every hope fails." In the meantime, he asked, would Netta, who in her September 4 letter had told him that although she wanted him to leave the army he should not do it in a way that would impair the high standing he had won for "courage and ability," write and "tell me whether I shall accept a leave of absence if I cannot get my resignation accepted?"

On September 18, his letter of resignation came back to him—disapproved.[3] This left him no practical choice, if he was to get home at all before the next campaign began, except to request a thirty-day leave; and as he notified Netta that same day, it was uncertain if even that would be approved. But obviously, he believed that chances were that it would be, for he also stated that he was refraining from writing a description of Atlanta, which he recently had visited for the first time, "because I expect to see you ere many days from the time you read this."

Taylor's optimism proved justified. Indeed, perhaps that very day he received the leave and at once set out for Ohio, as his diary abruptly ceases on September 17 and does not resume until October 24. Furthermore, since travel time did not count as leave time, in all likelihood he reached Georgetown on or about September 24. If so, then he probably arrived at almost the same time as his September 18 letter in which he not only had said that "I expect to see you ere many days" but also had declared that "I suppose I'll shine all over with glory when I return—Atlanta is taken—I'm one big halo." In any case, it can safely be assumed that once Taylor did return to Netta at their home on the hill outside Georgetown, he soon became a bigger halo.

No doubt the thirty days passed all too swiftly until October 24. Taylor's diary entry for that date reads:

> Bade adieu to house and friends. Arrived at Cinti. At 10¾ A.M. & stopped at the Phoenix [Hotel]. Went to barracks, saw [1st Lt. Adolph] Ahlers [of the Forty-seventh] and went around the city with him. At Davey's had photo taken [and] paid nine dollars for two doz. Ahlers to forward [the photos to him]. Continued sober. Visited Pike's Opera [House], saw Lucille Western in East Lynne—acting of high order but bore too strongly on several passages—making it in these unnatural. Abed at twelve at night. Had fortune told but forgot it all.

The following day he called on Colonel Parry's wife in company with Ahlers, purchased a pair of leggings, some novels, and a quart of "cocktails," and then, so supplied, boarded a steamboat to Louisville. From there, on October 26, he took a train to Nashville where he went to a play that night and on the afternoon of the next day resumed his journey, during which he had "a jolly company & time" with "songs & stories &c." The derailment of another train produced a five-hour delay and resulted in his not reaching Chattanooga until noon on October 28. But he could not continue to Atlanta and East Point to rejoin the regiment, as it no longer was there. In fact, only the XX Corps remained in Atlanta. Almost all the rest of Sherman's army was somewhere in northeastern Alabama, chasing Hood.

At the end of September, Hood, who had withdrawn his army to Palmetto, Georgia, on the West Point–Montgomery Railroad southwest of Atlanta, led it northward across the Chattahoochee with the purpose of compelling Sherman to abandon Atlanta by breaking his rail supply line from Chattanooga, defeating him in battle, and then invading Tennessee. It was a daring plan; it was also, unfortunately for Hood and the Confederacy, an impractical one. Sherman, who had expected such a move, promptly pursued with the bulk of his army and pressed Hood's much smaller force so closely that it was unable to do any significant damage to the Western & Atlantic Railroad and soon had to retreat into Alabama. On the other hand, Sherman, who could not bring Hood to bay and crush him, found himself faced with a potential strategic deadend; in effect he was placed on the defensive and thus prevented from taking the offensive.

How to escape it? Sherman's solution was to post Thomas in Tennessee with sufficient troops to deal with Hood while he, with the main part of his army, marched from Atlanta across Georgia to the ocean, a march that would serve the double purpose of demonstrating to the Southern people that the Confederacy had become a hollow shell and of putting him in position to join Grant at Richmond, where together they could overpower Lee and end the war. Grant, after some hesitation, approved this plan; and as October drew to a close, Sherman was merely waiting for the November elections to take place in the North before executing it.

Taylor, of course, knew nothing of these matters, and upon arriving in Chattanooga was unable, as he notified Netta, "to ascertain exactly where our command is," other than that "two days ago they were about seven miles below Ga[y]lesville [Alabama]" and that Sherman's base of operations was Rome, Georgia. Hence the following day, October 29, he took a train that carried him and his baggage to Kingston, where he spent the night sleeping on a floor, and then continued by the same mode of transportation to Rome. There, on October 31, he joined a wagon train carrying other officers in quest of their units, and at sundown found and rejoined the regiment at Cave Springs, Georgia, near the Alabama line.

He neither intended nor expected to remain with it long. On the way to Chattanooga, so he had informed Netta in his October 28 letter, "I saw several officers who have been recently discharged and from what they say I think I shall be able to be home by the 17th of January and perhaps much earlier. As soon as I settle my accounts I intend to make application to be mustered out." Moreover, although for the time being he refrained from telling Netta, while in Chattanooga he had met a quartermaster officer who offered him a position in his department that paid $125 a month and rations. What a lucrative, safe, yet honorable way to finish out the war!

It was not to happen. Soon after rejoining the regiment, he learned, as he notified Netta on November 7, "I could not be mustered out until the end of the present campaign, an order having been issued to that effect." This campaign, he added, "is involved in mystery but all agree in believing *that it looks seaward.*" Should this prove true, "I may not be able to get out [of the army] much before February," in which case "I shall not enter the Q.M. department," the offer to join he also reported in this letter, "but come directly home to you or rather have you and Carr meet me in New York and make a tour of our family and [home] county [in New Jersey]."

As for the present, he was "working on the records of a court martial of which I am the Judge Advocate. It seems that I have choice of positions. Gen'l. Hazen has solicited me to act as his Judge Advocate and I have been informed that when Gen'l. Logan returns [from campaigning for Lincoln's reelection in Illinois] I shall have a position on his staff suitable to my rank." Evidently, Hazen had taken favorable notice of Taylor's professional qualifications and intellectual qualities, and in turn Taylor's attitude toward the general probably had become more positive, owing to measures he had taken to tighten discipline in the division.[4] And it would seem that Taylor had forgiven Logan for having turned him into an "American slave"—after all, it was flattering to have one's services deemed indispensable by one's corps commander, especially if that commander was John "Black Jack" Logan.

Taylor wrote his November 7 letter at Ruff's Station, twelve miles north of Atlanta, where Sherman was concentrating his troops for the march to the sea. The following day, the presidential election took place, and the Ohio troops who were old enough and wished to vote did so. Taylor, according to his diary entry for November 8, "organized the election" in the Forty-seventh Ohio, but so few McClellan tickets showed up at the polling booth that he did not bother to cast a ballot himself. Contrary to his prediction to Netta that the Second Division was for McClellan, it went overwhelmingly for Lincoln, as did the army as a whole. The men believed that victory for "Father Abraham" guaranteed victory in the war.

The day after the election, Taylor again addressed Netta. This time there was no mention whatsoever of trying to obtain a discharge and returning home. His opening paragraph made the reason for this abundantly clear:

We are now about to sever our connection with the United States— to cast adrift upon this uncertain world. It is a glorious "old expedition" and I think will prove such a success as will cause the sun of the Confederacy to go down without leaving the faintest glimmer of light upon the political horizon. What a happy termination that will be. How amply will it repay us for all the blood that has been shed and the treasure expended in the suppression of this most nefarious rebellion. How gratifying it shall prove to my family and to me that I formed one of so glorious an expedition—that I was in the first blast of the bugles and remained until the horrid body of this rebellion shall have been quivering in the last agonies of death.

Taylor, who once had described himself to Netta as being an "enthusiast," again was feeling enthusiastic about the war. The prospect of marching through Georgia to the sea aroused this feeling in him. How far, far more exciting it would be than sitting in a quartermaster's office in Chattanooga tallying figures and filling out forms! And it truly would be a glorious expedition, one in which glory and perhaps promotion could be achieved, in which case he again would shine like one big halo.

The march was to begin soon—so soon that this might be the last letter he could send Netta before it began. "Dear," he advised her in the next and closing paragraph,

you will probably not receive a line of any description from me under two months. The reason is obvious. The railroad will be destroyed [from Atlanta] to Dalton, communications will have closed with America.[5] There will be no post in the rear—forward, forward—on all sides the enemy—our only safeguard our trusty rifles, our only hope success. We are going, going 'To the cottage by the sea'—and I shall write to you immediately upon crossing its threshold.

Nearly two months passed before Netta received another letter from her husband. And when it came, it was written in a different script and by a different hand.

A Scene of Destruction and Woe
November 10–December 13, 1864

THOMAS TAYLOR became "A.J.A." (Acting Judicial Advocate) of Hazen's division on November 10 and celebrated with a "small party at Div. Ors," during which "champaign [*sic*] and good whisky" flowed and those present had a "general good time." For the next several days, he presided at courts-martial, a task that he continued until after the division entered Atlanta along with the rest of the XV Corps on November 13. "Grand move began," he noted in his diary, adding, "Destruction of public works in Atlanta progressing rapidly—but how much to be regretted!"

Before setting out on his march, Sherman, who had expelled virtually all the civilian population soon after occupying Atlanta, was destroying everything in the city that possibly could be of use to the Confederates should they return after he left. Assembled in and around its environs, he had 62,000 troops. They consisted of the XV and XVII Corps, into which the XVI Corps had been absorbed in order to bring them up to full strength, and of the XIV and XX Corps. Howard commanded the first two, which were designated the Right Wing and retained the name of Army of the Tennessee. Maj. Gen. Henry W. Slocum headed the other two, which formed the Left Wing and had been labeled the Army of Georgia. Sherman's objective point, which he tried to conceal even from his own generals but which many of even the rank and file correctly guessed, was Savannah, almost three hundred miles distant. Reaching it would be no problem since the Confederates had only a few thousand cavalry and militiamen to oppose him. As for feeding his army, he issued an order to "forage liberally off the country," thereby granting permission to his soldiers to do what they would have done in any case.

On the morning of November 15 the XV Corps set out from Atlanta, its commander now Peter Osterhaus owing to Logan's inability to return in time from his political campaigning. Taylor, at his request, accompanied the Forty-seventh. It had become, in a sense, his home away from home. It also, thanks to the addition of 400 or so conscripts and substitutes, had become a full-sized regiment again (by 1864 standards), numbering 500-plus.[1] Most of the new troops, moreover, were (according to Taylor's diary for November 6) "good, large men, and apparently well satisfied with their fate." Once they learned the ropes and passed through such routine recruit illnesses as measles, they proved to be fine soldiers.

For a reason to be made known in due course, Taylor never wrote Netta a letter—it would have been another "large" one—describing what he saw, experienced, and did during the march to the sea. So we shall turn to his diary. It suffices, except at the very end.

TUESDAY 15TH. "Reveille at 3&½ A.M. Marched at 7 A.M. Passed through a very poor country, improvements of no account. Women decidedly displeased at our advent. Marching towards McDonough on the road over which Hood & the [Georgia] militia [that served with Hood's army in the defense of Atlanta] passed when they evacuated Atlanta. Marched to Tucker's Cabin—3rd Brig. 2 & 1st [a third brigade, consisting of a brigade of William Harrow's division, had been transferred to Hazen's division in order to bring it up to proper strength]. Wagon train divided in the 2nd and 1st Brig. Went into camp about six P.M. Recruits stood up admirably. Passed Rough & Ready [a village on the Macon railroad southeast of Atlanta]. Marched at least 18 miles. Day fine—roads good, country well watered.

WEDNESDAY 16TH. Marched at 6 A.M. About 8 A.M. passed Tucker's Cabin—a real old unchinked, rickety affair, situated in a pleasant grove and in good country. The country up to four miles from McDonough very poor. This morning indications of enemy; 47th next to front. On account of its large number of raw recruits and the few officers present [it] was permitted to take the rear of the brigade. This disliked [by the regiment] but as the Col [presumably Augustus Parry] was in command [it] gave an assent. Near McDonough the land improves—plantations present a more thrifty appearance and people look more intelligent. Cotton of a good quality for Upland—and [in] the swamp very good rice is grown. Large quantities of land is worn out, although it has not been cleared more than fifteen years. The dwellings are very indifferent. The village of McDonough is a small country village, with one school house or academy and two churches; it is the county seat of Henry, the court house is a commodious, plain two story brick—jail frame. Crossed today Cotton River and Walnut Creek—on the creek are some cotton factories. Camped five miles from Locust Grove having marched 17 miles.

THURSDAY 17TH. Awoke about 7 A.M., good breakfast, good smoke and long read. This morning a pocket book [wallet] was reported lost. A statement of fact was made to C[ompany] "A" & any one having found the same requested to hand it to the Commander [of the company]. None did so [and] a search was instituted. One man—[Pt. Christopher] Smith—took a pocket book from his pocket & put it in his sock. Sergt. Maj [Hiram W.] Durrell [of Company A] detected the move and it was then found. Man [Smith] claimed he had a hole in his pocket & it had slipped down. When pocket examined, he said there was no hole—there was not. He then offered the Col. all the money he had and swore he would never do so again if he would let him go.[2] Left our camp and took up line of march at 4 P.M. Wagon train moving double and troops on the flank—moving fast. Night presented a most shameful spectacle—burning buildings and smoking ruins—barns and cotton gins appeared the especial objects of the wrath of parties engaged. In what way will the destruction of so much property aid us in restoring peace, harmony and union to our distracted country? Cui bono? [For whose benefit?] Went into Camp four miles below Locust Grove . . . having marched 15 miles.

FRIDAY 18TH. Took up line of march at 7 A.M. and moved to Indian Springs. The country exhibited a good state of improvement. The soil, however, is perfectly exhausted—land generally red clay, occasionally a streak of sand loam. Very few men seen thus far. The country is gently undulating. Camped about noon at Indian Springs, Ga. Having marched nine (9) miles.

SATURDAY 19TH. Moved from Camp at four A.M., passed through Indian Springs, a small village, chiefly frame, with one very large boarding house. This place from its appearance I think possessed considerable notoriety in this area as a watering place. . . . Crossed [a] thin creek and after having marched about six miles through a pretty good country, struck the Ocmulgee river at "Planters Factory" and crossed on pontoons. . . . Marched about one mile from river and took the road to the right. Marching very difficult—roads wet and slippery with rain. Passed over rough country, soil naturally good but badly run. Camped at 3 P.M. Marched 14 miles.

SUNDAY 20TH. Marched in rear of 1st Division at 10 A.M. Roads wretched—country generally good—much worn out land. Sweet potatoes, hogs and chickens abundant. Improvements very fair. Passed through Hillsboro, a small village boasting a tavern, school house and two churches—town perhaps numbered a hundred souls. Saw three houses burn. The creek east from town almost impassable. Made a hard night march. Command straggled—mud, rain and darkness combined made a chapter of evils to rouse any one to the "horrors of war." Regiment twice today engaged in pushing teams up the hills. Divided my command into sections. Went into Camp five miles from H[illsboro] near a church at which Maj. Gen'l. Stoneman was captured—burned rails taken from his works. Camped at 9.5 P.M. Marched 14 miles.

The church was Sunshine Church, about one-half mile south of Hillsboro. There on July 31, 1864, Confederate cavalry intercepted a large Federal mounted force under Maj. Gen. George Stoneman that was trying to make its way back to Sherman's army after being foiled in an attempt to liberate the Union prisoners at Andersonville. Many of Stoneman's troopers managed to escape, but Stoneman and about 700 of his men were captured.

MONDAY 21ST. 6 & ½ A.M. orders recd. to march at 6 A.M. Coffee hurried but the assembly and forward [bugle calls] called us into saddle and again we struck out in mud & rain, everyone mad, especially I, poor devil, who had eaten no breakfast. Saw somebody treating somebody and cried out "Bully for me!" The fellow [yelled] "come down," ran along side and handing his flask said "drink hearty." I drank hearty. I did; and strove to engage his attention half an hour or so, until I could take a parting drink—but in vain. Rested one hour, then moved into Clinton, Jones Co. and halted about 1 & half hours. Clinton is pleasantly situated—is a county Seat, has a good C.H. and from the appearance of the ruins the best county jail I ever saw. From C[linton] we moved on road towards Whitaker. After moving about two miles turned into a field & by-road, passing through the finest young orchard of apples I ever saw; it was planted with that regard to order and regularity which made it appear more as though one was passing through the beautiful [geometrical] problems of Euclid, however there is one great error manifested in it. The trees set too close. Camped at 6 P.M.—marched 11 miles. Rain ceased—weather very cold.

TUESDAY 22ND. Marched about 8 A.M., crossed an unfinished grade and then struck the Macon and Savannah R.R. which was burning. Passed a short distance beyond and halted an hour—then moved up and Camped at a place according to [Surgeon Jacob] Huber [of the Forty-seventh Ohio) abounding in molasses, honey and yams [at] about 3 P.M. Marched only seven miles. Cleared up cold—water froze. Washed, shaved and changed. Towards night a sharp fight sprang up. Enemy repulsed.

The "sharp fight" occurred near Griswoldville, where three brigades of Georgia militia attacked Charles Walcutt's brigade, which was acting as rearguard of the XV Corps. What happened in this battle—actually, it was more akin to a massacre—is described with essential accuracy by Taylor in his diary entry for November 24. Readers who wish to skip ahead to read it have, like Sherman's soldiers, permission to do what they will do anyway, but they are advised to return promptly to the November 23 entry. Not only does it contain some highly interesting information, but it also provides the title for this chapter.

WEDNESDAY 23. Up quarter to five—regiment in line—tent down at seven but order changed, [and] now [we are] lying in the cold about 13 miles from Macon. Left encampment at 9 A.M. and marched towards Irwinton. . . . Country poor. At 11 ordered to wait for 2nd Div. Sup[ply] train and escort it. Huber found peanuts and we had a party baking. At 2 P.M. moved with the train. After marching about two miles witnessed a scene of destruction and woe, which beggars description. On yesterday a party of foragers under no officer entered the premises [of a plantation] and after robbing the family of every thing to eat, deliberately proceeded to break jars, dishes, [window] sashes, furniture &c. until not more than a dozen [and a] half sashes were left and not a single piece of furniture left undamaged—then robbed the beds of their bedding, wardrobes of their clothing and cut open mattresses even to the one on which the little children slept in their crib. To complete their inhuman and fiendish act [the foragers finished] by driving the lady [of the house who was] big with child, her innocent, little children and her aged mother from the house, saying Gen'l. Osterhaus said if she did not leave they would burn the house with them in it. Another incident must be added: Finding the graduating diploma of [a] Miss Bryan they tore the ribbon and seal from it and cast it on the floor. Such an act of barbarity I have never before witnessed in all the service, yet these fiends wore the Federal uniform. I could get no clue to them—some speedy retribution should surely overtake them. Col. Parry sent me a guard and a Surgeon of some regiment brought the lady [back to her house]. I labored to adjust affairs—but it was impossible to leave the family in any manner comfortable. The heart rending grief added to the other touching scenes around filled me too full for utterance. Our wagon [had] passed a long time before and I had no blankets with me. Our mess rations [also] were by [us] and I could not contribute aught of them. I called the A.G.S. [?] and he said they could not furnish any. I took a comfort from my [saddle bag?] and wrapped one child up. And thus I was compelled to leave them. What a black page for American history! Camped about 4 P.M. at a X [cross] roads eight miles from Irwinton and nine miles from Mile's Mills, having marched 8 miles.

THURSDAY 24TH. Court [martial] met. Sent all unarmed men to brigade Hd Qurs. Marched at 9 A.M. and moved without much effort or meeting with any unusual incident to within ¾ of a mile of Irwinton where we camped about 3 P.M. and constructed light works. . . . The engagement which occurred two days ago [at Griswoldville] resulted very disastrously for the rebels, they having left 353 dead on the field, whom the 1st Div. 15 A.C. buried. Walcutt's brigade was formed in a hollow and perfectly screened by brushwood from the enemy who charged our works on opposite side of the hollow, not anticipating any force in front of the works. They rushed in their three line formation almost upon Walcutt's line before he opened on them with his murderous vollies [sic].

Taylor probably derived his assertion that the Confederates "left 353 dead on the field" at Griswoldville from officers of Walcutt's brigade, which now formed part of the First Division of the XV Corps, having been transferred to it from the Fourth Division. Brig. Gen. Charles Woods, commander of the First Division, stated in his report that the "rebel loss, as near as could be ascertained without actual count, was 300 killed and from 700 to 1,200 wounded." The actual Confederate loss, according to the report of Maj. Gen. Gustavus W. Smith, commander of the First Division, Georgia Militia, was "a little over 600," but this constituted "more than one-fourth of the effective muskets we had in the engagement." Casualties in Walcutt's brigade totaled, according to Woods's report, "13 killed, 79 wounded, and 2 missing." Griswoldville was the largest encounter to take place during the march to the sea. It merely demonstrated the utter, pathetic inability of the Confederates to resist the Federal legions as they moved toward Savannah.[3]

> FRIDAY 25TH. Marched at 10 A.M., passed through Irwinton and took the Balls Ferry road. Country as yesterday very sandy. Pine forests abound in excellent timber. Camped about one mile from the river in a swamp said to be the "Great Dismal Swamp," having marched 12 miles. [The Great Dismal Swamp lies in Virginia and North Carolina.] Rested only once and marched very rapidly—the men stand it finely. Trains of the 15th & 17th A.C. in road. The troops of those corps on either side.
>
> SATURDAY 26TH. Laid in Camp until 6 P.M. at which time moved to [Balls] Ferry and crossed the Oconee. Was agreeably surprised to find that after traveling one mile east of the river we entered a dry rolling country. Camped at 10 P.M. two miles & half east of river, having marched four miles. The much dreaded swamp is now passed. Its surface is flat and cut by sloughs which are very bad, is covered by a heavy growth of pine—the sub stratum is a sort of quick sand— several wagons sunk in it. Swamp not to exceed four miles long. No improvements.

Taylor's diary entries for the final four days of November contain little of interest other than that the weather turned warm and that the march was taking place on the direct road to Savannah. On December 1 the XV and XVII Corps' columns struck another "big swamp" and made "slow progress" through "very poor country." During the next several days, swamps and lagoons became increasingly numerous, with the intervals between consisting of "very poor" and "piney country." On December 4 the advance reached Statesboro, "the county seat of Bullock Co.," a hamlet of "about half doz. cabins & frame C.H." Here a "lively skirmish" occurred when a "battalion of the rebels charged our foragers. . . . Foragers fell back to the 76th Ohio

V. V. I. which repulsed the enemy." Taylor recorded that the Seventy-sixth "lost 22 wounded & 2 captured." The foragers' casualties he did not state and probably did not care about.[4] This was the first semblance of enemy resistance since Griswoldville, but rarer still was what Taylor reported in the entry for the following day—the court-martial of a soldier for plundering.

MONDAY 5TH. Last night began work on Drum Head Court [Martial]. This morning Court met and took up the case of Newton K. Campbell for "Pillaging a house." Pros[ecution] closed & Court adjourned to give C[ampbell] an opportunity to obtain a witness. Marched at 9&½ A.M. in rear of third brigade. Crossed fewer swamps than heretofore, but more Creeks where the crossing was not capacious enough to make easy crossing. Camped at 7 P.M. having marched thirteen miles. Worked again on D.C.M. [Drumhead Court Martial].

TUESDAY 6TH. Marched at 9 A.M. [and] crossed one wretched swamp and camped, having marched one & half miles. Last night passed a good looking mansion. The country more open—passed one cotton field in which there were stalks eight feet high. . . . Col. [James S.] Martin gave invitation to all parties present to join him on the 12th at Fort Pulaski for dinner. [Located at the mouth of the Savannah River, Fort Pulaski had been captured and occupied by Federal forces in April 1862. Evidently Martin, who commanded the 111th Illinois in Taylor's brigade, expected Sherman to march to that fort and arrive there by December 12. Sherman had other plans.]

WEDNESDAY 7TH. Marched at 8 A.M. At 8&½ began to rain—heavy shower continued until about 11. Passed through numerous lagoons—saw more wagons stuck than ever before, near the swamps roads have no bottom. In afternoon passed through a country [a] little better improved—but few sloos [slews]—timber live oak, pine and some ash. Saw the most beautiful hollies I ever beheld. At night a shower [and] in an hour a clear sky with bright gleaming stars and an atmosphere as balmy as a May morning. Marched 11 miles.

THURSDAY 8TH. Marched at 8 A.M. In half mile struck Big Black Creek, and quarter further struck Little Black. Saw considerable cypress and passed through the longest swamps, always excepting the Little Ohoopee or the Great Dismal. I have yet to see the water waist deep—men ford for a quarter of a mile. Heat rather oppressive. The country flat and marshy [and] filled with little brooks—very few

improvements. Moving in Bryan Co. Camped at the County Seat—
nothing but the C.H. to be seen. No other buildings. Cypress trees
have smooth bark and square, flat tops. Heard by rebel papers of
Hood's repulse [in an attack on a Federal army headed by Schofield
at Franklin, Tennessee, on November 30]. 3 Brig. skirmishing at
ferry, rebs reply with art[illery]. Marched 13 & 12 miles.

FRIDAY 9TH/64. Left camp at 8 A.M. At 11 A.M. had an alarm—brigade fell in. Were soon dismissed. Marched to the . . . Canoochee
[Canouchee] river. . . . Crossed part of the regiment in pontoons and
then moved out . . . about one mile & took a road to the right, on
which we continued about one mile and then at 5 "live oaks" . . . again
turned to the right. This road we left when we reached a building
containing books with McCallister's name [in them and] where the
direction was changed to the left and [we] moved to the Savannah
or Albany & Gulf [Railroad]. . . . Struck the railroad about two miles
east or to the left of Fleming's Station near a lagoon about three
hundred feet wide—the trestle across which we burned, then
destroyed. Marched up the railway destroying the bridges as we
marched, three in no., the first 50, second 150 and third about 75 feet
long. Between the 2nd, & first is the Hine's plantation—on which is
a neat modern two story residence. Hine was a Capt. of Cav[alry]
in C[onfederate] A[rmy] & killed [in] Va. On this plantation are
numerous fields which are subdivided in squares in dimensions to
the extent of the water privileges—between each of these is a canal—
this series of canals intersect each other at right angles—around each
square is an embankment with a small inlet or gate on the upper and
[an] outlet on the lower. Above these fields is a dam with races leading to the fields through which the water is conveyed to the fields.
The live oaks before mentioned are the grandest trees I ever saw—
lofty spreading branches, forming beautiful oval heads, towering
from eighty to one hundred feet. . . . When near Way's Station we
took the regular Savannah road and when opposite the station turned
to the left and marched towards Eden, Bryan Co. and camped on
the East side of [the] Cannonchie [sic] about one mile & half from
the river at 9 P.M. having marched eighteen miles.

SATURDAY 10TH. Marched at eight A.M.—crossed the river. On
east side of the river is a swamp about ½ mile wide, which the road
crosses on a fill and trestle. The rebs had attempted to destroy this
but were prevented by the opportune arrival of the 3rd Brig. 2nd Div.

after they had set fire to the river bridge—the bridge was consumed, but the trestle did not burn. After crossing the river the troops marched the river road to Dillon's bridge, just below the mouth of the Ogechee [Ogeechee] canal and crossed the Ogechee river on strings [planks] laid on the ruins of the burnt bridge. The mounted officers went up to an old road and crossed a short distance above the canal. . . . At one P.M. we marched down the river, passing one road leading in the direction of Savannah, and camped a short distance beyond in a field of cotton at 4 P.M. having marched eleven miles.

SUNDAY 11TH. Convened Drum Head C. M. and disposed of Newton K. Campbell's case.[5] Saw Palmetto, Century plant, and other rare exotics. Read East Lynne and made up the records. Day cold—living any thing but good. Col. got whisky. . . . Kilpatrick's force pass[ed].

Brig. Gen. Judson Kilpatrick, commander of Sherman's cavalry, was on his way to reconnoiter the approaches to Fort McAllister, a Confederate bastion located on the south bank of the Ogeechee River near where it emptied into the Atlantic. Before taking Savannah, which he proposed to do by investing and besieging it, Sherman first needed to open a way by which the Union fleet lying off the coast could transport supplies to his troops, many of whom were subsisting solely on rice. To this end, he instructed Howard on December 12 to have one of his divisions storm Fort McAllister the next day. Howard selected for this purpose Hazen's division.[6] What ensued is described in the last entry in Taylor's Civil War diary:

TUESDAY 13TH. Left Camp at 6¾ A.M. [and] crossed King's bridge [the bridge referred to as having been burnt by the Confederates in the December 10 entry], which was rebuilded yesterday/last night, [a] little before sunrise. Coming to a cross-road on Judge McLaw's Plantation, we took the road to our left. We then crossed the A. & G. [Albany & Gulf] R.R. and marched down near to McAllister's plantation where we took a road to the right, [and after] marching on it for about ¾ of a mile we again turned to the left on a road leading directly to Fort McAllister. Coming within one mile of the fort, we halted & the brigade massed. A few hundred yards further, near the rebel outpost, several torpedoes [the equivalent of today's land mines] were [found] buried in the road. However they were dis-

Fort McAllister.
Miller, ed., Photographic History, *3: 231.*

covered before doing any mischief. We then moved on again with
the 54th Ohio & 111 Ill. of our Brig. (the other 3 Regts. being left back
in reserve) until we came within about 1100 yards of the fort, when
a line of battle was formed in which we advanced 300 yards & halted,
this was about 1 P.M. The skirmishers moved up to the front as close
as possible, so as to prevent [with sharpshooter fire] the rebel artillerists to work the [fort's] guns, this was done very successfully. We
remained in this position until 4:50 when Orders for an assault were
given; during this interval the rebels opened on us with their artillery, however without doing any damage. Capt. [John H.] Groce,
A[cting] A[ssistant] A[djutant] Gen'l. 2nd Brig. was killed, & Col.
W. S. Jones was wounded in the side about 4 P.M. At 4:55 the advance was sounded, the column moved steadily forward without
flinching, notwithstanding the obstructions in our way & the heavy
firing from the enemies guns & Infantry & in less than 10 minutes
the celebrated fort McAllister was in Yankee possession. About 200
yards from the fort, we discovered that there were no obstructions
below the river bank, our Regiment being in line next to the river
bank, took immediately advantage of this, slided down it & moved
up to the fort under cover of the bank. Being fairly along side the
fort we rushed up on the parapet our Colors being the first stand of
U.S. colors on the Fort.

Here ends the account of the storming of Fort McAllister in Taylor's diary. Furthermore, it is written in a different script from any of the previous entries. The explanation can be found in a description of the battle by a *New York Herald* correspondent:

> Maj. Taylor and some of his command [upon entering the fort] engaged a squad of rebels and drove them into the magazine, from which they discharged their pistols. The Maj. decided to cage the fiends by shutting the door upon them, but in doing so had two fingers shot off.[7]

More accurately, he lost the index finger of his right hand, which meant that for the time being he no longer could write with that hand but would have to use the left, which he did in the preceding diary entry. It also was what in later wars would be called a "good wound," one that was not serious but that would take him out of combat and enable him to obtain a medical discharge.

If he wanted it.

14

A Brigadier General or Dead
December 15, 1864–August 30, 1865

THE DECEMBER 26 *Cincinnati Commercial* brought Netta the first news, in a reprint of the *New York Herald*'s account, of her husband's being wounded in the storming of Fort McAllister. Then, evidently, came a War Department telegram, which confirmed this report but provided a more accurate statement of the extent of his injury. On December 27, she wrote Taylor: "Last evening I received the account of your sad misfortune and oh how deeply grieved in my heart." Yet at the same time she was relieved to learn that he had lost only one finger instead of two, as reported in the *New York Herald* story, which she then quoted. But even so, "This is sad enough, especially if it is your good right hand." She concluded, as might be expected, by urging him to "see if you can get home to us once more, perhaps they will now let you resign, now that you are crippled."

Long before this plea could make its way to Savannah, which Sherman's army occupied on December 21, Taylor received a letter from Netta dated November 16 in which she described what she had done with respect to various financial and household affairs that he had asked her to take care of prior to his setting forth on the march to the sea. Replying from "Headquarters 2nd Div., 15th AC, Army of the Tennessee, Ft. McAllister, Ga.," on December 20, he praised her "sound discretion" and "judicious reasoning," which were of such a high order that "I think I shall be justified in appointing you my General Agent." As to his own situation, "At present I am at Headquarters. Here everyone strives to increase my comfort. One brings oysters, another sends a fish and a third a buggy. Calls I have immeasurable and thus my time passes most pleasantly. When not engaged in conversation I am deeply plunged in the delightful labyrinths of my favorite poet, Byron."

"I shall not," he continued, "attempt a description of my wound—suffice it to say that I esteem it a proud souvenir of the storming of Fort McAllister by the 2nd Division, 15th A.C. For which affair our division has been complimented by Maj. Gen'ls. Sherman and Howard."

Then, after describing the wounds of two soldiers from Brown County and stating that his own wound "is very healthy" but that "it will prove a most tedious one because it is bruised & lacerated," he wrote,

> I shall start for home as soon as all danger of inflammation is over. This will probably be the latter part of next week. I cannot speak with certainty as I cannot read the future. I shall perforce come by way of New York [and] Philadelphia. Stop at Columbia (Pennsylvania] and bring Mother home with me. When I get to Pittsburg [sic] will [take a] steam[boat] to Ripley [Ohio, the closest Ohio River landing to Georgetown]. My traveling will not be swift as I shall lay up by night to avoid catching cold.

This was, he remarked in closing, "my first attempt with my left hand. Please preserve." Netta, of course, preserved the letter, with its most-welcomed message that her husband would be coming home soon and this time, surely, to stay. The original is with Taylor's other Civil War letters, and the first thing that strikes the reader is that although it was the first he wrote with his left hand, before writing it he obviously had done considerable practicing: it is easier to read than many of the letters he enscribed with his right hand!

Netta received the letter on January 4; by then she also had been informed by Dr. Stephen J. Bonner, surgeon of the Forty-seventh Ohio, in a December 15 message that "my friend Major T. Taylor" was "doing well" after the operation he had performed to remove the remnants of the severed index finger and that he would "have a good hand except for the finger mentioned." The next day, Netta replied:

> I am much relieved to hear directly from you. . . . How sad I feel at your loss, but gratified it is no worse. Some may think it is trifling, but when I think it is your dear hand and that you are the sufferer it grieves me deeply. I hope my dear that you will settle up your business with the army and when you do come [home to me] you will come to stay. I never want to see you leave again for the field of battle. I hope the storming of that Fort will be your last engagement during this war.

In all likelihood this letter did not reach Taylor before he was on the way by ship, train, and steamer to Ohio. Assuming what seems probable, he began the journey shortly after Christmas and arrived in Georgetown, along with his mother, sometime during the second week of January. Since no correspondence between Netta and him exists for most of that month, presumably he remained at home until his sick leave expired, whereupon he reported to a medical board in Cincinnati to have his fitness for further service evaluated. In any case, his next extant letter to Netta, dated January 28, 1865, was written at the Grant Officers Hospital in that city and reveals that he had hoped, even expected, to obtain an extension of his leave, only to be disappointed:

> It seems that I am a creature of circumstances, that God in his infinite wisdom is consistently displaying to me evidence of His unequaled might [for on January 25] I was much surprised at after the examination by the Medical Board to be ordered to this place to await orders from the Secy. of War. Extensions [of leave] except through the S. W. [secretary of war] have ceased—I know not what will be done in my case.

There is no surprise in Netta's February 1 reaction to this unexpected news: "I cannot express to you the sad feeling of disappointment I experienced last evening when instead of clasping my dear husband and brother [Carr White, who had accompanied Taylor to Cincinnati] to my bosom and giving them the soldiers kiss of welcome I received the letter informing me of your detention in the city."

Could he not, she plaintively asked, as she had so many, many times during the past four years, resign? "I am so *weary* of this way of living."

Taylor's reply, dated February 5, took the form of a long and profuse love letter:

> My sweet one, my adored, my angel, the light of my footsteps, the joy of my life and the well spring of my happiness, how I miss you, how I dream of you and how I linger over those glorious, those memorable days of our earlier years. Oh those visions of ineffable bliss! How I doat [*sic*] on them! How my mind revels in their contemplation! Oh this delightful joy, oh heaven of my existance [*sic*]. . . . Oh my dearest one, life of my life and the darling of my existance,

how I long to have you with me, to embrace thee and tell thee of my
love.

And so forth and so on. It is unlike any other of the nearly three hundred letters Taylor wrote Netta during the war in that although many of them
contained words of adoration, this one contained nothing else. Why? The
almost certain answer is that he wished to prepare the way for and soften the
impact of what he told her ten days later when he arrived home—that he could
not stay, that the next day he had to leave for Washington, D.C. Orders from
the secretary of war had come; he was to proceed to the nation's capital, there
to serve on a general court-martial. Lack of a right index finger did not dis-
qualify an officer for service in the field—he could still grip and wave a
sword—but since he could not rejoin his regiment, which by then was marching northward through South Carolina with the rest of Sherman's army, the
army would make use of his skills as a lawyer.[1]

Netta's heart sank on hearing this news. Her hated "way of living" was
to resume and continue for who could tell how much longer? She also felt
betrayed. Instead of seeking to resign if not to be discharged, as he so often
had promised, her husband was remaining in the army and, moreover, doing
so willingly and with obvious delight at receiving such an assignment. But
she saved her reproaches for later, for future letters, letters that would be punc-
tuated by periods of silence, a tactic she had abundant cause to know would
make more of an impression than any words she might write.

Taylor arrived in Washington by train on the night of February 17, a
night that his comrades in the XV Corps saw Columbia, South Carolina,
turn into a giant bonfire. In the morning he met the other members of the
court-martial, whom he found to be "excellent, sociable gentlemen" and
caused him to conclude that he "had at length found my refining school"
in legal affairs. The judge advocate presiding over the court helped him
obtain a "good room" in the court building itself that cost only five dollars
a week, and he discovered a place where he could dine for a mere dollar a
day—a "very economical arrangement for this city." As to Washington itself, it was "the muddiest city I ever saw, every street, every crossing and
every thoroughfare is floating with mud." However, the work of the court
was "light," "meeting at 11 A.M. and adjourning at 4 P.M." and frequently
having a "roll call only." In sum, Maj. Thomas Taylor liked being in Wash-

ington despite the muddy streets. Besides, so he had been told, the soil there "quickly absorbs the moisture."

Then came a letter from Netta written the day after he left Georgetown for Washington. One short sentence presented its essence: "I experienced sad feelings of disappointment on the previous evening on learning that you were being detained in the service."[2]

On February 21, probably the same day he received this epistolary shot across the bow, Taylor attempted to placate "My Dear Wife" with more of his standard boilerplate about how although they were again "traveling life's beaten pathway and breasting the fierce storms of the world alone," instead of "growing gloomy and disheartened" they should "thank a beneficent Providence for His gracious kindness to us." Thus, had he left the army to return home, they soon would have been unable to "live as we desire, nor at all" but "would have been compelled to begin business anew"; and the result would have been "my ruin," for "I am now so ignorant of law that I would have created no sensation except of commiseration for my ignorance" and of being "scoffed at." Furthermore, "The amount of cash on hand would only have been sufficient to liquidate existing liabilities"; hence, they would have had to resort "to that odious credit system" and so become "inextricably involved" in debt, "something we both wish to avoid."

As it was, by serving on the court-martial in Washington, he was drawing a salary of $280 a month, an income surpassing that of all except perhaps four other Georgetown men, and from which he had left, "after supporting your family at home and paying my own expenses," the "snug little sum of $150 per month." And, last but not least, the court-martial was providing him with "an opportunity to read up [on the law] before resuming practice in Georgetown and so preparing him "for the conflict which is to come."

Then, having employed God and mammon as allies, he again summoned cupid to his aid:

> Most gladly I would hasten to thy hearthstone were I not convinced that it would be most monstrous folly for me to abandon such a post and such prospects as I now possess. Hourly thou art with me, I see thy smiles, feel thy breath and hear thy sweet voice falling in softest tones upon my ear. Dear, rest satisfied in my love, rejoice with me in the day of our prosperity and prepare for that joyful future which I am convinced kind nature has reserved for us.

What Netta thought of this when she read it cannot be described, but it can be surmised; during the ensuing three weeks, she sent him only one letter. And that, dated February 27, dealt almost exclusively with her having been bedridden by a cold and with his instructions for managing their farm. Regarding the latter, she wrote: "Your letter containing advise [*sic*] and directions about the place would do very well for a person that had a plantation of negroes but to one situated as I am it is rather perplexing, however I shall use my utmost ability to comply with your every wish."

The sarcastic tone of these words must have made it clear to Taylor that Netta still resented his "detention" in the army. He responded on March 3 by stating that the news of her illness had "saddened" him and by imploring her not to "expose yourself to any inclement weather or go into the mud." But then, in signing the letter, he could not resist in engaging in some sarcasm of his own: "I have the honor to subscribe myself, madam, Your very affectionate husband, Thomas T. Taylor."

The very next day, he attended Lincoln's inauguration to a second term as president, an event ensured and perhaps made possible by the capture of Atlanta; for prior to its fall, most Republicans, including Lincoln himself, believed, as did the Democrats, that a war-weary North probably would turn to the Democratic party, with its promise of restoring the Union by means of peace instead of continuing to wage a war that could not be won. Moreover, possibly because of Lincoln's reelection and the overwhelming support of the soldiers for it, Taylor's attitude toward the president, whom he had denounced as a "usurper" and a "tyrant," had begun to soften, causing him to go so far as to purchase, soon after his arrival in Washington, a portrait of the "Railsplitter" to send, along with likenesses of Grant and Sherman, to Netta. "I do not admire Lincoln," he explained to her on February 21, "but he is and ever will be a prominent historical character."

Taylor had hoped to obtain a "privileged place" from which to view the inaugural ceremonies from Chilton White, who now was a lame duck congressman, having been defeated (as Netta had predicted) in his bid for a third term; but his brother-in-law already had given away all his passes. Even so, Taylor managed to secure a position, albeit standing in an inch of mud, only thirty feet from the Capitol terrace, where the swearing in took place, and directly in front of it and so was able to observe Lincoln closely. What he saw and heard, along with his reactions, he described to Netta on March 9:

After the applause of the multitude was hushed, he [Lincoln] arose & bowed—rather ungracefully—and read his address. His countenance was radiant with hope, though furrowed with wrinkles, [and] sparkling with life, full of freshness—beaming with humor and smiling with the greatest complacency as though he perfectly understood that every one in that vast assembly appreciated his efforts and meaning. No shade of melancholy rested on his features—no expression of care or sad reflection of the past flitted o'er his brow but all was as serene and joyous as the face of nature on the loveliest morning of May. When he spoke of peace his upturned eyes, his depth of tones was [*sic*] as of the heart ascending in suppliant words to the throne of the mighty Ruler of nations. He is not care worn, is not sad—his whole condition indicates a healthy, cheerful state of mind and body and that he is full of compassion for the suffering incurred [by the war].

After his address there was considerable applause and he sat down. When it subsided he again rose up and Chief Justice [Salmon P. Chase] likewise. Chief Marshall Goodlor held the Bible, the President and Chase each placed a hand upon it while Chase read from the Constitution the oath of office which the President repeated aloud—when it was concluded the President kissed the sacred book and was qualified as President four years more.

The Hon. Andrew Johnson [the vice president elect] was then called, he bowed and wanted to speak but his [condition] would not let him—he was drunk—could not articulate distinctly and had all subjects so conglomerated that he could not recollect or call up any particular thing or names. He forgot who is the Secretary of Navy when attempting to speak of that Department and after stammering over it two or three times asked—sotto voce—who the devil is he? He was sworn and delivered his address in the Senate Chamber—what I have written I got from a party—a reporter—who was present. But his intoxication was patent to every one—was mirrored on his face.

A few minutes before the President appeared the morning which had been overcast and rainy—dismal and damp—cleared up and the sun shone out in its most glorious effulgence.

The procession was decidedly poor, almost a failure. . . . The military display consisted of an admixture of whites and blacks—veteran Reserve Corps and colored troops, negros [*sic*], Masons and Odd

Fellows. [It] did no credit to any one & [I] was shocked by it. A section of flying artillery [horse-drawn light cannons] looked much better, but the cavalry was poor.

There was an immense concourse of persons in attendance. The audience could be counted by the tens of thousands and though not noisy, boisterous and demonstrative, was highly satisfied and murmurs of approval ran through the whole assembly.

Another week then passed without any letters from Netta. On March 14 and again two days later he wrote her complaining of her failure—or was it refusal?—to write him. Finally, on March 17th, a letter did come. In it she explained that family illnesses had prevented her from writing, but she also once more harped on the subject of his remaining in the army, this time reproaching him for being in so happy a mood when he stopped off at home before going on to Washington, a place she had "heard so much against" that she had "a dread" of his being "led off by gay companions."[3]

That same day, Taylor replied. She must understand, he declared, that he was emotionally dependent on her letters:

Notwithstanding my exuberance of spirit, living apart from you weighs heavily upon me. . . . Am I gay? Ask the world. Balls, soirees, parties, operas, concerts and the stage have no attraction for me—a ladies [*sic*] face receives a passing glance, a nod of recognition, a bow. In large audiences I am lonely, a feeling of loneliness depresses my spirit and I hasten to the quiet of my room, where I read your letters and converse with your spirit.

Having thus done his best to demonstrate that he was not living a life of licentious debauchery in wicked Washington, Taylor next turned to how he had acted on his last night at home. The assignment to court-martial duty in the capital, he admitted, had indeed given him "great pleasure and satisfaction." Moreover, "I was not prepared to be mustered out and I was thankful it [the assignment] came. Most willingly did I determine to obey its mandate, to endure the pain and discomfort of another separation from family and house and my heart overflowed with gratitude to the great Omnipotent for it." Motivating him was a sense of duty to both his family and his country. Concerning the first, Netta and he had children to rear and educate and hence could not "lie still in pleasurable dalliance." As to the second, "love of my country and the regret I [would] feel in apparently abandoning her in this hour of perils" left him no other choice than to do as he did.

Taylor should have made such a forthright declaration to Netta as soon as he received the order to report for court-martial duty in Washington. It would have stopped before it started what this statement now ended—their final wartime marital quarrel. By the same token, Netta should have realized that after three years during which her husband had repeatedly spoken of leaving the service but somehow never managed to do so, he was not going to try to do it again upon obtaining a choice assignment and with the war obviously approaching a victorious termination. It would have meant his throwing away all chances of securing, if they ever were to be secured, the honors and perhaps the promotions for which he had so long sought and fought, labored and intrigued, suffered and aspired. Taylor, as Netta also should have recognized, was no more capable of performing this sacrifice, given his obsession with triumphing in his "battle with the world," than he was of accepting defeat in that battle.

Union victory came clearly in sight on April 3 when Grant's troops occupied Richmond, following Lee's evacuation of the city when his last supply lines to the south were severed. "The third of April is a day which should be enshrined in the heart of all loyal Americans," Taylor joyfully proclaimed to Netta the next day. It made him "proud that I am an American and one of those who suffered that it [the nation] live. In this struggle I behold the harbinger of our future greatness. We now realize that we are a nation, mighty, powerful beyond all conception and feared." At the same time victory, now merely a matter of time and little of that, recompensed all soldiers like him for "our toilsome and exhausting marches, our nightly vigils, our days of fasting and nights of unrest," along with the "firey [*sic*] ordeals" through which they had passed and the "countless hours of harrowing suspense" that they had endured. So, "Praise God from whom all blessings flow."

Two days later, he received a request that from a purely personal standpoint pleased him even more than the news of the fall of Richmond. It was a short letter, actually just a note, from William Hazen, who had been promoted to the long-deserved rank of major general as the reward for storming Fort McAllister. It was dated "March 30th, 1865," written from "Goldsboro, N.C.," which Sherman's army had reached, and addressed to "My dear Maj.":

I would very much like to have you along the coming campaign. It will be necessary to join up the 10th Prox. in case you come. I wish to have you at Hd. Qurts.

If agreeable, apply for relief to join in the field. You will have no trouble getting off. Have you recovered [?] Try and come.

Your Friend
W. B. Hazen
M. G.

If the fall of Richmond produced exultation in Taylor, reading this brought exaltation. It was clear that he had made a most favorable impression on Hazen, who in his official report on Fort McAllister had singled him out for praise, stating that "Maj. Thomas T. Taylor, Forty-seventh Ohio, acting judge advocate of this division, preferring to serve with his regiment on the campaign, was severely wounded while fighting in the fort."[4] By the same token, Taylor's initial low opinion of Hazen had long since given way to a high regard for him both as a soldier and a man. To be asked by him to serve on his staff in a permanent capacity and in such a fashion not only was very pleasing, but it also was an honor. Even more, it proved to him, and should demonstrate to others, that his wartime career had been a success, that during it he had achieved victory in his self-proclaimed "war with the world"—a victory that would be a prelude and a springboard to further victories in the peacetime soon to come.[5]

At once he sat down to write Netta. He began by again acknowledging that his joining and remaining in the army had imposed great stress on her as well as on himself and that it had set back his professional advancement by four precious years.

Yet I cannot repine—I elected this course. The vast world was before me—[an] easy life with obscurity and poverty [or] distinction and riches through labor and anxiety were before me. My election compelled me to strike boldly out into the world and toil and battle with the raging elements. I am fairly launched into the struggle, to pause, to halt, involves disaster. I must move on and on, hourly, daily, yearly. With what anxiety, with what exhaustion God alone knows. But I have ever, in all my doubts through all of my discouragements and through all my fatigue been steadfast to my purpose and everything [else] has been as an auxiliary to its attainment. This incessant toil, this concomitant anxiety, is inseparably connected with my choice, but in my election I espoused it all, believing it to be a sacred duty. How well I am succeeding my general reputation will show, both in civil and military life. I point with pride to this. And at my early age I have made such progress, won such friends and amassed such a clean estate without either wealth [or] resources [other] than a fertile brain and determined spirit [that it] is truly remarkable. Had Parry not been in the way I would have been a B[rigadier] G[eneral] or dead. Once in that position there would have been more than one youthful M[ajor] G[eneral] made. You know that nothing made me deviate from my fixed course of action. I fear nothing and early determined to make my temper and predilections subservient to my interests. This very energy and determination will carry me sooner to the goal of my ambition.

Gen'l. Hazen sends the inclosed letter. Save it my darling. I cannot get to him by the time stated. It just reached me today. But oh, how wedded I am to the field. However give yourself no uneasiness. I shall not go—but I admire the Gen'l. and am devotedly attached to the old officers.

Taylor followed this statement with a sentence in which he asked, rhetorically, "Shall I tell you how much I long for your society?" and then did so in his customary fashion. It is doubtful that Netta was impressed. Why should she have been? It was manifest from what he had written that had Hazen's message arrived sooner he already would be on the way to join him for the "coming campaign." Netta also surely realized that as much as her husband loved her—and there is no reason to doubt his essential sincerity in this respect—he loved what he termed the "goal of my ambition" even more.

Taylor's letter makes it clear that this goal, at least when it came to military status, was high, very high. How realistic was it? In answering this question, three observations are in order. First, throughout the Civil War only one Union officer under thirty and lacking West Point credentials attained the rank of major general and only a handful became brigadier generals.[6] Second, Taylor seems to have forgotten or ignored the fact that had it not been for Augustus Parry he would not have achieved promotion to major, much less major general. And third, despite his proud words about Netta's knowing that "nothing made me deviate from my fixed course of action," once he entered the army, the truth was that he often had felt frustrated in his aspirations to glory and higher rank, that he had made repeated and sometimes elaborate efforts to leave the army, and that no one was more aware of this than Netta. So elated was Taylor at being asked by Hazen to join his staff that his spirits soared, taking with them his mind until it ascended beyond the realm of reality.

On April 9 Lee surrendered the remnant of his army to Grant at Appomattox Court House, and the Confederacy became the Lost Cause. Taylor's reaction to the culminating event of the war, as conveyed to Netta on April 12, took the rather anticlimactic form of describing the celebratory illumination of Washington that had taken place the previous night and of commenting sardonically on a division of public opinion as to the

> disposition of the leading rebels. Many of the most rabid abolitionists and all the copperheads are shouting "Mercy, Mercy," and one correspondent of the N.Y. Times suggested the propriety of obtaining permission for Robert E. Lee to come to N.Y. City and be greeted by a reception of the people and thus would lionize all those traitors who have deluged this country in blood and devastated a portion of the fairest of God's creation with fire and sword.

Three days later, the North's rejoicing gave way to shock, grief, and outrage: on the evening of April 14, at Washington's Ford Theater, the pro-Confederate actor John Wilkes Booth shot and killed Abraham Lincoln. Early the next morning (the letter is misdated April 14) Taylor addressed Netta:

> Today I believe is universally recognized as the gloomiest which it has been the fate of our nation to experience. In the midst of his vigor and full health our chief, our President was stricken with death— not wasted by disease, nor worn with toil but cut down by the dastardly hand of an assasin [sic]. To say that the nation mourns is too mild—it shrieks with anguish. Our best defender is gone—

Most of the rest of this lengthy letter is taken up with an account, derived from newspaper reports, of Lincoln's assassination and of an attempt by one of Booth's henchmen on the life of Secretary of State William H. Seward. But the most interesting, because most significant, passage is the preceding one. After years of sharply criticizing Lincoln for what he deemed to be his incompetent conduct of the war and abuses of power, and only two months after telling Netta that he did not admire him, Taylor now regarded him as "our best defender" whose death was a national calamity.

What brought about so complete a transformation? The answer lies in Taylor's April 5 letter reacting to Hazen's note:

> I shall try to come home about election time. I believe I might set the republican party on their toes and the copperheads heels up were I to come home before the election and make a speech. I guess I have crossed the Red Sea of politics. I won't have anything to do with any set of men opposed to the war. My entire and radical change has been progressing during the last four years.

In short, lifelong Democrat Taylor had turned Republican. To him preservation of the Union came first, and he fervently believed that this could be achieved only by the North's fighting and winning the war. Hence, in 1862, his letters increasingly deplored the growing antiwar stance of the Democratic leadership; in 1863 he engaged in regimental ballot-box stuffing in order to help prevent the election of the Ohio Democratic gubernatorial candidate, the arch-Copperhead Clement Vallandigham; and in 1864, despite having stated that he would for family reasons support Chilton White's reelection, he refrained from distributing Democratic tickets when the Forty-seventh went to the polls, thereby contributing to his brother-in-law's defeat, which, according to *The History of Brown County,* was brought about by the soldier vote.[7] By then, in all likelihood, the presidential platform of the Democrats, declaring the war a failure and calling for a suspension of hostilities, had caused him to equate them with the Copperheads. And when the fall of Richmond ensured the salvation of the Union, he felt free to announce to Netta his change of political allegiance, a change that many other Northern Democrats underwent during the war, among them Gen. John Logan, whose example conceivably influenced Taylor to follow the same course. How Netta, who in 1862 had hoped the army would depose the Republicans from power, reacted to his switch cannot be determined from her extant letters, but it is indicative that in writing to him on April 16 she said that she had "no doubts" that Lincoln's assassination was "planned in Richmond."

Taylor's correspondence for the rest of April and most of May offers little of historical or personal interest. Concerning the first, his letters mainly contain prolix, banal, and often factually skewed comments on such events as the surrender of the remaining Confederate armies (so-called), the tracking down and killing of John Wilkes Booth, and the capture of Jefferson Davis. As to the second, the predominant theme of what he wrote Netta continued to be the loneliness of his life in Washington and his longing to return home.

Return, though, he could not until released from his court-martial assignment, and there was no chance of this occurring until he could rejoin his regiment, which now was on the way to Washington with Sherman's army to participate in a grand review of the triumphant Union hosts. During winter and early spring, the regiment had marched through South Carolina and into North Carolina, where it had fought in the March 19–21 Battle of Bentonville, helping to repel an attack by a motley enemy force headed by Joe Johnston and consisting in part of the pathetic remnants of the once puissant Confederate Army of Tennessee. That army, under the indefatigable but ill-starred Hood, had been crushed by Thomas at Nashville December 15–16 after all but slaughtering itself in a desperate, valiant, but suicidal assault on a smaller but strongly entrenched Federal force under Schofield at Franklin, Tennessee, November 30. Far more than Sherman's well-publicized march through Georgia and the Carolinas, these battles sealed the fate of the already doomed Confederacy.[8]

On May 23 the Army of the Potomac and then, the following day, the Army of the West, as Sherman's troops now were designated, paraded down Pennsylvania Avenue. Among the thousands of joyful spectators was Taylor, who as soon as the Army of the Potomac's review ended returned to his room, by then in a boarding house, and related to Netta what he had seen, despite feeling "quite fatigued" from "having passed the whole morning and until after 2 P.M. standing in one place," i.e., across from the Treasury building and near the reviewing stand on which sat President Johnson, the cabinet, and other dignitaries, including Sherman, who, according to Taylor's account, took his place there belatedly:

> Major General [George M.] Mead[e], [commander of the Army of the Potomac] led the column—he is a man past beyond middle age, with gray hair and blue eyes, his head does not exhibit a fine development nor anything above an ordinary mind. His manner this morning displayed great affectation, as though he was striving to let every one know "I command this army." He rode hat in hand bowing and smiling—I don't like him.

[I then beheld] . . . , accompanied [only] by three or four Staff officers and orderlies . . . Sherman [mount the reviewing stand] and mentioned audibly his name. It was taken up and the multitude rent the air with their shouts [illegible] deafening and overshadowing the plaudits to Mead. But Sherman was as frigid . . . as an arctic winter. The wrinkles upon his face and brow are more deeply furrowed than when I last saw him and his head was drawn close down upon his shoulders. I thought of the arrow which is through his heart—Stanton's vicious reasons—and the deep and implacable hatred he [Sherman] feels for him. He looked like a caged lion. Verily I never saw him look so gloomy before. [Sherman bitterly resented Stanton having publicly condemned a surrender agreement that he negotiated with Johnston shortly after Lee's surrender and for issuing orders directly to generals under his command without notifying him. He believed that Stanton had deliberately sought to humiliate him, and on mounting the reviewing stand, he ostentatiously refused to shake the secretary of war's outstretched hand. Taylor, of course, totally sympathized with Sherman.]

Major General [George A.] Custer's division of cavalry led the column of cavalry. He is a young looking man, with light hair hanging in ringlets upon his shoulders, sharp featured, prominent nose and chin and had a brigandish look. Those who have seen him before say he was trying to make all out of this display he could. He kept his horse prancing and frothing and led his staff almost fifty yards as though to show Major Gen'l. Custer thoroughly to all. Finally in catching a wreath [thrown to him], his horse I think was permitted [by him] to run off. This made his display ridiculous and it seemed to react upon him. I saw him and his wife riding yesterday morning.

The Cavalry was poorly mounted and wretchedly clothed—the most of them were very dirty and slovenly in appearance. In their rear came the horse artillery brigade composed of three United States batteries and one volunteer. This was a splendid exhibition. The artillerist[s] all [were] mounted upon good horses and their sabers, clothing and equipment in the most perfect order.

Taylor scrawled several more pages describing the Army of the Potomac's parade, but they are of little interest, being poorly and sometimes incoherently written, with numerous missing, misspelled, and illegible words. He clearly was very tired when he wrote this and so did it in a hasty, careless

The Grand Review in Washington: The XVII Corps, Army of the Tennessee (General Frank Blair on lead horse).
   Miller, ed., Photographic History, *3: 345.*

manner. Two days later, when he provided Netta with an account of his own army's review, he plied his pen with his customary vigor, being fully rested and inspired by a subject nearer and dearer to his heart than the easterners of General "Mead":

> Yesterday was another grand day and I never felt prouder except when I lay in McAllister conscious of our victory and that I had helped win it.
>   Our old Fifteenth corps marched as though that weight was one thousand pounds per man. I don't think that I ever beheld them

when they look[ed] more immovable and more formidable. With very little music, no attempt at display and that quick, steady, swinging step which much marching gives men they moved regularly, grandly and rapidly by, eliciting vociferous cheers. . . . Of the regiments ours marched decidedly better than any in the brigade. The ranks were well aligned and the men uniformly dressed—the regiment too was the largest in the brigade and hence showed to much better advantage. . . . Following this [the XV Corps' infantry] came the artillery in most excellent trim. DeGress and his twenty pounder Parrots were in capital condition and it did me great good to point them out and speak of his fine shooting and most excellent discipline. . . .

Hardly had the rumbling of the artillery grown faint ere the blast of bugles and bands announced the coming of Blair. His corps [the XVII] was close behind him and like the 15th was loudly greeted, the same fighting trim was manifested by them and the marching was so good it would be difficult to tell which was the best. This corps bore ample evidence of its severe service and as it passed what glorious recollections were revived in my mind. The hard fought fields which crossed my vision displaying their horrors but faintly and their glories most vividly. How proud I am of the clustering memories. . . .

Then next, though at a long interval, came the Army of Georgia [XIV and XX Corps] preceded by Major General Slocum, and considerable time after him appeared the 20th A.C. led by its most fearless leader, Major General John H. Mower. The corps marched very well, that is, kept good time and very good alignment, but the intervals between the brigades and divisions were shocking and in a measure to a military man marred the whole movement. Each brigade of the corps was followed by its pack animals in perfect order. These were packed just as you would see them on a campaign. On top of the pack you would behold some pet, a gamecock, goat, lamb, pup or little Negro. They constituted a very pleasant feature of the parade and relieved the monotony. . . .

After another long interval came the 14th A.C. headed by the gallant and skillful Major General Jeff C. Davis. This corps marched well and looked well. Everything was in most excellent order and each man showed to good advantage. I was glad to point out our Western boys and especially those from our section—among good soldiers they are preeminent, they are the best.

Taylor concluded his account by expressing an opinion, which would be surprising only if it were other than what it was: "In the judgement of the vast multitude of lookers on and also of *soldiers* The Army of the West excelled The Army of the Potomac and the 9th A.C. in marching and soldierly bearing."[9]

Following the review, Taylor went with friends from the Forty-seventh to visit its camp on the outskirts of Washington; and on May 9 Colonel Parry in turn called on him in Washington, where they went together to the War Department and inquired about a brevet (honorary) brigadier general's commission that Parry understood had been bestowed upon him. Much to the colonel's chagrin, they discovered that the brevet had been issued to Edward A. Parry, not Augustus C. As they left the War Department, Parry told Taylor that he intended to go home in a few days, which he did after submitting his resignation. Reporting the incident to Netta on May 27, Taylor commented, "I am not surprised at the non-recognition of his merit. He is very brusque in his manner, profane, &c., nor does he take any pains to disguise his dislikes. This injures him."

The court-martial now had only one case remaining, and Taylor looked forward eagerly to leaving Washington, a place he had come to find "very disagreeable," even "revolting" (or so he told Netta on June 6). Furthermore, he not only hoped but also expected to be able to go home soon for at least a short stay because Hazen had applied to the War Department for his services as judge advocate with the Army of the Tennessee, whose headquarters were in the process of being transferred to Louisville. Indeed, so confident was he that his stay in the capital was about to end that early in June he had his mother come there from Columbia, Pennsylvania, so that she could accompany him directly to Georgetown on his way to Louisville.[10]

Again, when it came to such matters, he experienced disappointment and frustration. The presiding judge of the court-martial fell ill, the trial of the last case dragged on and on, and so did the days—sweltering, interminable days.[11] Not until June 22 was he able to notify Netta that the court had recessed and that he was going to visit his mother, who in the meantime had returned to Columbia. He dared not try to predict when he would arrive home, but he assured his wife that "I think you will find me one of the most earnest and indefatigable kissers in the world. I feel as though my system is surcharged with them [kisses] and any pair of pouting lips I pass calls out some expression upon the kissable quality of the *article,* but nonetheless I am saving all of my precious embraces for your bonnie self and shall take the greatest pleasure in giving you measure for measure."

Three days later, Taylor sent Netta a short but happy letter from Columbia:

> Last evening I received a dispatch . . . informing me that the Court was dissolved on Friday [June 23]. I shall, therefore, leave here with Mother tomorrow for Washington which place I will leave on Thursday night [June 27] for "Home, sweet, sweet home." I think I shall arrive in Georgetown on Thursday or Friday night and not later than Saturday.

Exactly when Taylor and his mother reached Georgetown is unrecorded and hence unknown. Whatever the date, his stay was brief—although presumably not so much so that he failed to make good on his promise to give Netta "measure for measure." On July 5, he went to Cincinnati, from where once more, but for the last time in uniform, he traveled to Louisville by steamboat, arriving on the morning of July 6. He received, so he informed Netta the following day, a "very cordial" welcome from Hazen, who now headed the XV Corps, Logan having assumed command of the Army of the Tennessee as a result of Howard's having been placed in charge of the Freedmen's Bureau, a government agency designed to assist Southern blacks in their transition from slavery to freedom.

The entire Army of the Tennessee had been ordered to be mustered out, Taylor notified Netta on July 7, yet "a great diversity of opinion" existed as to whether the order applied to the Second Division (and thus to the Forty-seventh Ohio) because it had been sent to Arkansas "beyond the confines of General Logan's Department." Hazen thought it did but could "make no promises or predictions on this matter." In any event, Taylor promised Netta, he would remain in Louisville, for he had no desire to rejoin the Forty-seventh, which, with Parry's resignation, had come under the command of its senior captain, an incompetent who had allowed the regiment to degenerate into a "wretched condition." Besides, he had certain goals in mind that could be best pursued at army headquarters. Having on June 16 been promoted to lieutenant colonel as a consequence of John Wallace's being physically unfit to serve because of hardships suffered while in Confederate prisons, he hoped next to secure a colonel's commission and then a brevet brigadier generalship. Had he not, as division skirmish officer, commanded the equivalent of a brigade and done so most capably? He believed he should be rewarded accordingly and that with the backing of Hazen and Logan there was a good chance that he would be.[12]

In later years, Taylor claimed that he served as Hazen's "chief of staff"— presumably this was while he was in Louisville as it could not have been at any other time or place. But if so, then his duties seem to have been quite light. From his July letters one gains the impression that he passed most of the month reading law books, enjoying "gay times" with fellow staff officers, and attending various social functions. Among the latter was a grand ball held at Hazen's headquarters, a mansion located three miles south of Louisville. Here he played a half-dozen games of cribbage and lost them all, drank a mint julep that "sickened me," and danced with some of the ladies, but, as he took care to tell Netta in a long July 25 description of the affair, "though surrounded by the gayest of the gay," he was "inexpressibly sad" in her absence, he who had always in the past greatly enjoyed "a party, especially a 'hop.'" "The ladies who dance," he commented in a PS, "have cards and when they accept your hand for a set you register and place the number after your name. It is a good practice—but I believe I would despise it."

On July 28 he mailed Netta a note that doubtless she read with the greatest of delight:

> Our corps organization is destroyed. Nothing remains. Head Quarters and it [the corps] will disband on the 31st inst. On same evening I think I shall start for "Cincinnati," O. Whether I come home on Tuesday or will have to proceed to Columbus on regimental business I am unable to say.
>
> To determine is with me to act. The terms in my dictionary are synonomous.
>
> I shall not write again unless disappointed.

Evidently he was not disappointed, as this was his last communication from Louisville. He did, however, travel to Columbus on regimental business but presumably not before he had spent most of August in Georgetown. The reason for believing this is that when the Forty-seventh, which had been mustered out at Little Rock on August 12, arrived by steamboat in Cincinnati on August 21, he was on hand to greet it, as were a large, cheering crowd, cannons firing salutes, and brass bands.

From the landing, "the Cincinnati Regiment," as it was dubbed for the occasion, marched to the South Street Market House where, to quote Joseph A. Saunier's history, it was "served with the finest dinner ever served in the city of Cincinnati." At the head of the banquet table sat Parry, Taylor, Mayor Charles Wilstach, a congeries of other dignitaries, veterans of the regiment who had been discharged for medical reasons, and widows of those members who had died. The Forty-seventh now numbered only 250 officers and men, despite the large accession of recruits prior to the march to the sea and having had a total of 1,550 enlistments during the course of the war. It was not an elite outfit but a good one that saw long, arduous service and paid the price.[13]

After spending the night at the Market House, the Forty-seventh traveled by train to Camp Dennison, where on August 24 it received back pay and discharge certificates.[14] The latter were obtained in Columbus by Taylor, or so it would seem from the letter he sent Netta from the "Spencer House, Cinti., Ohio" on August 30 in which he also indicated that he had contracted to take care of some other matters, not only for the Forty-seventh but also the Seventieth Ohio, most of whose troops came from the Brown County region:

> Yesterday I received my discharge but not my pay. The adjutant in making out my record on the muster out roll neglected to state the distance to be travelled [from Cincinnati to Georgetown?]. The mustering officer promised to call last night or this morning and rectify it but he has failed to do so and I cannot afford to wait any longer. The business I got from the 47th & 70th will net me about $1,100, if I succeed. At Columbus I did admirably—procured certificates for all the men except one. Wrote them myself and the Adjutant General signed them. In that office it is almost like home I know them [the personnel] so well.

He then closed the letter by writing the words that Netta had been waiting and hoping to read for four years: "I will be coming home Friday or Saturday"—coming home, that is, to stay.

So ended Taylor's Civil War correspondence and with it his military career. It had been a successful one, it's success being crowned on September 4, soon after his arrival home, by the receipt of a colonel's commission from Gov. John Brough of Ohio. Nor was that all. Six days later, he became a brevet brigadier general (as did Parry, Wells S. Jones, and Carr White), to rank from March 13, 1865. To be sure this was not the same as achieving the actual rank of brigadier and exercising it in the field. Yet it was good enough. It provided official, formal recognition that he had served his nation well and that if the war had lasted longer, his circumstances been more favorable, or both, he might well have realized his aspiration to be a general or die in the attempt. Moreover, it gave him for the rest of his life the right to use, and be addressed by, the title "General Taylor." Above all, it signified personal victory and vindication in what might be termed the military phase of his "battle with the world" and provided him with a potentially valuable asset as he resumed that battle in the civilian arena.[15]

No doubt he entered this fray confident of success—a success in peacetime greater in scale and at a higher level than he had achieved in wartime. Reestablish his law practice. Rise to the top of his profession. Secure a seat on the bench or in the legislature. Make his mark as a leader, a coming man. Win election to the House of Representatives, to the governorship, to the U.S. Senate. Perhaps take up residence in the White House. Why not? Had he not the requisite qualities in abundance: intellect and initiative, courage and determination, enormous energy—oh, such energy!—and an ability to calculate, manipulate, and dominate? Thomas Thomson Taylor, in order to ascend to the very zenith of power and prestige, needed only the right luck at the right times and places.

Would he have it? Would he do it? The years ahead offer the answer.

Epilogue: Section 1, Lot 19

WOULD THOMAS TAYLOR reach the zenith of power and prestige? The answer is no. Taylor resumed the practice of law in Georgetown, and presumably he did well enough at it, given his exceptional intelligence and awesome industry. But when it came to his political aspirations, it was a different story. To quote from his memoir, "My Family and I," which he wrote in the third person, "very much to his displeasure," he was elected justice of the peace for Georgetown in fall 1865. Not only was this a humiliating comedown for one who before the war had held the far more important post of prosecuting attorney for Brown County, but it also was an insult to a man who had commanded the equivalent of a brigade on the battlefield. Neither did he relish the prospect of becoming a district judge, refusing in 1866 a nomination by the governor to that position. Instead, he sought and secured, thanks to a recommendation by Carr White and the endorsement of Gen. Grant, an appointment as assistant assessor of internal revenue for the Sixth District of Ohio.[1]

The appointment brought additional income but led nowhere politically. This hardly mattered, however, for as a Republican he had no political future in Brown County anyway. Although the Republicans controlled Ohio as a whole and would for a long time continue to do so, the Democratic party remained dominant in the county, and many of its leaders were unrepentant Copperheads not in the least impressed by young "General Taylor," whom no doubt they viewed as a turncoat. Somewhat belatedly realizing this, Taylor early in 1867 did what he so often proposed doing back in the dark days of 1862 out of disgust with Georgetown; he left it to migrate beyond the Mississippi to the vast plains of the West. In April he moved to Edina in Knox County, Missouri, later to be followed by Netta and their five children, two having been added, Sarah Elizabeth and Hiram Chilton.

Why Taylor chose to go there, probably no one other than he could have explained, and he never did, at least in no source I have found. Possibly a good guess as any is that he scouted Missouri for a town capable of supporting a newspaper but that did not have one, for in Edina he established and edited a weekly, *The Sentinel.* In any event, his choice of location, not to mention vocation, could scarcely have been worse. Situated in the northeastern corner of Missouri, a region that to this day remains predominantly rural, Edina was smaller than Georgetown and even more isolated, being without rail or nearby river communication and about 150 miles from the nearest city accessible by steamboat, St. Louis. Possibly, too, the inhabitants of Edina looked upon the former Union army officer from Ohio as little better than a carpetbagger, for a large minority of Missourians were of Southern origin and had sympathized with, or, if young men, fought for the Confederacy as soldiers or guerrillas. One cannot help but think that Taylor would have been wiser to have gone to Cincinnati. There he had influential friends and contacts, his war record and honors would have been an asset rather than a liability, and he would have had abundant opportunities in law, politics, business, or all three while the "Queen City" grew in majesty, as it rapidly did throughout the last third of the nineteenth century. By settling in Edina, Taylor most definitely chose the wrong place to attain the success he craved.

He did not enjoy any luck there, either. He published his paper but apparently not enough people subscribed to it, for after a while he again resorted to government jobs to supplement his income, one as swampland commissioner and the other as an assistant U.S. marshal, in which capacity he took the census for Knox County in 1870. He could not have derived much pay or satisfaction from these posts, and to make matters worse, his health began to fail. This, at any rate, is what he claims in his memoir, but one suspects that the actual failure was his will to continue struggling to succeed in a place where success was impossible; there was a limit even to his vaunted determination. Consequently, he shook the dust—or should it be the swamp water?—of Knox County from his feet and moved to Hutchinson in Reno County, Kansas, in May 1874. By this time his family included another son, Bruce, born in 1871.

Hutchinson at this time had been in existence less than two years and was just a village. But unlike Edina, or for that matter Georgetown, it had a future that soon saw it become, thanks to railroads, cattle, wheat, and salt mining, what it remains: a prosperous small city. Furthermore, Taylor's Republican affiliation was an advantage in Kansas, where the party of Lincoln totally dominated the state politically, and so too was his service in the Union army, which he made known by joining the Grand Army of the Republic, a veterans' organization so closely tied to the Republican party that the two were virtually identical. Thus it is neither remarkable nor surprising that Taylor, who opened a law office in Hutchinson, won election to the lower house of the Kansas legislature in fall 1874 and in the following year obtained an appointment as deputy prosecuting attorney of Reno County. In the latter post, he secured indictments against some corrupt local officials that led to their "permanent exit from the County and the State," to quote his own account of the affair. Then, after serving another term in the Kansas house and a four-year hitch in the state senate, he became president of the State Board of Charities, a director of the Kansas State Historical Society, and a life member of the State Horticultural Society.

Unfortunately, these advances were accompanied, through no fault of his, by a circumstantial setback. In 1875, Indians raided Kansas's southwestern frontier settlements, and U.S. troops had to be employed against them. Wishing to forestall a repetition of the raids, in 1876 Gov. Thomas Osborn appointed Taylor a brigadier general in the state militia and placed him in charge of preventing further forays. This he successfully accomplished by the novel means of recruiting several bands of veteran buffalo hunters to patrol the frontier. But then Osborn gave way to a new governor, George T. Anthony, who promptly ordered Taylor to disband his buffalo hunters and revoked his general's commission, thereby preventing him from reaping the potential political benefits of the favorable publicity he would have received had his defense system proved effective on a long-term basis.[2]

In 1887, Taylor again became a member of the Kansas house, where he successfully led a campaign to grant women the right to vote in municipal elections. This, however, terminated his political career. By then he was in his early fifties—not old, yet no longer young enough to harbor any realistic hope of gaining higher offices in the future than he had in the past. By the same token, the time also had come to ensure the financial status of his family, which now numbered eight offspring, George and Edgar having been born in 1874 and 1877. To this end, he devoted himself to his law practice and to his 1,120-acre farm near Hutchinson, on which he raised cattle and hogs and lived in what a 1917 *History of Reno County* described as a "most substantial house."[3]

Then in 1893, J. B. Watkins, a Lawrence, Kansas, entrepreneur, offered Taylor the job of general counsel for the St. Louis, Watkins, and Gulf Railroad, his office to be in Lake Charles, Louisiana. He promptly accepted. Not only did the position offer financial security, but it also would put him in proximity to the Louisiana branch of the Taylor clan, contact with whom already had been restored when his older brother Ziba, the blockade runner, came to reside with him in Kansas before he died in 1881, the same year, coincidentally, that his mother and Carr White died. Putting his farm up for sale, he traveled alone to Lake Charles to acquire a suitable house. On the way, he stopped off in New Orleans, where he was greeted by his cousin and namesake, the Confederate Tom Taylor, who also had survived the war and become a planter, an inventor, and an author. On meeting at the New Orleans depot, where the Louisiana Taylor and his family had waited for hours with growing anxiety as train after train had arrived but none bearing the Kansas Taylor, the two Toms embraced. What once had divided them, the war, now united them, for both had fought, bravely and well, for what they believed in, and each had experienced the glories and miseries of being a soldier and so shared an experience that obliterated any past difference.[4]

In Lake Charles, Taylor soon acquired the respect of many friends among the community's social elite, an outcome no doubt facilitated by his Louisiana family connections and, as a local newspaper put it at the time of his death, by his staying "pretty well out of politics."[5] Although the townspeople did not hold his service in the Union army against him, they would have looked askance at any attempt by a Republican from Ohio by way of Kansas to secure election to a public office, a reality he was intelligent enough to recognize. He also knew that as a Republican he would stand absolutely no chance of being elected in solidly Democratic Louisiana, in any case. Therefore, he confined himself to his legal work for the railroad, serving as a bankruptcy referee; to various community projects; and, during his last years, to church activities. When, on January 17, 1908, Netta and he celebrated their golden wedding anniversary, well-wishers crowded their house, and the *Lake Charles Weekly American* published a long account of the career of "General Taylor."[6]

Less than a month later, on February 15, he suddenly died, having contracted the "grippe," which aggravated an asthmatic condition.[7] Following his death, Netta lived for a while with her daughter in Washington, D.C., and then with her son Carr, who had taken over his father's law practice in Hutchinson, until she died on September 29, 1913.[8] Thus ended the odyssey through life of Tom and Netta Taylor.

With respect to Taylor, it can be said that by normal standards this odyssey was not a failure. Both in the army and in civilian life he always occupied positions of superior status, and although he probably suffered some financial stress while in Edina, he otherwise always enjoyed at least a modest affluence and during his latter years more than that. Yet at the same time, he clearly fell far short of achieving the triumph in his "battle with the world" that he desired and that he believed was his destiny, given his intellectual and personal qualities.

Why? Part of the answer lies in an unfortunate talent for choosing the wrong, or else not the best, place to wage that battle. But the main reason, as readers in all likelihood have already perceived, was Taylor himself. Manifestly, he possessed a superior intellect, erudition, and energy fueled by a driving ambition to achieve glory and promotion as a soldier, fame and prestige as a civilian. These were impressive qualities, especially when complemented by his courage and coolness in times of crisis, and they did impress. Making due allowance for the archaic language and concepts, his obituary in the *Lake Charles Weekly American* spoke the truth when it said of him that "during a life of activity and energy lasting almost three quarters of a century, in every situation and aspect of life, Thomas T. Taylor was every inch a man; and man can give no higher praise."

But if he impressed, he also could and did offend and antagonize. His sense of his own superiority was flagrant, his ambition blatant, and his penchant for manipulation extravagant. It is small wonder that Lyman Elliott, at first friendly, came to regard him as a threat to his authority until they reached an "understanding"; or that Augustus Parry, who opened the way to the key event in Taylor's military career, promotion to major, sometimes resented him. Likewise, it probably is safe to surmise that in Kansas other ambitious politicians soon saw in him a dangerous competitor and so took countermeasures that prevented him from rising higher than he rose. His very appearance, as revealed in a photograph taken when he was a member of the state legislature (see page 233), was so formidable that he was bound to gain an opponent for every supporter acquired by that appearance and by the very real ability that went with it.

By the time he moved to Louisiana, Taylor had realized, as did so many men of his generation, a generation "touched by fire" in the words of another Union officer, Oliver Wendell Holmes Jr., that his war years had been and

Taylor the Legislator.
Kansas State Historical Society.

always would be the high point of his life, that during them he had enjoyed his most gratifying tastes of glory and won his most satisfying triumphs in battling with the world. The evidence for this, although indirect, is overwhelming. Thus in 1885, eight years before that move, he published in Cincinnati *A Sketch of the Operations of the Forty-Seventh Ohio Volunteer Infantry from May 3, 1864 to September 8, 1864,* a fifteen-page pamphlet that presumably was distributed to veterans of the regiment.[9] Further, nearly two decades later, he (in all probability) arranged for and subsidized in whole a part of the compilation and publication of the *History of the Forty-Seventh Ohio* by Joseph Saunier, a Georgetown friend and former noncom in his company. Printed by a small-town press in Ohio, its numerous typos and misspellings, erratic syntax, and sometimes awkwardly worded text must have embarrassed someone as articulate and meticulous as Taylor. Yet he had provided, by transcripts from his letters and diaries, much if not most of the source material, with the foreseeable and no doubt foreseen outcome that he figured prominently in the story of the Forty-seventh. More space was devoted to him than to Elliott or even to Parry, neither of whom were in a position to complain, both having died shortly after the war, as did Lt. Col. John Wallace.[10] Author Peter Finley Dunne, speaking through his fictional Chicago saloon keeper, Mr. Dooley, commented that Theodore Roosevelt's *With the Rough Riders in Cuba* should have been called "Alone in Cuba." By the same token, an appropriate title for Saunier's book would have been "Through the Civil War with General Thomas T. Taylor and the Forty-Seventh Ohio."

If more evidence is required to demonstrate what his participation in the Civil War meant to Taylor during his latter years, it is provided by his choice of a burial place: Arlington Cemetery. There the remains of his mortal being, and also those of Netta, who was interred beside him, lie in Section 1, Lot 19. He, who when alive so often spoke of leaving the army and on occasion attempted futilely to do so, is with it forever in death.

Notes

All citations of letters by Taylor to his wife Netta and of Netta's letters to her husband refer to letters by them in Taylor's papers at the Ohio Historical Society. Likewise, all commentaries accompanying Taylor's accounts of military events during the Atlanta Campaign derive from the pertinent sections of the author's *Decision in the West: The Atlanta Campaign of 1864* (Lawrence: University Press of Kansas, 1992), unless otherwise indicated. This is not because what is written about that campaign in this book is infallible but simply because the notes for *Decision in the West* contain the sources for what is written there and thus for the commentaries.

Prologue: The Heavy Tramp of Thousands

1. *The History of Brown County, Ohio* (Chicago: W. H. Beers and Company, 1883), 47, 336–37.

2. The description of Taylor is based on the photographs of him, especially the one of him taken during the Civil War, and on references to his appearance in his letters.

3. Thomas T. Taylor, "My Family and I: Being a Genealogical and Biographical Sketch of Thomas Thomson Taylor," 1–21, Taylor (Miles and Family) Papers, Hill Memorial Library, Louisiana State University, Baton Rouge. This is a typewritten transcript of the original, which Taylor wrote c. 1903 at the request (so he noted) of the Kansas State Historical Society, which had been sent to him by "its late Secretary," Franklin G. Adams. My attempt in May 1994 to locate the original at the Kansas State Historical Society in Topeka met with failure.

4. Hiram Taylor to wife, June 12, 1836, Taylor (Hiram and Thomas Thomson) Papers, Hill Memorial Library, Louisiana State University, Baton Rouge.

5. Taylor, "My Family and I," 1–46, passim.

6. Ibid., 45–46.

7. Ibid., 22; *Lake Charles (La.) Weekly Press*, Feb. 21, 1908.

8. Taylor, "My Family and I," 21–22, 28, 46–47; *Lake Charles (La.) Weekly Press*, Feb. 21, 1908; *History of Brown County*, 336, 339; U.S. Census, 1860: Brown County, Ohio (microfilm, Ohio Historical Society); Netta Taylor to Thomas Taylor, Sept. 7, 1861, Thomas Thomson Taylor Papers, Ohio Historical Society (OHS).

9. Taylor, "My Family and I," 21, 28, 46–47; *Biographical Directory of the American Congress, 1774–1971* (Washington, D.C.: Government Printing Office, 1971), 1796.

10. Taylor to Netta, June 18, 1861.

11. Taylor to Netta, undated, but evidently written in late August 1861.

12. Letters of Taylor to Netta and of Netta to Taylor for which the date is given in the text will not be cited in the notes, as to do so would be redundant.

13. Taylor to Netta, June 18, 1861.

14. Taylor to Netta, June 22, 28, 1861.

15. Joseph A. Saunier, ed., *A History of the Forty-seventh Regiment Ohio Veteran Volunteer Infantry* (Hillsboro, Ohio: Lyle Printing Company, 1903), 8–9; Witelaw Reid, *Ohio in the War: Her Statesmen, Her Generals, and Soldiers,* 2 vols. (1867; rpt., Columbus, Ohio: Bergman Books, 1995), 2: 291.

16. Taylor to Netta, July 28, 1861. Ulysses S. Grant, who spent most of his boyhood in Georgetown, stated in his *Personal Memoirs of U. S. Grant,* 2 vols. (New York: Charles L. Webster and Company, 1885), 1: 35, that during the Civil War, "if the opportunity could have been afforded," Georgetown would have "voted for Jefferson Davis for President of the United States, over Mr. Lincoln, or any other representative of his party," so predominantly and intensely Democratic were its inhabitants. If so, then perhaps this was the reason for the failure of Taylor's recruiting effort. On the other hand, by October 1862 Brown County had supplied 5,127 soldiers to the Union army from a population of slightly under 30,000 (Reid, *Ohio in the War,* 1: 77).

17. Saunier, ed., *Forty-seventh Ohio,* 9–11.

18. Ibid., 12–14; Taylor to Netta, Aug. 7, 1861.

19. Saunier, ed., *Forty-seventh Ohio,* 12–14.

20. Ibid.

21. Taylor to Netta, Sept. 1, 1861; Saunier, ed., *Forty-seventh Ohio,* 16. According to the latter source, the train carrying the Forty-seventh Ohio hit the wagon "within one mile" of Columbus, and Davis was "stripped of his uniform and marched off to some guard house." Since Taylor's account of the trip to Columbus was written only three days afterward and he was personally involved with Davis, it must be considered the more reliable one. Presumably because he never was formally mustered, Davis is not listed in the roster of the Forty-seventh Ohio that appears in the *Official Roster of the Soldiers of the State of Ohio in the War of the Rebellion,* 8 vols. (Akron, Ohio: Warner Printing and Manufacturing Company, 1897), vol. 4. (This work, which is on microfilm at the Ohio Historical Society, hereinafter is cited as *Ohio Official Roster.*) Unlike Reid's *Ohio in the War,* which lists only the officers of regiments, the *Ohio Official Roster* lists all the soldiers who officially served in Ohio military units during the Civil War. Most of the actual volumes of this compilation are on an open shelf in the reading room of the Ohio Historical Society but because of their fragile condition are not available for photocopying.

22. Netta to Taylor, Aug. 28, 1861.

Chapter One. I Want to Distinguish Myself

1. Jacob D. Cox, "McClellan in West Virginia," in *Battles and Leaders of the Civil War,* ed. Robert U. Johnson and Clarence C. Buel, 4 vols. (New York: Century Company, 1887), 1: 125–37. Nominally, the Union commander at Rich Mountain was Maj. Gen. George B. McClellan, but apart from agreeing to Rosecrans's plan he contributed noth-

ing to the Federal success and almost turned it into a failure by not carrying out his part of the operation.

2. Ibid., 142–44.

3. Netta responded to her husband's complaints by writing him on September 14: "Your life is more to your family than all the world. . . . I feel that our men are throwing away their lives for naught, for what will it avail them in the end?" Her attitude toward the war and Taylor's participation in it definitely was not that of the legendary Spartan wives who told their husbands, when they went off to war, to "return with your shield or upon it."

4. U.S. War Department, *The War of the Rebellion: A Compilation of the Official Records of the Union and Confederate Armies* (Washington, D.C.: Government Printing Office, 1880–1901), ser. 1, vol. 5: 128–32, 14648 (hereafter cited as OR, with all references being to series 1 unless otherwise indicated; whenever a volume consists of two or more parts, the volume number will precede OR and the part number will follow). See also Cox, "McClellan in West Virginia," 145–48; Douglas Southall Freeman, *R. E. Lee: A Biography*, 4 vols. (New York: Charles Scribner's Sons, 1934–1935), 1: 562–69; and Terry Lowry, *September Blood: The Battle of Carnifex Ferry* (Charleston, W. Va.: Pictorial Histories Publishing Company, 1985), 74–121. Floyd had been secretary of war in Pres. James Buchanan's cabinet prior to the Civil War, and according to an erroneous but widespread belief in the North he had used his position to transfer armaments to Southern arsenals in order to facilitate the establishment of the Confederacy. Consequently, he feared that if captured he would be tried and condemned as a traitor.

5. Lowry, *September Blood*, 96–100.

6. In a September 27, 1861 letter to Netta, Taylor asserted, rather vaguely, that while in Weston "I had occasion one night to fix a disguise and go out to look [for Confederate conspirators]. I made a Catholic priest out of myself—put on a long, black gown, black pants, etc. and made a good true appearance." If this be true—and it is difficult to believe that it is—Taylor could not have made himself more conspicuous, given the small number of Catholics in western Virginia at this time, had he clanked about Weston in a suit of medieval armor.

7. Taylor to Netta, Sept. 25, 27, 30, and Oct. 11, 1861; Saunier, ed., *Forty-seventh Ohio*, 42–44.

8. Taylor to Netta, Sept. 27, Oct. 11, 1861.

9. For a good account of guerrilla warfare in West Virginia, see Richard O. Curry and F. Gerald Ham, eds., "The Bushwhackers' War: Insurgency and Counter-Insurgency in West Virginia," *Civil War History* 10 (1964): 416–33.

10. Cox, "McClellan in West Virginia," 147–48; Freeman, *Lee*, 7: 588–602; William M. Lamers, *The Edge of Glory: A Biography of William S. Rosencrans, U.S.A.* (New York: Harcourt, Brace and World, 1961), 52–62.

11. Taylor to Netta, Oct. 24, 1861.

12. Taylor to Netta, Dec. 16, 1861; Netta to Taylor, Jan. 26, 1862.

13. Saunier, ed., *Forty-seventh Ohio*, 63.

14. Taylor to Netta, Dec. 4, 16, 22, 1861.

15. The German artist was Corp. J. Nep Roesler, whose *Portfolio of Lithographs of the War in Virginia and West Virginia*, a collection of twenty lithographs "Sketched from nature & drawn on stone," to quote the title page, was published by a Cincinnati firm (Ehrgott, Forbriger, and Company) in 1862. These pictures, several of which are among the illustrations for this book, are highly proficient technically and offer some artistically striking views of the mountain scenery of West Virginia. On the other hand, their depiction of Union soldiers (among whom the Forty-seventh Ohio always is included) and of combat are so stylized as to be little more realistic than the famous Currier & Ives lithographs of Civil War battles.

Chapter Two. What Have I Accomplished?

1. Taylor to Netta, Jan. 8, Feb. 9, March 13, 1862.

2. Taylor to Netta, Feb. 14, 1862. Mrs. Steinbarger, in her transcripts from Taylor's letters, did not include this passage.

3. Taylor to Netta, March 19, April 17, 1862.

4. 12 OR 1: 4–8; Jacob D. Cox, 2 vols., *Military Reminiscences of the Civil War* (New York: Charles Scribner, 1900), 1: 202–20.

5. Taylor to Netta, April 28, 30, June 10, 1862.

6. Taylor to Netta, undated but probably written c. May 9, 1862; Taylor to Netta, May 12, 15, June 10, 1862; Saunier, ed., *Forty-seventh Ohio*, 57–77.

7. 12 OR 1: 10–12, 804–13; Cox, *Reminiscences*, 1: 202-20.

8. Taylor's account was incorporated into a letter to Netta dated June 10, 1862.

9. Taylor to Netta, June 24, 1862.

10. Kenneth W. Noe, "Exterminating Savages: The Union Army and Mountain Guerrillas in Southern West Virginia, 1861–1862," in *The Civil War in Appalachia: Collected Essays*, ed., Kenneth W. Noe and Shannon H. Wilson (Knoxville: University of Tennessee Press, 1997), ably describes the increasingly vicious nature of the guerrilla war in West Virginia. Unfortunately, a passage (112–13) based on Taylor's letters contains numerous inaccuracies in its references to Taylor.

11. See also Taylor to Netta, July 2, 1862.

12. See Netta to Taylor, May 27, 1862; Taylor to Netta, June 10, July 2, 1862.

13. Mrs. Steinbarger's transcriptions of Taylor's July 31 and August 3 letters omit, understandably enough, the sexual references. Unfortunately, Netta's letters to Taylor during July are either missing or are for the most part so faded as to be illegible, thus making it necessary to surmise their contents and, when possible, to ascertain their dates from Taylor's letters in reply.

14. Cox, *Reminiscences*, 1: 222–25.

15. Taylor to Netta, August 7, 10, 13, 17, 19, 1862.

16. Taylor to Netta, July 26, 28, 1862; Saunier, ed., *Forty-seventh Ohio*, 89.

17. Taylor to Netta, July 26, 1862.

18. Taylor spelled Hesser with one "s," but in the *Ohio Official Roster* it is spelled as presented in the text.

19. 19 OR 1: 1057–59, 1068–70, 1070; Jacob D. Cox, "Forcing Fox's Gap and Turner's Gap," Johnson and Buel, eds., *Battles and Leaders of the Civil War*, 2: 583–90; Cox, *Reminiscences*, 1: 392–93.

20. 19 OR 1: 1057–60, 1070, 1073–74.

21. Cox, "Fox's Gap and Turner's Gap," 586–90; Jacob D. Cox, "The Battle of Antietam," Johnson and Buel, eds., *Battles and Leaders of the Civil War*, 2: 651–56. In the fighting at South Mountain and Antietam the Kanawha Division suffered 611 casualties.

22. Undated and anonymous sketch of Thomas Taylor, son of Miles Taylor of Louisiana, in Taylor (Miles and Family) Papers.

23. Col. Samuel A. Gilbert, acting commander of the brigade to which the Forty-seventh belonged, Colonel Crook having accompanied Cox to Maryland, singled out not Elliott but Lt. Col. Augustus C. Parry of the Forty-seventh for special praise in his report on the fighting at Charleston (see 19 OR 1: 1067).

24. Taylor to Netta, Oct. 1, 20, 1862; Saunier, ed., *Forty-Seventh Ohio*, 109; Cox, *Reminiscences*, 1: 408.

25. Cox, *Reminiscences*, 1: 408–14.

26. Ibid., 414–17. Clayton R. Newell, *Lee vs. McClellan: The First Campaign* (Washington, D.C.: Regnery Publishing, 1996), 267–69, contends that the Federals could have used their control to "press outward out of the mountains" to ravage the Shenandoah Valley, "breadbasket of Virginia." This was a logistical impossibility.

27. Taylor to Netta, Oct. 23, 29, 1862.

28. For Netta's contention that the war was being fought for the "equality of the negro," see her letter of June 1, 1862. Taylor shared his wife's racial attitudes and opposed emancipation of the slaves (see Taylor to Netta, May 15, 29, 1862). But his main criticism of Lincoln was for failing to use the North's full strength and for not waging a harder war against Southern civilians (see Taylor to Netta, Sept. 2, 8, 1862).

29. OR 21: 940; Saunier, ed., *Forty-seventh Ohio*, 114.

Chapter Three. The Almighty Will Preserve Me

1. Some of the Cincinnatians in the Forty-seventh became so angry when told that they would not be allowed to go ashore to visit families and friends that they cut the tiller ropes of their boat, causing it to float out of control for several miles before the damage was repaired and the craft lashed to another steamer (Saunier, ed., *Forty-seventh Ohio*, 115).

2. Ibid., 118.

3. This is a surmise based on two facts: first, since Taylor' s assignment to recruiting duty in December 1862 required the approval of departmental headquarters, it would seem to follow that his being relieved of that assignment required the sanction of the same headquarters; and second, as his Feb. 27, 1863 letter to Netta demonstrates, Taylor did join the remnant of the Forty-seventh at Camp Gauley Mountain, and this was also where he went in December 1862 when waiting to learn whether departmental headquarters would approve his assignment to recruiting duty.

4. Reid, *Ohio in the War*, 2:293; *Ohio Official Roster*, 4: 389.

5. The assumption that Taylor's request to be relieved from recruiting duty and permitted to rejoin his regiment was denied is derived from the fact that in March 1863 he returned to recruiting service in Ohio, as indicated in his March 10 and April 13 letters to Netta. For his support of conscription, see his Aug. 7, 1862 letter to Netta.

6. Saunier, ed., *Forty-seventh Ohio*, 120–35.

7. Taylor to Netta, April 17, 1863.

8. Taylor to Netta, April 13, 17, 1863. For the attempt by Taylor and other officers of the Forty-seventh to make Parry rather than Elliott colonel, see Taylor to Netta, July 26, 1862, and Saunier, ed., *Forty-seventh Ohio*, 89. According to Saunier, (118), "Captain Taylor, who enjoyed a personal acquaintance with Governor Todd [*sic*] . . . on Feb. 26th [1863] secured the appointment of Lieutenant Colonel Parry" to be the colonel of the Forty-seventh Ohio. Taylor was not a personal acquaintance of Tod and played no role whatsoever in Parry's promotion.

9. A notice of Taylor's promotion appeared in the April 15, 1863 *Cincinnati Commercial* beneath the heading "From Columbus," p. 3.

10. Taylor, "My Family and I," 49. Saunier, ed., *Forty-seventh Ohio*, 118, repeats this claim, no doubt on the basis of a statement supplied to him by Taylor.

11. Saunier, ed., *Forty-seventh Ohio*, 118; Taylor to Netta, June 25, 1863.

12. Saunier, ed., *Forty-seventh Ohio*, 99–100; in the two assaults the Forty-seventh lost ninety-two killed or wounded and eight captured or missing (151).

13. Taylor's criticism of Confederate engineering skill may have been justified, although he scarcely qualified as an expert on the subject, but it overlooked the obvious fact that Vicksburg's fortifications served their purpose. Had the Confederates stored a six-month's supply of provisions in Vicksburg, quite possibly they would have held the place that long. Likewise, although the cotton uniforms of the Rebel soldiers were dirty, one suspects that they were better suited to Mississippi's summer climate than were the wool uniforms of the Federals.

14. This and the succeeding quotations and descriptions pertaining to Taylor that appear in this chapter are from a letter he wrote to Netta starting on July 19 and headed "Headquarters 47th Ohio Infantry, State Auditors Office, Jackson, Miss."

15. Sherman's report on the Jackson expedition, 24 OR 2: 536; Kenneth P. Williams, *Lincoln Finds a General: A Military Study of the Civil War*, 5 vols. (New York: Macmillan, 1949–1959), 5: 54–60.

16. Taylor to Netta, July 26, 29, 1863; 24 OR 2: 536–37.

Chapter Four. We Will Achieve Mighty Victories

1. Presumably the George referred to here was Taylor's former camp servant in West Virginia. Statements in other letters by Netta indicate that he had a job in the drugstore of which Taylor was half-owner.

2. Taylor to Netta, July 8, 1863.

3. 30 CR 2: 545–52.

4. Grant, *Memoirs*, 1: 578–81.

5. See pertinent portions of Steven E. Woodworth, *Six Armies in Tennessee: The Chickamauga and Chattanooga Campaigns* (Lincoln: University of Nebraska Press, 1998).

6. Shelby Foote, *The Civil War: A Narrative*, 3 vols. (New York: Random House, 1954–1978), 2: 763–65.

7. Taylor to Netta, Sept. 3, 1863; Saunier, ed., *Forty-seventh Ohio*, 182–85.

8. Taylor to Netta, Oct. 16, 1863. Taylor's account of the attack on the train carrying Sherman agrees in all essentials with the one that Sherman gives in his *Memoirs of Gen. W. T. Sherman*, 2 vols. (New York: Charles L. Webster and Company, 1891), 1: 377–78.

9. Taylor to Netta, Oct. 16, 1863.

10. Ibid.

11. Grant, *Memoirs*, 2: 17–18, 23.

12. Sherman, *Memoirs*, 1: 383.

13. Grant, *Memoirs*, 2: 36–38.

14. Maj. Gen. Patrick Cleburne's Report, 31 OR 2: 745–48. Where not otherwise indicated, the commentary on Sherman's attack on Missionary Ridge and the Battle of Chattanooga in general is based on the pertinent passages of Wiley Sword, *Mountains Touched with Fire: Chattanooga Besieged* (New York: St. Martin's Press, 1995), the best detailed account of the Battle of Chattanooga.

15. Cleburne's Report, 31 OR 2: 747–49.

16. Ibid., 749–52; for Lightburn's report (which was written by Taylor), see 629–30. Buschbeck in his report (ibid., 360–61) stated that his brigade had only two regiments fully engaged in the fighting and that two other regiments that were not part of his brigade also participated in the action. Sherman in his official report actually praised Buschbeck's brigade for displaying "a courage almost amounting to rashness" (ibid., 581).

17. This description of the culmination of the Battle of Chattanooga derives mainly from Sword, *Mountains Touched with Fire*, chapters 31–38. Sherman's report on his attack at Tunnel Hill (31 OR 2: 574–76) conceals more than it reveals.

18. I have taken the liberty of correcting, without what otherwise would have been an excessive amount of pedantic scholarly baggage, some errors of content and word usage in this quoted passage. Taylor obviously wrote it hurriedly, under adverse conditions, and while very fatigued. Thus, as written, he states that this was his twenty-eighth birthday. It was his twenty-seventh, unless he lied about his birthdate before and ever afterward.

Chapter Five. I Have Calculated, Worked and Talked

1. This is a different letter from the one containing Taylor's long account of Sherman's attack at Missionary Ridge quoted in chapter 4. Although that letter also is dated Dec. 20, 1863, Taylor did not complete it until Dec. 31.

2. Grant, *Memoirs*, 2: 92–95; Sherman, *Memoirs*, 1: 390–92; Thomas T. Taylor diary, OHS, Nov. 26, 27, 1863; Taylor to Netta, Dec. 20, 1863 (the long letter).

3. Sherman, *Memoirs*, 1: 394; Foote, *The Civil War*, 2: 862–65.

4. Taylor to Netta, Dec. 20, 1863 (the short letter).

5. Taylor diary, Dec. 21–22, 1863; Grant, *Memoirs*, 1: 573. For Logan's Civil War career, see Albert Castel, "'Black Jack' Logan," *Civil War Times Illustrated* (November 1976): 4–10, 41–45.

6. Taylor diary, Jan. 2, 4, 16, 1864.

7. Ibid., Jan. 29, 1864.

8. Taylor to Netta, Dec. 27, 1863, Jan. 16, 1864.

9. Taylor diary, Jan. 8–10, 25–28, 1864.

10. Taylor diary, Feb. 10, 1864.

11. Ibid., Feb. 11, 1864.

12. Taylor to Netta, Jan. 29, 1864.

13. Taylor diary, Feb. 14, 1864.

14. Ibid., Feb. 13, 15, 1864; Taylor to Netta, Feb. 19, 1864.

15. Taylor's description of Thomas is generally accurate except for stating that he was "compactly built." About six feet tall, Thomas weighed well over two hundred pounds. He was forty-seven in February 1864 but owing to a mainly white beard looked older.

16. Whipple's order to Matthies, dated February 15, 1864, is found in 32 OR 2: 397. Thomas sent Matthies's "temporary division" to Cleveland and then to Knoxville in response to instructions from Grant, who on the basis of what proved to be erroneous reports, believed that Longstreet was moving against Knoxville. As a consequence, a planned demonstration by Thomas against the Confederate Army of Tennessee at Dalton, Georgia, that Grant also had ordered had to be postponed. This in turn enabled troops from that army to reinforce Lt. Gen. Leonidas Polk's forces in Alabama against a much larger army headed by Sherman, which had advanced eastward through Mississippi and was threatening Montgomery, Selma, and (so the Confederates believed) Mobile. See Albert Castel, *Decision in the West: The Atlanta Campaiqn of 1864* (Lawrence: University Press of Kansas, 1992), chap. 2, passim.

17. Taylor diary, Feb. 16, 1864; Taylor to Netta, Feb. 19, 1864.

18. Taylor diary, Feb. 17–21, 1864.

19. This letter is not dated but its contents make it clear that Taylor at least began it on March 5.

20. For enlisting of Alabama Unionists in the Forty-seventh Ohio, see Taylor diary, Jan. 30, 1864. An entire regiment of Alabamians, the First Alabama Cavalry, served with Sherman's army.

21. Taylor to Netta, March 16, 1864. While stationed in Cleveland, Tennessee, Taylor asked a young woman to accompany him to a party to which he and two other officers of the Forty-seventh Ohio had been invited, but she refused, saying that she was "Secesh." Taylor recorded this incident in his diary (Feb. 26, 1864) but for obvious reasons did not mention it in a description of social life in Cleveland that he included in his March 5, 1864 letter to Netta.

Chapter Six. Once More Into the Breach

1. Castel, *Decision in the West*, 68, 112–14. Unless otherwise indicated, all descriptions and interpretations of the Atlanta Campaign appearing in this and subsequent chapters are based on the pertinent sections of this work, where they are fully documented.

2. Taylor diary, April 26–30, 1864; Taylor to Netta, May 1, 1864.

3. Taylor diary, May 1–4, 1864.

4. Thomas P. Lowry, *The Story the Soldiers Wouldn't Tell: Sex in the Civil War* (Mechanicsburg, Pa.: Stackpole Books, 1994), 77.

5. Taylor diary, May 5–8, 1864; Taylor to Netta, May 8, 1864.

6. Taylor diary, May 9–10, 1864.

7. Ibid., May 22, 1864.

8. See also Taylor to Netta, June 2, 1864.

9. 38 OR 3: 95–96; Castel, *Decision in the West*, 246 and pertinent endnotes.

10. Taylor to Netta, June 7, 1864.

Chapter Seven. Oh, Jerusalem, Jerusalem

1. The actual attack was made by Brig. Gen. Charles Walcutt's brigade of Harrow's division. In his report (38 OR 5: 317) Walcutt put his own casualties at 63 and claimed to have taken "about 400 prisoners." Although it is possible that Taylor witnessed this affair, the positions of Harrow's and Morgan Smith's divisions, plus his failure to mention that Walcutt's troops waded a creek in order to get at the Confederates, make it probable that he based his account on what others told him.

2. On June 22, following the repulse of Hood's attack at Kolb's Farm, Thomas recommended to Sherman that he take advantage of the weakening of the Confederate right by having McPherson strike toward Marietta from the east, but Sherman ignored this proposal for the same reason he decided not to use the Army of the Tennessee to turn the Confederate left flank—fear of exposing Big Shanty and the railroad to an enemy thrust. So thinly stretched were the Confederate forces on and about Big Kennesaw that Johnston found it necessary to station a large portion of his cavalry, dismounted, in trenches covering Marietta on the east (see Castel, *Decision in the West*, 296, 300–301). There is, of course, no way of knowing, much less demonstrating, that a full-fledged Union assault on Big Kennesaw would have succeeded; but judging by Taylor's account,

it could have, the chances of success being enhanced by the likelihood that it would have caught the Confederates by surprise in the same manner as the Army of the Cumberland's charge up Missionary Ridge had done.

3. The Confederates overrun in their rifle pits belonged to the Sixty-third Georgia, which suffered 123 casualties. Lightburn's attack actually was directed at Pigeon Hill, not Little Kennesaw as implied by Taylor. Walcutt's brigade and the First Brigade of Morgan Smith's division assailed Little Kennesaw over ground so rugged that it would have been difficult for troops to pass over it even if there had been no enemy resistance. For a full description and analysis of the Battle of Kennesaw Mountain, see Castel, *Decision in the West*, 306–21.

4. Some historians, notably Herman Hattaway and Archer Jones in *How the North Won* (Urbana: University of Illinois Press, 1983), 526–32, contend that Grant did not expect to be able to defeat Lee in 1864 and hence entrusted Sherman with the task, in effect, of winning the war in Georgia by means of a "raiding strategy." If this was so, then Sherman was unaware of it, as demonstrated by his letter of April 24, 1864 to McPherson in which he stated: "Of course the movement in Virginia is principal and ours [in Georgia] secondary, and must conform" (32 OR 3: 479).

Chapter Eight. Hell, Stranger, This Is No Place for Me to Halt!

1. Fuller personally directed this brigade during the encounter with Walker's division. He had headed it until July 17, when as a result of the illness of Brig. Gen. James C. Veatch he became the acting division commander. Normally a single brigade consisting of only four regiments would not have been able to repel an attack by a full division so easily as was the case on this occasion. However, Walker was killed by a Union rifleman just prior to the assault; his division had suffered heavy losses at Peachtree Creek; some of its units failed to advance; and many of its officers and men were of poor quality, including the general who took command upon Walker's death. In contrast, Fuller's troops were battle-hardened veterans, they enjoyed strong artillery support, and one of their regiments possessed repeating rifles that enabled it to beat back an enemy thrust that threatened to turn the brigade's right flank. Following the battle, Walker's Division was dissolved and its brigades assigned to other divisions.

2. The figure for the number of men left in the Forty-seventh Ohio after the July 22 battle was taken from Taylor's diary, July 28, 1864.

3. See Col. Wells Jones's report, 38 OR 3: 223–24, and *Ninth Reunion of the 37th O.V.I., St. Mary's, Ohio, Tuesday and Wednesday, September 10 and 11, 1889* (Toledo: Montgomery and Vroom Printers, 1890), 49–50. The latter source states that Maj. Charles Hipp, commander of the Thirty-seventh Ohio, also suggested to General Smith that the railroad cut be barricaded and the nearby house and outbuilding be burnt but that Smith refused, saying that the buildings would be useful as a hospital and that barricading the railroad cut would be "labor lost, as he was confident that we would take dinner in Atlanta."

4. 38 OR 3: 180.

5. Logan in his report on the July 22 battle estimated Confederate casualties to be "at least 10,000" (38 OR 3: 21), and Sherman in his report on the Atlanta Campaign put them at "a full 8,000 men" (ibid., 1: 75). See Castel, *Decision in the West*, 412, for reasons why the Confederate loss probably was c. 5,500.

Chapter Nine. We Had Another Big Fight

1. 38 OR 3: 799–800, 927.

2. Ibid., 41–42, 179. Taylor's description of the fighting on the Union right is confirmed in all essentials by John K. Duke, *History of the Fifty-third Ohio Volunteer Infantry During the War of the Rebellion, 1861–1865* (Portsmouth, Ohio: Blade Printing Company, 1900), 150–51. For calculations of Confederate casualties and an analysis of the Battle of Ezra Church, see Castel, *Decision in the West*, 434–36.

Chapter Ten. I Am an American Slave!

1. Taylor to Netta, Aug. 22, 1864.

2. Taylor diary, Aug. 5, 1864. The statement that Taylor received a copy of the recommendation for a colonelcy of a regiment is based on the assumption that the original of this document would, of necessity, have gone to Logan.

3. 38 OR 3: 42, and 5: 610; Taylor diary, Aug. 18, 19, 1864.

4. Writing Netta on July 4, 1864, Taylor accused the Army of the Cumberland of claiming successes gained by the Army of the Tennessee. Obviously, he was ignorant of the fact that until that point in the campaign the XX Corps alone of the Army of the Cumberland had done more hard fighting and put out of action more Confederates than the entire Army of the Tennessee.

5. William B. Hazen, *A Narrative of Military Service* (Boston: Ticknor and Company, 1885), 281, 283–85.

6. Ibid., 282–84.

7. This document is undated, but its contents indicate that Taylor began writing it on August 24 and completed it the following day.

Chapter Eleven. The Enemy Charged Upon Our Lines

1. 38 OR 3: 183; Hazen, *Narrative of Military Service*, 289.

2. Hazen, *Narrative of Military Service*, 284–85.

3. In fairness to Howard it should be noted that Hazen also believed, to quote his journal, portions of which are reproduced in his *Narrative,* that "a strong [Confederate] infantry force intrenched" defended Jonesboro (290).

4. Saunier, ed., *Forty-seventh Ohio*, 321–22, contains an account, doubtlessly supplied by Taylor, which describes Taylor as overhearing a conversation between Sherman

and Thomas while they surveyed the Confederate line from near the Forty-seventh Ohio's position, during which they agreed that it was time to move out of range of Confederate sharpshooters; viewing Sherman as he looked at his watch, "which was lying in his open hand and which marked 3 P.M."; and then having heard Sherman say to Thomas: "General, we ought to hear Stanley's firing over there [the right rear of Hardee's defense line]"; and finally seeing Thomas ride off to order the XIV Corps to attack immediately without waiting for the IV Corps to arrive on the battlefield. To put it as gently as possible, this is nothing but an "old soldier's tale." Had Taylor observed and heard these things, he surely would have recorded them in his diary or described them in his letter to Netta relating the August 31 Battle of Jonesboro or both. Moreover, they are factually false.

5. Hazen, *Narrative of Military Operation,* 297, states that "the failure to capture or completely destroy Hardee on this occasion was the finest opportunity lost by the Union forces under my observation during the war." Sherman's order, sent but not delivered by Thomas, for the IV Corps to cease tearing up railroad track and to march rapidly to the Jonesboro area did not reach Stanley, the IV Corps commander, until 3:30 P.M.— the exact time at which, according to Taylor's account and most others, the XIV Corps' attack got under way (see 38 OR 1: 932).

Chapter Twelve. I'm One Big Halo

1. Taylor to Netta, Sept. 14, 1864.

2. Presumably by the time Taylor wrote this he had received a letter from Chilton White written on September 4 (but erroneously dated August 4) in which his brother-in-law predicted that McClellan would be elected president on a Democratic platform calling for "a temporary cessation of hostilities and a convention of the States to the end that the Union may be restored upon the basis of the Federal Constitution"—that is, with no emancipation of slaves (letter in Taylor Papers, OHS). White also expressed confidence that he would be reelected to Congress but asked Taylor to campaign on his behalf among "the Boys of the 89th or 59th" Ohio regiments because his Republican opponent was counting on the soldier vote to unseat him. (This was a peculiar request, given that both of these regiments were in the Army of the Cumberland.) Probably this explains why Taylor in his September 14 letter to Netta also stated that he would continue to support White politically and asserted that his defeat in the election would be detrimental to the whole family.

3. In his letter of resignation, dated September 14, Taylor gave as his reasons for wishing to leave the service: "The delicate health of my family"; "embarrassments in my business connections"; and "have served three years and five months." Taylor had good cause to "fear" that Logan would reject his application. In fact, so contrary was the last reason to Logan's order stipulating that service time would be counted from the date on which an officer's unit was mustered that one is tempted to conclude that he not only expected but desired to have his resignation disapproved and that in submitting it he merely was engaging in a pretense designed to appease Netta.

4. On September 8, immediately after the arrival of the Army of the Tennessee at East Point, Hazen issued an order: "Loud and boisterous shouting on frivolous occasions is prohibited in the division." The order was aimed at the practice of the troops yelling "hard-tack" and "sow-belly" and also (to quote from Hazen's memoirs) of "making cat calls and other disrespectful demonstrations" in the presence of generals. There is no positive evidence that Taylor approved of the order (which proved highly effective), but he did not criticize it in his diary, as he had previous orders by Hazen to improve the efficiency and discipline of his division, and there are numerous indications in his diary and letters that he disliked the rowdy character of the Army of the Tennessee's soldiers. They were, as Hazen observed, splendid on the battlefield but tended to be obnoxious off of it (*Narrative of Military Operations*, 299–301).

5. Actually, the railroad remained intact from Chattanooga to Kingston and from there to Rome. This was done in order to facilitate a movement by Thomas into Georgia should Hood turn south in pursuit of Sherman.

Chapter Thirteen. A Scene of Destruction and Woe

1. "Substitutes" were hired by men who faced possible conscription to serve in their place.

2. According to the *Ohio Official Roster*, 4: 394, Pvt. Christopher Smith enlisted on June 15, 1861, but under "Remarks" there is nothing about when he left the army—possibly an indication that he received a dishonorable discharge.

3. Woods's report, 44 OR 1: 98; Smith's report, ibid., 414. During the engagement Walcutt was wounded and Col. Robert F. Catterson of the Ninety-seventh Indiana assumed command of the brigade. In his report (ibid., 105–6) Catterson gave the loss of the brigade as fourteen killed and forty-two wounded, with the latter number being "only those sent to hospital." He estimated the Confederate casualties at no less than "1,500, about 300 of whom were killed," and also stated that the militia numbered "between 6,000 and 7,000 men."

4. In his report (ibid., 110) Hazen stated that the foragers from his division were attacked by Confederate cavalry and lost twenty-seven captured and eight wounded. Possibly all the foragers were from the Seventy-sixth Ohio, but that seems unlikely. The *Official Records* contain no report for that regiment during the Savannah Campaign, and the commander of the brigade in which that regiment served made no mention of this incident in his report.

5. Evidently Campbell, a private in Taylor's former company, received a lesser punishment, if found guilty and punished at all, than a dishonorable discharge, for the *Ohio Official Roster*, 4: 413, records him as being mustered out with the regiment in August 1865.

6. 44 OR 1: 10, 72; Sherman, *Memoirs*, 2: 671–74; David Power Conyngham, *Sherman's March Through the South* (New York: Sheldon and Company, 1865), 284–85.

7. Newspaper clipping in Taylor Papers, OHS, Box 2, "Miscellaneous" folder. The clipping was taken, almost surely by Netta, from the *Cincinnati Commercial*, which re-

printed the *New York Herald* reporter's account of the storming of Fort McAllister in its December 26, 1864 issue. (Since writing this endnote I discovered, on November 12, 1999, that this clipping and the folder housing it no longer are in Box 2 of Taylor's papers— a circumstance that I promptly reported to the staff of the OHS. On that same day I confirmed, by a microfilm of the *Cincinnati Commercial* for 1864, that the *New York Herald* account of Fort McAllister appeared in its December 26, 1864 issue.) Hazen's division, which numbered close to 4,500, lost only 6 killed and 110 wounded in the attack. The Confederate garrison, which consisted of about 250 troops, was captured along with twenty-three cannons and suffered some forty to fifty casualties. The Forty-seventh Ohio lost one killed and seventeen wounded (44 OR 1: 72, 95, 117). Fort McAllister was situated and designed to prevent Union warships from moving up the Ogeechee River to assault Savannah and had successfully done so. Its defenders simply were too few to muster the firepower needed to repel an attack by a force as large as Hazen's.

Chapter Fourteen. A Brigadier General or Dead

1. The dates of Taylor's arrival at and departure from home, as well as what occurred while he was there, are derived from Netta's February 16 and March 13, 1865 letters to him and his letters to her of February 19, 21, and March 17, 1865.

2. Netta to Taylor, Feb. 16, 1865.

3. Netta to Taylor, March 13, 1865.

4. 44 OR 1: 111.

5. Quite possibly Hazen saw in Taylor many of the same qualities, in particular intelligence, that had caused him to make another young officer a member of his staff and a personal protégé—the future author Ambrose Bierce, whose short stories are classics of American literature.

6. The exception was Francis J. Herron, a non–West Pointer who became a major general on March 10, 1863 at the age of twenty-six as a result of an outstanding performance as a division commander in the Prairie Grove Campaign in Arkansas in December 1862 (Ezra J. Warner, *Generals in Blue: Lives of the Union Commanders* [Baton Rouge: Louisiana State University Press, 1964], 228–29). Had Taylor served in the Confederate army his chances of becoming at least a brigadier general would have been much better. Not only was there a greater turnover among Confederate generals owing to a higher casualty rate than among Union generals, but the Confederates usually promoted colonels to brigadier general when they took command of a brigade on an indefinite basis; in the Union army, as can be seen in the case of Wells S. Jones, colonels commanded brigades for long periods of time without being assigned the appropriate rank (see xx–xxi).

7. *History of Brown County*, 48.

8. The Civil War probably would have had the same outcome in the same way and in the same place had Sherman's march to the sea and then through the Carolinas never taken place. Sherman made the march as a consequence of his failure to obliterate the

Confederate army during the Georgia campaign, something that he should and could have done.

9. The IX Corps, although it served with the Army of the Potomac, officially was not part of that army because its commander, Burnside, was senior in rank to Meade and the object of misplaced pity by Lincoln, thus Taylor's referring to it as a separate entity from the Army of the Potomac.

10. Taylor to Netta, May 29, 31, June 2, 6, 1865.

11. Taylor to Netta, June 13, 15, 18, 1865.

12. Taylor to Netta, July 11, 17, 19, 21, 1865; *Ohio Official Roster,* 4: 389; Reid, *Ohio in the War,* 2: 295.

13. Saunier, ed., *Forty-seventh Ohio,* 469, 471–72, 474. The official date of the Forty-seventh's mustering out was August 11, 1865, but it actually occurred on August 12, 1865 (469). According to the *Ohio Official Roster,* 4: 389, Taylor was "mustered out with regiment Aug. 11, 1865," but obviously that was not literally the case as by then he was in Ohio and the mustering out occurred in Arkansas.

14. Saunier, ed., *Forty-seventh Ohio,* 472.

15. Reid, *Ohio in the War,* 2: 290, 295; Warner, *Generals in Blue,* 587, 594. Parry died of "consumption" in December 1866 shortly after being elected treasurer of Hamilton County, wherein lies Cincinnati. Both Elliott and Wallace also died shortly after the war (Reid, *Ohio in the War,* 1: 980).

Epilogue: Section 1, Lot 19

1. This account of Taylor's postwar career is based mainly on his c. 1903 memoir, "My Family and I," 21–23, and on the obituaries about him that appeared in the *Lake Charles (La.) Weekly Press,* February 21, 1908 and the *Lake Charles (La.) Weekly American,* February 22, 1908. The obituaries were based on information Taylor had supplied, and for the most part repeat, when it comes to him personally, what he states in the memoir. Hence, unless otherwise indicated, all statements in this epilogue pertaining to him and the birthdates of his children derive from these sources. When the obituaries present information about him not contained in the memoir, this too will be indicated. According to the *Weekly American* obituary, that newspaper published four weeks before Taylor's demise an "extended biographical sketch" of him in an issue that unfortunately is unavailable on the microfilm of the *Weekly American* that is at the Hill Memorial Library, Louisiana State University, and efforts to find it elsewhere have proved unavailing. However, much of what it contained probably appears in the *Lake Charles Weekly Press's* obituary.

2. According to Taylor's obituary in the *Lake Charles Weekly Press,* February 21, 1908, "Shortly after his removal [from command] another Indian raid occurred and the frontier was mercilessly devastated," with the result that Governor Anthony "was beaten at the next election." This assertion, which almost surely came from Taylor or a member of his family, is false. No other Indian raid took place in Kansas until 1878, and it had

little or nothing to do with Anthony's defeat in the gubernatorial election of that year, which was caused mainly by his mishandling of a railroad strike in which militiamen unintentionally killed a preacher. See William Frank Zarnow, *Kansas: A History of the Jayhawk State* (Norman: University of Oklahoma Press, 1957), 132, 160.

3. Sheridan Ploughe, *History of Reno County, Kansas: Its People, Industries, and Institutions* (Indianapolis: B. F. Bowen and Company, 1917), 444–45.

4. Memorandum by Thomas Taylor of Louisiana, in Taylor (Miles and Family) Papers.

5. *Lake Charles Weekly Press*, Feb. 21, 1908.

6. *Lake Charles Weekly American*, Feb. 22, 1908.

7. Ibid.

8. *Hutchinson Gazette*, Sept. 30, 1913; Ploughe, *History of Reno County*, 446. Carr Taylor died in Hutchinson on September 29, 1947 (*Hutchinson News-Herald*, Sept. 30, 1947).

9. As the dates in the title suggest, this pamphlet consists of the report that Taylor wrote on the role of the Forty-seventh Ohio in the Atlanta Campaign. It is not available at the Ohio Historical Society, but the text is found in 38 OR 3: 243–49.

10. Saunier's book is a mishmash of his own stumbling prose; paraphrases or quotations (sometimes not indicated as such) from various sources, notably those supplied by Taylor from his letters and diaries; and reports culled from the *Official Records*. The book itself disappeared some years ago from the holdings of the Ohio Historical Society but is available there on microfilm. For the writing of this book I used a microfilm copy of this microfilm, purchased from the Ohio Historical Society and then photocopied on a microfilm reader at the Hillsdale College library.

Index